AF251280

SOMETHING
EXTRAORDINARY

*A Short History of
the Manhattan Project, Hanford,
and the B Reactor*

ROBERT L. FERGUSON
and C. MARK SMITH

BOOKS BY ROBERT L. FERGUSON

Nuclear Waste in your Backyard:
Who's to Blame and How to Fix It (2014)

The Cost of Deceit and Delay: Obama and Reid's Scheme
to Kill Yucca Mountain Wastes $Billions (2012)

BOOKS BY C. MARK SMITH

Congressman Doc Hastings:
Twenty Years of Turmoil (2018)

In the Wake of Lewis and Clark:
From the Mountains to the Sea (2015)

Community Godfather: How Sam Volpentest shaped
the history of Hanford and the Tri-Cities (2013)

Raising Cain: The Life and Politics
of Senator Harry P. Cain (2011)

SOMETHING EXTRAORDINARY

*A Short History of
the Manhattan Project, Hanford,
and the B Reactor*

ROBERT L. FERGUSON
and C. MARK SMITH

BOOK PUBLISHERS NETWORK

Book Publishers Network
P. O. Box 2256, Bothell, WA 98041
(425) 483-3040
www.bookpublishersnetwork.com

Copyright © 2019 by Robert L. Ferguson and C. Mark Smith

All rights reserved by author including, but not limited to, any media now known or hereafter devised. No part of this book may be reproduced, stored in, or introduced into a retrieval system or transmitted in any form or by any means (electronic, mechanical, photocopying, recording, or otherwise) without the prior written permission of the author.

10 9 8 7 6 5 4 3

LCCN: 2019908463
ISBN: 978-1-948963-27-5
ISBN: 978-1-948963-28-2 (eBook)

Names:	Ferguson, Robert L. (Robert Lewis), author.	| Smith, C. Mark (Of Richland, Washington), author. | B Reactor Museum Association, sponsoring body. | Washington State University at Tri-Cities. Hanford History Project, sponsoring body.

Title:	Something extraordinary : a short history of the Manhattan Project, Hanford, and the B Reactor / Robert L. Ferguson and C. Mark Smith.

Description:	First edition. | Bothell, WA : Book Publishers Network, [2019] | "In cooperation with the B Reactor Museum Association and the Hanford History Project, Washington State University Tri-Cities."--Cover. | Includes bibliographical references and index.

Identifiers:	ISBN: 978-1-948963-27-5 | 978-1-948963-28-2 (eBook) | LCCN: 2019908463

Subjects:	LCSH: Manhattan Project (U.S.)--History. | Hanford Site (Wash.)--History. | B Reactor National Historic Landmark (Wash.)--History. | Atomic bomb--United States--History--20th century. | Plutonium industry--Washington (State)--Hanford--History--20th century. | Nuclear weapons--Materials. | Hanford (Wash.)--History--20th century. | Washington (State)--Economic conditions--20th century. | Hazardous waste site remediation--Washington (State)--Hanford Site. | Nuclear weapons plants--Waste disposal--Environmental aspects--Washington (State)--Hanford Site. | Environmental monitoring--Washington (State)--Hanford Site.

Classification:	LCC: QC773.3.U5 F47 2019 | DDC: 355.8/251190979751--dc23

Manufactured in the United States of America

First Edition

Cover design: by Laura Zugzda
Editor: Julie Scandora
Book design: Melissa Coffman
Production: Scott Book
Maps: Chris Picken
Diagrams: Dr. Delmar Larsen/Libre Texts
Index: Cher Paul
eBook production: Marcia Breece

*To the hundreds of thousands who worked on the
Manhattan Project, at Hanford, and at the
B Reactor, advancing the fields of science
and keeping the rest of us safe.*

*Bob Ferguson would further like to
dedicate this book to "Katie,
who made my life possible."*

CONTENTS

Introduction . . . . *ix*

Chronology . . . . *xiii*

1. Brave New Worlds 1

2. An Uncertain Race 15

3. The Manhattan Project 33

4. "A Free Sort of Place to Live" 53

5. Hanford and the B Reactor 71

6. War and Peace 99

7. A New Threat Arises 111

8. New Challenges and Missions 119

9. Hanford Cleanup and Beyond 139

Acknowledgments 169

Appendix: Atoms to Fission 171

Notes 187

Bibliography 197

Index 203

About the Authors 219

About Our Partners 221

INTRODUCTION

THIS BOOK IS WRITTEN TO COINCIDE with four important anniversaries. Eighty years ago, in September 1939, World War II broke out in Europe. Scientists who had escaped from Hitler's Germany were concerned that it would be the first to acquire the atomic bomb. They enlisted the eminent physicist Albert Einstein, himself a German refugee, to help draft a letter to President Franklin D. Roosevelt expressing their concerns. The result was that Roosevelt approved America's own research effort, which resulted in the Manhattan Project—America's monumental effort to develop and deploy the atomic bomb during World War II.

As a result of that decision, beginning in 1942, the Hanford Engineer Works (HEW) was built in remote Washington State, providing the massive plutonium production and processing facilities that were required to help win the war and preserve the peace during the Cold War that followed.

Seventy-five years ago, on September 26, 1944, the first of the plutonium production reactors—designated as the B Reactor—went critical for the first time. The reactor was involved in many firsts before it was deactivated in 1968. Its historical significance was properly recognized in 2015 when it was included as one of the facilities of the new Manhattan Project National Historical Park administered by the National Park Service.

This year also marks the thirty-fifth anniversary of the startup of WNP-2, the only nuclear power plant that survived the collapse of the ill-fated Washington Public Power Supply System, better known as WPPSS. The reactor is now known as the Columbia Generating Station and is operated by Energy Northwest on the Hanford Site. The dream of a nuclear energy park that could supply electricity throughout the West and return the profits to the Tri-Cities community was once believed to be the future alternative to plutonium production at Hanford when production reactors were deactivated. While both WPPSS and the dream of a nuclear energy park are long gone, a new vision of a clean, or green, energy park at Hanford has taken its place.

Finally, 2019 is the thirtieth anniversary of the signing of the Tri-Party Agreement between the US Department of Energy, the US Environmental Protection Agency, and the state of Washington in 1989 that changed Hanford's mission from production to cleanup. That effort is estimated to have cost at least $323 billion by 2019 and will almost certainly cost more, and take longer, than anyone anticipated.

On a more human level, this book is a story of the triumph of physics, chemistry, engineering, construction, and most of all, the human willpower of the scientists, soldiers, and companies that developed the bomb and built the facilities to produce it and the visionaries, community leaders, environmentalists, construction workers, and politicians who have had to deal with its aftermath. It is, in the words of one of those who lived through the Manhattan Project, "something extraordinary was happening here."* This book is dedicated to each of them.

Not surprisingly, the Hanford Site also played an important role in the economic growth and community culture of the nearby communities. Following President Johnson's decision to deactivate the reactors in 1964, those communities experienced decades of alternating booms and busts before the last production reactor was shut down in 1988. The decades that followed resulted in a continuing saga of incredibly complicated, expensive, and time-consuming efforts to clean up the Hanford Site and eliminate the roughly fifty-six million gallons of nuclear waste remaining at the site after forty-five years of production.

---

* Katrina R. Mason, "Something Extraordinary Was Happening Here," in The Manhattan Project: The Birth of the Atomic Bomb in the Words of Its Creators (New York: Black Dog & Leventhal, 2009), 178.

THIS HISTORY NECESSARILY INVOLVES a number of events and activities that took place at different times and places. Limiting the narrative to include only the scientific discoveries or the geopolitics or the military history would not tell the whole story. We've chosen, instead, to focus each chapter and the appendix on a major theme, and as a result, there is some unavoidable overlap in the timing and sequence of events. What remains, we hope, is a chronological thread that flows from one chapter to the next. A chronology is provided to help the reader better understand the flow of events, but it should be noted that the information comes from various sources that do not always agree. We apologize in advance for any confusion this may cause.

TO BETTER UNDERSTAND the Manhattan Project, Hanford, and the B Reactor, it is useful to review the history of atomic research that led to the development of the atomic bomb. We originally provided this information as the second chapter of the book but have been persuaded that placing it there interrupts the flow of the story of the Manhattan Project, so we have included it as an appendix. We should note that it is written for the general public and is not intended to be scientifically precise in its descriptions of certain technical details. Those who wish to know more about the scientific history that led to the events described in this book can begin by reading the appendix before starting chapter 1.

THIS YEAR'S ANNIVERSARIES are sure to generate a flurry of new books and magazine articles about the Manhattan Project, Hanford, and the B Reactor. New research is being conducted by the Atomic Heritage Foundation, the Hanford History Project at Washington State University Tri-Cities, the National Park Service, and the historical arm of the Department of Energy, but the past research upon which this book is based deserves mention.

This book draws on the body of excellent existing sources and the authors' own experiences to produce a concise history of the Manhattan Project, Hanford, and the B Reactor. For more information, we recommend Richard Rhodes's Pulitzer Prize–winning book, *The Making of the Atomic Bomb*, which describes the Manhattan Project and the events leading up to it in rich detail. There is also Cynthia Kelly's *The Manhattan Project*, which tells the story using the words of those who lived and wrote about it. Hill Williams, whose father was the editor of the *Pasco Herald* newspaper when the Hanford Site was acquired, has written an excellent account, *Made in Hanford: The Bomb that Changed the World*. French historian Pap Ndiaye has written about the crucial role the DuPont Corporation played in developing the Hanford Site. University of Washington professors John M. Findlay and Bruce Hevley have written about the impact of the Manhattan Project and Hanford on the local communities in *Atomic Frontier Days: Hanford and the American West*. Locally, Michele Gerber has written about the legacy of the Hanford Site in *On the Home Front: The Cold War Legacy of the Hanford Nuclear Site*. Other excellent books describe the very interesting geology and paleontology of the region, the history of the local Native American tribes, the exploration and development of the Mid-Columbia, and those hardy pioneers who lived along the Hanford Reach before it became the Hanford Site. These and other sources are listed in the bibliography of this book.

More information about the Manhattan Project, Hanford, and the B Reactor is also available at The Reach, the twelve-million-dollar interpretive center for the Hanford Reach National Monument that opened in 2014, the Manhattan Project National Historical Park Hanford Unit Tour Center from which all current tours originate, and at area museums and historical societies.

We wrote this book in the hope that it would provide a useful supplement to the visitor experience for those who visit the Tri-Cities and, more particularly, the B Reactor and the parts of the Hanford Site now open to the public on guided tours, providing an inexpensive memento of their tour.

CHRONOLOGY

1897	**APRIL**	J. J. Thomson discovers the electron, the first subatomic particle.
1904		Thomson formulates his "plum pudding" model of the atom with negative electrons floating in a positive central core of the atom.
1905		Albert Einstein publishes a paper expounding his theory of relativity. $E=mc^2$ the most relevant aspect of the theory because it states that there an equivalency between mass and energy.
1911		Ernest Rutherford formulates a new model of the atom with electrons orbiting the nucleus.
1913		Niels Bohr formulates an atomic model that depicts the atom as a small, positively charged nucleus surrounded by electrons that travel in elliptical orbits.
1914		H. G. Wells publishes *The World Set Free*, in which he imagines an atom bomb.
1918	**NOVEMBER 11**	Armistice ends the fighting in World War I.
1919		Ernest Rutherford discovers proton.

1929	**OCTOBER 24**	The American stock market crashes, starting the Great Depression.
1932	**FEBRUARY 22**	James Chadwick discovers neutron.
	NOVEMBER 8	Franklin D. Roosevelt elected president of the United States.
1933	**JANUARY 30**	Adolf Hitler appointed chancellor of Germany. Two months later, Enabling Act gives him dictatorial power.
	SEPTEMBER	Hungarian physicist Leó Szilárd conceives the idea of nuclear chain reaction using recently discovered neutrons.
1934	**OCTOBER**	Enrico Fermi splits the uranium atom but fails to recognize his achievement. Frédéric Joliot and Irène Curie discover artificial radiation.
1935	**SEPTEMBER 15**	German Jews stripped of rights as a result of Nuremberg Decrees.
1936	**MARCH**	Germany reoccupies the Rhineland in violation of the Versailles Treaty. Allies do nothing to stop it.
	NOVEMBER 3	Roosevelt elected to second term as president.
1938	**MARCH 12**	Germany annexes Austria.
	NOVEMBER 9	Kristallnacht begins in Germany.
	DECEMBER 16-17	Otto Hahn and Fritz Strassman discover the process of fission in uranium atom.
	DECEMBER	Lise Meitner and Otto Frisch confirm Hahn-Strassman discovery and pass on their findings to Niels Bohr.
1939	**MARCH 16**	Germany invades Czechoslovakia.
	AUGUST 2	Léo Szilárd and Albert Einstein complete the first draft of their letter to Roosevelt.
	SEPTEMBER 1	Germany invades Poland, beginning World War II in Europe.
	SEPTEMBER 3	Britain and France declare war on Germany.

	October 11	Alexander Sachs delivers Einstein's letter to President Roosevelt.
	October 21	First meeting of Advisory Committee on Uranium appointed by Roosevelt.
1940	**April 9**	Germany invades Denmark and Norway.
	April 10	British MAUD committee meets for first time.
	May 10	Germany invades France, Belgium, Luxembourg, and the Netherlands. Winston Churchill appointed prime minister of Great Britain.
	June 27	National Defense Research Committee (NDRC) replaces the Advisory Committee on Uranium with Vannevar Bush named as its chairman.
	September 7	German aerial blitz against Britain begins.
	November 5	Roosevelt elected to third term as president.
1941	**January**	Germany chooses heavy water as a reactor moderator over impure graphite, resulting in its failure to achieve a nuclear reaction or build an atomic bomb.
	February 25	Glenn Seaborg's research group discovers plutonium at University of California.
	March 28	Seaborg demonstrates that plutonium is fissionable.
	June 22	Germany attacks Soviet Union.
	June 28	Roosevelt creates Office of Scientific Research and Development (OSRD), encompassing NDRC. Uranium Committee becomes the S-1 Committee of OSRD.
	July 2	British MAUD Committee Report concludes that an atomic bomb is feasible.
	July 14	Bush and Conant receive British MAUD Committee Report.
	August 30	Churchill approves British "Tube Alloys" program.
	October 9	Bush briefs Roosevelt and Vice President Wallace on status of US atomic bomb research.
	November 27	American scientists announce they agree with findings of the MAUD report.
	December 6	S-1 Committee authorizes American research on plutonium for an atomic bomb.
	December 7	Japan attacks United States at Pearl Harbor.

	DECEMBER 10	Germany and Italy declare war on United States.
1942	**JANUARY 19**	Roosevelt approves production of atomic bomb.
	JUNE 17	Roosevelt orders all types of atomic research proceed at the same time.
	JUNE 19	S-1 Committee of OSRD becomes the S-1 Executive Committee.
	JUNE 20	Roosevelt and Churchill agree to share atomic research during Churchill's second wartime visit to the US.
	MAY 8	US forces in the Philippines surrender to Japan.
	MAY 23	S-1 Executive Committee recommends construction proceed with all methods of producing uranium-235 and plutonium.
	AUGUST 7	Americans go on offense by landing at Guadalcanal in the Pacific.
	AUGUST 13	The Manhattan Engineer District (MED) of US Army Corps of Engineers created.
	SEPTEMBER 17	Col. Leslie R. Groves appointed to head MED.
	SEPTEMBER 19	Groves selects Oak Ridge, Tennessee, as location of pilot uranium separation plants.
	SEPTEMBER 21	First flight of Boeing B-29 bomber in Seattle.
	OCTOBER 15	Groves selects Robert Oppenheimer to direct US research into bomb design.
	NOVEMBER 8	Allies land in North Africa.
	NOVEMBER 25	Groves selects Los Alamos, New Mexico, as atomic bomb research laboratory.
	DECEMBEr 2	First nuclear chain reaction achieved at University of Chicago.
	DECEMBER 12	DuPont signs contract to undertake plutonium production.
	DECEMBER 14	Col. Franklin Matthias, scientists from Met Lab in Chicago, and DuPont engineers meet to determine criteria for plutonium production site.
	DECEMBER 22	Matthias and DuPont representatives inspect the Hanford Site in Washington State and agree it is the most promising site, forwarding their recommendation to General Groves.
1943	**JANUARY 16**	Groves approves the Hanford Site.

	February 22	War Department announces its intent to acquire land for the Hanford Site, dissolving the towns of Hanford, White Bluffs, and Richland.
	March	Construction begins on the building of Hanford Camp to house construction workers at the former Hanford town site.
	March 22	Local residents and property owners receive letters condemning their land while construction begins at Hanford.
	June	Construction begins on 4,000 "alphabet" houses in Richland to house approximately 17,500 workers.
	June 10	Site preparation begins for start of construction of the B Reactor—the first full-scale nuclear reactor. Dates differ depending on sources, from August 27 to October.
	August	The United States, Great Britain, and Canada agree to consolidate future atomic research The Quebec Conference.
	September 8	Italy surrenders to Allies.
1944	**June**	Hanford reaches peak employment of approximately 48,000 workers.
	June 6	D-Day. Allies land in Normandy.
	July 23	A B-17G Flying Fortress, named "Day's Pay," in recognition of contribution of a day's pay from Hanford workers, dedicated at an airstrip on Hanford Site.
	August 19	Construction of B Reactor completed.
	August 25	Paris liberated by Allies.
	September 26	The B Reactor goes critical for the first time, but then quickly dies.
	November 7	Roosevelt elected for fourth term as president.
	December	Construction of the T Plant chemical separation facility completed. Plutonium processing begins at Hanford.
	December 16-27	Germans launch counteroffensive in Battle of the Bulge in France.
	December 28	B Reactor restarted after xenon poisoning discovered and finally reaches full power.

1945	**FEBRUARY 3**	First shipment of plutonium leaves Hanford for Los Alamos.
	APRIL 12	President Roosevelt dies in office. Vice President Harry Truman becomes president of the United States.
	APRIL 23	Americans obtain confirmation that Germany never attempted to build an atomic bomb.
	MAY 7	German armed forces surrender.
	JUNE 11	Atomic scientists release report correctly predicting post-war arms race.
	JUNE 21	Japan defeated in battle for Okinawa.
	JULY 16	First full-scale Trinity test of plutonium device takes place in New Mexico.
	JULY 24	President Truman informs Stalin that US has tested a powerful new weapon.
	JULY 25	Truman approves use of atomic bomb against Japan.
	JULY 26	Allies issue Potsdam Proclamation calling on Japan to surrender. Japan rejects their demand three days later.
	SEPTEMBER 3	Allies finally victorious in battle for Philippines.
	AUGUST 6	"Little Boy" uranium bomb dropped on Hiroshima, Japan.
	AUGUST 8	Russia declares war on Japan, invades Manchuria.
	AUGUST 9	"Fat Man" plutonium bomb dropped on Nagasaki, Japan.
	AUGUST 15	Japan surrenders after Emperor addresses nation.
	SEPTEMBER 2	Japan signs Articles of Surrender on board *USS Missouri*.
1946	**FEBRUARY 22**	"Long telegram" regarding Russian postwar intentions sent to US State Department by George Kennan.
	MARCH 12	Truman announces Truman Doctrine to protect Greece and Turkey.
	JUNE 2	DuPont contract with the Manhattan Project expires nine months after end of hostilities.
	JULY 1-25	US tests nuclear weapons at Bikini Atoll in the Pacific.
	AUGUST 1	Truman signs Atomic Energy Act of 1946 creating Atomic Energy Commission (AEC).

	AUGUST 15	Manhattan Engineer District is abolished.
	SEPTEMBER 1	General Electric Company officially replaces DuPont as primary contractor at Hanford.
1947	**JANUARY 1**	AEC assumes control of nuclear program from the Army.
	AUGUST	AEC announces it will add five new plutonium reactors at Hanford by 1955 and modernize existing reactors as Cold War intensifies.
	AUGUST 15	Manhattan Engineer District disbanded.
1948	**APRIL 3**	Truman signs European Recovery Plan (Marshall Plan).
	JUNE 19	Richland Community Council holds its first meeting in response to AEC initiative to "normalize" atomic cities.
	JUNE 24	Russians block Allied access to Berlin. US responds with Berlin Air Lift that lasts until May 1949.
	AUGUST 19	Richland holds its first Atomic Frontier Days celebration.
1949	**JULY 5**	Plutonium Finishing Plant at Hanford begins operation.
	AUGUST 29	Soviet Union tests its first atomic bomb.
	OCTOBER	GE completes H production reactor in first phase of postwar expansion at Hanford. DR Reactor follows in October 1950.
	OCTOBER 1	People's Republic of China established after Chinese nationalists defeated.
	DECEMBER 2-3	AEC intentionally releases radioactive iodine into the atmosphere ("Green Run") at Hanford for national security reasons to see if Russians can detect it.
1950	**JANUARY**	Truman approves development of hydrogen (fusion) bomb.
	JUNE 25	North Korea invades South Korea, initiating Korean War.
	NOVEMBER	Chinese communist forces intervene in Korea.

1952	**January 2**	REDOX separation plant begins operation at Hanford.
	November	C Reactor comes online in second phase of Hanford postwar expansion.
	November 1	US tests first hydrogen bomb at Enewetak Island in the Pacific.
1953	**July 23**	An armistice signed ending fighting in the Korea.
1955	**January**	K-W Reactor comes on line in third phase of Cold War Hanford expansion. K-E follows in April.
	August	President Eisenhower signs legislation authorizing sale of property and transfer of municipal government to citizens of Richland and Oak Ridge.
1956	**January 12**	PUREX chemical separation plant begins operation at Hanford.
	September 1	GE forms Hanford Laboratories to undertake research and development.
1957	**January 31**	Washington State Legislature authorizes creation of Washington Public Power Supply System (WPPSS).
	June	Federal government begins to sell Richland homes and businesses to private owners.
1958	**April-August**	US conducts more than twenty tests at Bikini and Enewetak.
	July 1	Joint Center for Graduate Study transferred from AEC to University of Washington.
	October 31	US announces unilateral halt to nuclear testing.
	December 10	Richland formally incorporates as a first-class city.
1959	**May 13**	Construction begins on dual-purpose N Reactor.
1961	**March 15**	Richland wins All-America City award for its efforts to incorporate.
1962		WPPSS agrees to build Hanford Generating Plant and market electricity it generates.

	OCTOBER 16-28	Cuban Missile Crisis brings US to edge of nuclear war with Soviet Union.
1963	**FEBRUARY**	Tri-City Nuclear Industrial Council (TCNIC) created.
	SEPTEMBER 26	President Kennedy visits Hanford to break ground for construction of Hanford Generating Station nuclear power plant to be built in conjunction with dual-purpose N Reactor. WPPSS agrees to build plant and market electricity it generates.
	DECEMBER	N Reactor starts up for first time.
1964	**JANUARY 8**	President Johnson announces in his State of the Union message that the plutonium production reactors at Hanford will be shut down, precipitating a major economic crisis in the Tri-Cities.
	JANUARY 21	GE announces its withdrawal as Hanford's prime contractor. AEC announces a program of "segmentation" and "diversification" at Hanford, splitting work between multiple contractors.
	NOVEMBER 9	N Reactor begins operation.
	DECEMBER	Production reactors at Hanford shut down between 1964 and January 1971.
1965	**JANUARY 4**	Battelle assumes responsibility for operating Hanford Laboratories.
	AUGUST	Contracts to replace GE as prime contractor at Hanford begin to be awarded, the first going to Battelle. Others were awarded to United Nuclear, Douglas Aircraft, and eventually, to Atlantic Richfield. Most contractors make efforts to provide local diversification projects.
1967	**JANUARY 23**	AEC chooses Hanford as the site of Fast Flux Test Facility (FFTF), a sodium-cooled research reactor.
	APRIL 8	First electricity produced at Hanford Generating Plant.
1968	**FEBRUARY 12**	B Reactor deactivated.

1969   **JANUARY** — Hanford is not selected as location of prototype US Breeder Reactor.

1970   **JANUARY 1** — President Nixon signs National Environmental Policy Act (NEPA).

FEBRUARY 1 — Work on FFTF reactor program is transferred from Battelle to Westinghouse.

JULY — Construction of FFTF research reactor begins.

DECEMBER 2 — US Environmental Protection Agency (EPA) is created.

1971   **JANUARY** — President Nixon announces closure of final production reactors, as well as the dual-purpose N Reactor.

1972   **MAY** — WPPSS announces it will build new nuclear power plant (WNP-2) at Hanford.

1973   **SEPTEMBER** — WPPSS announces start of construction to begin on first of three nuclear power-generating reactors to be built at Hanford.

1975   **JANUARY** — US Energy Research and Development Administration (ERDA) replaces AEC.

1976 — Basalt Waste Isolation Project (BWIP) begins to develop an underground repository for nuclear waste at Hanford. Project terminated in 1987.

1977   **OCTOBER** — ERDA is replaced by the Department of Energy. Work begins on the construction of WNP-2 nuclear power plant.

1978   **DECEMBER** — FFTF reactor completed at cost of $647 million.

1979   **MARCH 28** — A nuclear accident at Three Mile Island in Pennsylvania triggers growing anti-nuclear sentiment.

APRIL — Washington governor Dixy Lee Ray supports Hanford as site of nation's nuclear waste depository.

1980	**MAY 18**	Mount St. Helens erupts causing massive work delays for WPPSS.
	NOVEMBER 4	Washington State voters pass Initiative 393 banning import of nuclear waste into the state of Washington. The measure overturned in June 1981.
1982	**APRIL**	FFTF reactor begins operation.
1983	**JANUARY 9**	Nuclear Waste Policy Act passed. It requires BWIP to meet NRC licensing requirements.
	JULY-AUGUST	WPPSS defaults on $2.25 billion in bonds, causing the largest municipal bond default in US history and another major recession in the Tri-Cities.
	NOVEMBER	President Reagan orders the PUREX plutonium processing plant to restart as part of his defense buildup during the Cold War.
1984	**SEPTEMBER**	WPPSS WNP-2 nuclear power plant dedicated at Hanford. Estimated cost $3.2 billion.
1985	**MARCH**	Civic leaders create the Tri-Cities Industrial Development Council (TRIDEC), replacing TCNIC, which had been created in 1963, and broadening local economic development efforts.
1986	**FEBRUARY 27**	DOE releases 19,000 pages of documents detailing history of Hanford Site, creating massive environmental concerns.
	APRIL 26	Massive nuclear accident occurs at Chernobyl in Ukraine.
	MAY 28	BWIP nominated as one of three sites for nation's first underground nuclear repository.
	NOVEMBER 3	More than 2,000 in Tri-Cities rally in opposition to Referendum 40.
	NOVEMBER 4	Washington voters overwhelmingly approve Referendum 40, which authorizes state officials to veto the storage of outside nuclear waste at Hanford.

1987 JANUARY — N Reactor shut down, ending Hanford's role in producing weapons-grade plutonium.

DECEMBER 8 — President Reagan and Soviet President Gorbachev sign the Intermediate Nuclear Forces (INF) treaty.

DECEMBER 22 — Nevada's Yucca Mountain site elected as sole underground repository for nation's high-level nuclear wastes, ending consideration of Hanford as a site and terminating Basalt Waste Isolation Project and 1,200 jobs.

1989 MAY — Hanford Site named one of five possible sites for the Superconducting Magnetic Energy Storage (SMES). The project is promptly killed by the administration of newly elected President G. H. W. Bush.

MAY 15 — Tri-Party Agreement (TPA) signed by DOE, EPA, and Washington State Department of Ecology, setting the framework for the future cleanup of the Hanford Site.

AUGUST 1 — Energy Secretary Watkins says Hanford will be flagship of agency's cleanup efforts and releases five-year plan that estimates cleanup will cost $57 billion and be completed by 2018.

OCTOBER — N Reactor permanently shut down.

NOVEMBER — DOE awards a $550 million construction contract to build high-level waste treatment plant (WTP) with construction planned to begin in 1991 and plant operations beginning in 1999.

1990 OCTOBER — DOE Energy Secretary Watkins announces the PUREX plant will not reopen for further plutonium production.

DECEMBER 12 — DOE informs Washington State that tank waste safety issues might delay start of construction of WTP. Signatories to the Tri-Party Agreement (TPA) reluctantly agree.

1991 JANUARY — DOE announces two-year delay in building WTP and pre-treatment plants.

	JANUARY 22	B Reactor Museum Association (BRMA) incorporated as nonprofit organization to save the B Reactor.
	AUGUST 14	DOE Energy Secretary Watkins announces the closure of N Reactor.
	DECEMBER 21	Final collapse of Soviet Union.
1992	**APRIL**	FFTF reactor shut down after no more missions could be found for it.
	MAY	Groundbreaking ceremonies held marking start of construction of the WTP.
	JUNE	B Reactor listed on the National Register of Historic Places.
1993	**OCTOBER**	Signatories to the TPA negotiate delays for TPA, overall cleanup, and action to clean up groundwater. New target to vitrify all tank waste is 2028.
1994	**JULY 6**	Groundbreaking for the Laser Interferometer Gravitational-Wave Observatory (LIGO) takes place at Hanford.
	NOVEMBER	The Spokane *Spokesman-Review* publishes an eye-opening series on money that had been wasted at Hanford.
1995		Pacific Northwest Laboratory, operated by Battelle, is officially designated as a National Laboratory.
	FEBRUARY	Newly elected Congressman Doc Hastings is instrumental in helping form the House Nuclear Cleanup Caucus in Congress.
	JULY 22	Groundbreaking for the Volpentest Hazardous Materials Management and Emergency Response Training Facility (HAMMER).
	SEPTEMBER	Energy Secretary O'Leary announces DOE will pursue privatization of tank waste treatment program.
1996	**JULY 28**	Kennewick Man discovered during Water Follies weekend.

	August 4	Fluor Daniel Hanford Company named prime contractor at Hanford, replacing Westinghouse.
	September	DOE awards contracts to private firms, BNFL and Lockheed Martin, for tank waste vitrification.
	October 16	DOE's Environmental Molecular Science Laboratory (EMSL) is dedicated at Pacific Northwest National Laboratory.
1997	**January**	FFTF reactor is placed in standby condition after being deactivated since 1993.
	June	PUREX chemical separation facility is deactivated.
	September 6	DOE announces 14-month delay in removing spent fuel from K basins.
	September 24-27	Volpentest HAMMER Federal Training Facility dedicated.
1998	**May**	DOE rejects Lockheed Martin's bid to construct and operate the WTP.
	July	N Reactor is deactivated.
	August	British Nuclear Fuels Ltd. (BNFL) is awarded contract to build and operate the WTP.
	September	World War II-era B Separation Plant deactivated. TPA signatories agree to delays in cleaning up K basins.
	October	Congressman Hastings inserts language into 1999 National Defense Authorization Act, creating DOE Office of River Protection.
1999	**April**	DOE determines the federal government will retain control over the Wahluke Slope.
2000	**February**	DOE selects Hanford and other sites as disposal locations for waste from other DOE facilities.
	April	BNFL estimates the WTP will cost $15.2 billion. Energy Secretary Richardson calls estimate "outrageously expensive and inadequate" and terminates contract.
	June 10	Vice President Gore announces the creation of 195,000-acre Hanford Reach National Monument, transferring land from DOE to the US Fish and Wildlife Service.

	JULY	Huge range fire blackens much of Hanford Site, threatening numerous waste storage facilities.
	DECEMBER	DOE awards 20-year, $4 billion contract to Bechtel National to construct the WTP.
2002	**JULY**	Construction begins on the WTP. The estimated cost of the facility is $5.8 billion.
2003	**MARCH**	The State of Washington files suit in federal court to stop DOE from shipping transuranic waste to Hanford.
	JUNE	A coalition of citizens groups files ballot measure to ban most nuclear waste from being sent to Hanford.
2004	**MARCH**	Most of the work at Hanford tank farms is halted due to worker safety issues related to tank vapors.
	JULY 4	DOE stops work on the WTP to study seismic concerns.
	AUGUST	Workers complete the pumping of free liquids from single-shell tanks.
	SEPTEMBER 28	Congress approves Congressman Hastings legislation to study creation of a Manhattan Project National Historical Park.
	OCTOBER	The last spent fuel is removed from K basins.
2005	**AUGUST**	DOE awards a $1.9 billion contract to consortium of Hanford contractors for the cleanup of contamination along the Columbia River.
2006	**JUNE**	Bechtel releases new cost estimate of $11.5 billion to build the WTP, along with further time delays.
	JULY	Federal court rules Initiative 297 is unconstitutional. It would have prohibited shipping nuclear waste to Hanford.
2007	**JANUARY**	Work resumes on the WTP. Estimated cost has risen to $12.2 billion.
	AUGUST	A range fire burns most of Arid Land Reserve portion of Hanford Reach National Monument.

	SEPTEMBER	The state of Washington agrees to further delays in the startup of WTP in return for increased effort to clean up groundwater contamination.
2008	NOVEMBER	DOE notifies other TPA signatories that multiple milestones under the agreement are at risk because of funding shortages. Washington State files suit in federal court.
2009	FEBRUARY 17	President Obama signs the American Recovery and Reinvestment Act (ARRA), making $1.9 billion in anti-recessionary funding available for Hanford cleanup. Oregon follows Washington in suing DOE over missed milestones.
	AUGUST	DOE, Washington, and Oregon announce a tentative settlement of litigation over WTP.
2010	OCTOBER	Federal district court decrees new schedule for receiving and treating tank waste at Hanford.
2011	MAY	TRIDEC requests 1,341 acres of Hanford land for economic development purposes.
	SEPTEMBER	Large numbers of Hanford workers are laid off as ARRA funds are spent.
2012	JUNE	Cocooning of N Reactor, last of production reactors completed.
	AUGUST	Work slows on WTP, now more than 60 percent complete, to more technical issues.
	SEPTEMBER	Workers remove the first of highly radioactive sludge from K-West basin.
	OCTOBER	The first postwar double-shell tank identified as leaking from inner tank.
2013	MARCH	DOE says it would prefer to send 3.1 million gallons of tank waste to New Mexico for disposal.
2014	JANUARY 22	Plutonium Recycle Test Reactor and more than 180 buildings removed from 300 area north of Richland.
	DECEMBER	Congress passes the 2015 National Defense Authorization Act, which includes language

establishing the Manhattan Project National Historical Park.

2015	**May 15**	The twenty-fifth anniversary of signing of the TPA. More than $30 billion has been spent on cleanup with the latest DOE estimate of remaining cost at about $113 billion. DOE estimates that 8 billion gallons of contaminated groundwater have been cleaned, and 7.5 million gallons of liquid waste from leak-prone underground tanks and 1.25 million gallons of highly radioactive sludge and salt-cake waste have been removed.
	November 10	Manhattan Project National Historical Park is officially created.
2016	**February 3**	DOE and local officials sign documents transferring 1,631 acres of federal land to local entities for economic development purposes. Federal court imposes deadline of 2023 to start treating tank waste. The estimated cost now $17 billion. Total cost of remaining cleanup estimated to be $107.7 billion.
	February 11	Congress orders DOE to conduct review of waste treatment options with results to be reviewed by the National Academy of Sciences. LIGO confirms detection of first gravitational waves.
2017	**May 9**	Some radiation is released and Hanford workers take cover after a portion of a tunnel containing buried nuclear equipment collapses at the decommissioned PUREX separation plant.
	June 1	LIGO detects new gravitational waves.
2018	**October 9**	DOE announces it is reconsidering how it defines high-level waste. Waste resulting from fuel processing would not be considered as high-level if it can meet certain criteria. Such waste might be able to be disposed of onsite without having to be sent to an underground repository.

	September 28	DOE announces it will fill in collapsed tunnel at PUREX plant.
	December 12	DOE announces delays in demolition of Plutonium Finishing Plant.
2019	**January 28**	DOE awards $4.8 million second-phase contract to study mixing concrete-like grout with tank waste and then ship off-site for disposal.
	February	DOE estimates the cost of remaining Hanford cleanup is now $323.2 to $677 billion. It also announces that one manager will oversee both DOE's Richland Operations Office and the Office of River Protection.
	April	DOE releases draft of report on waste treatment options ordered by Congress in 2016. It indicates there are less costly options to treating tank waste.
	June 5	DOE announces that it will allow what had previously been considered high level waste to be reclassified based on its radiological content rather than on how it was produced, allowing DOE to expand its potential disposal options.

Chapter One

BRAVE NEW WORLDS

THE WEATHER HAD CLEARED in Washington, DC, after early morning showers, offering a pleasant, if breezy, fall day with temperatures in the low seventies. It was Wednesday, October 11, 1939, and the mood of President Franklin D. Roosevelt and his advisors inside the White House was decidedly worse than the outside weather.

Just five weeks earlier, on September 3, Britain and France had jointly declared war on Germany after it ignored their ultimatum not to invade Poland. The world crisis had forced the White House staff to postpone a number of important previously scheduled meetings with the president. A meeting with Alexander Sachs, a noted economist and vice president of Lehman Brothers, the prominent Wall Street investment house, was one of them. Roosevelt and Sachs were old and close friends. Earlier, Sachs had led the research division of the National Recovery Administration (NRA), an important and controversial New Deal agency, and he remained one of Roosevelt's seemingly endless supply of unofficial advisers.

Sachs carried with him a letter dictated by the Hungarian-born physicist Leó Szilárd in consultation with his fellow countrymen and physicists Edward Teller and Eugene Wigner, but the letter was signed by the famous German physicist Albert Einstein in the hope that his name would help focus Roosevelt's attention to the importance of its contents.

Back in 1933, Szilárd had been the first to imagine that great energy might be released by bombarding the nucleus of an atom and splitting it into smaller and lighter nuclei. All that was needed was to find the element in which that process might take place. Now the answer to that question was known. The element was uranium.

Szilárd and the others were all refugees who had fled from Nazi Germany. They were aware that nuclear research was taking place in Germany and felt the only way to stop the Nazis from developing an atomic bomb was for the United States to develop it first.

The letter they had written said in part:

> It may become possible to set up a nuclear chain reaction in a large mass of uranium, by which vast amounts of power and large quantities of new radium-like elements would be generated. Now it appears almost certain that this could be achieved in the immediate future.
> . . . This new phenomenon would also lead to the construction of bombs, and it is conceivable—though much less certain—that extremely powerful bombs of a new type may thus be constructed.[1]

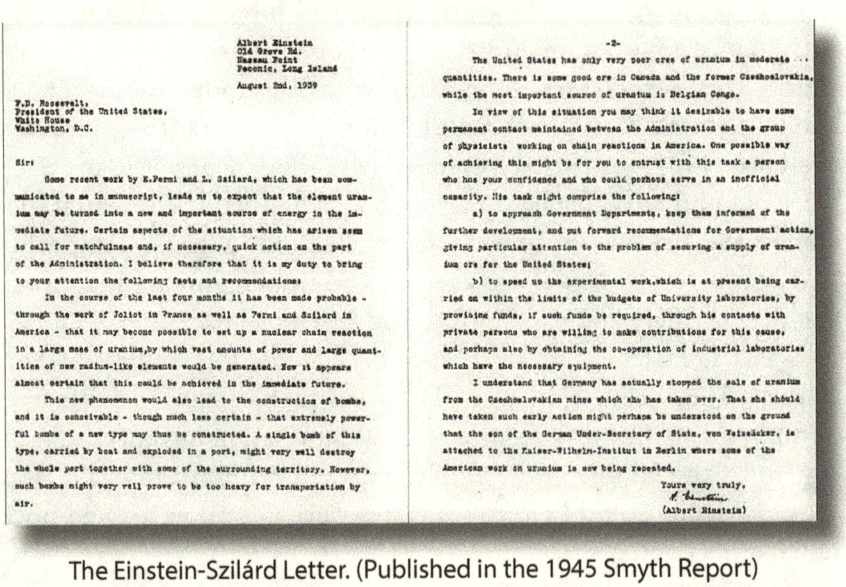

Albert Einstein
Old Grove Rd.
Nassau Point
Peconic, Long Island

August 2nd, 1939

F.D. Roosevelt,
President of the United States,
White House
Washington, D.C.

Sir:

Some recent work by E.Fermi and L. Szilard, which has been communicated to me in manuscript, leads me to expect that the element uranium may be turned into a new and important source of energy in the immediate future. Certain aspects of the situation which has arisen seem to call for watchfulness and, if necessary, quick action on the part of the Administration. I believe therefore that it is my duty to bring to your attention the following facts and recommendations:

In the course of the last four months it has been made probable - through the work of Joliot in France as well as Fermi and Szilard in America - that it may become possible to set up a nuclear chain reaction in a large mass of uranium,by which vast amounts of power and large quantities of new radium-like elements would be generated. Now it appears almost certain that this could be achieved in the immediate future.

This new phenomenon would also lead to the construction of bombs, and it is conceivable - though much less certain - that extremely powerful bombs of a new type may thus be constructed. A single bomb of this type, carried by boat and exploded in a port, might very well destroy the whole port together with some of the surrounding territory. However, such bombs might very well prove to be too heavy for transportation by air.

-2-

The United States has only very poor ores of uranium in moderate quantities. There is some good ore in Canada and the former Czechoslovakia, while the most important source of uranium is Belgian Congo.

In view of this situation you may think it desirable to have some permanent contact maintained between the Administration and the group of physicists working on chain reactions in America. One possible way of achieving this might be for you to entrust with this task a person who has your confidence and who could perhaps serve in an inofficial capacity. His task might comprise the following:

a) to approach Government Departments, keep them informed of the further development, and put forward recommendations for Government action, giving particular attention to the problem of securing a supply of uranium ore for the United States;

b) to speed up the experimental work,which is at present being carried on within the limits of the budgets of University laboratories, by providing funds, if such funds be required, through his contacts with private persons who are willing to make contributions for this cause, and perhaps also by obtaining the co-operation of industrial laboratories which have the necessary equipment.

I understand that Germany has actually stopped the sale of uranium from the Czechoslovakian mines which she has taken over. That she should have taken such early action might perhaps be understood on the ground that the son of the German Under-Secretary of State, von Weizsäcker, is attached to the Kaiser-Wilhelm-Institut in Berlin where some of the American work on uranium is now being repeated.

Yours very truly,
(Albert Einstein)

The Einstein-Szilárd Letter. (Published in the 1945 Smyth Report)

Sachs's meeting with the president, and the message he carried, would lead to the Manhattan Project, the American effort to develop the atomic bomb.

There is now new evidence that Einstein later changed his mind about signing the letter to Roosevelt. In May 2019, a never-before released audio tape recorded in 1951 went to auction. On it, Einstein says that the letter "was a great mistake," adding "I regret it very much." Einstein then declares his belief that if FDR had lived, he would never have used the atom bomb. "This I am convinced," he said.[2]

The scientists' sense of urgency was motivated by their own experiences in their native Europe following the end of the First World War. That war had resulted in the fall of the German, Austro-Hungarian, Russian, and Ottoman Empires. The winners, led by Great Britain and France, had survived—due to the late intervention of the United States—but barely, ending the war exhausted, deeply in debt, and shocked by the loss of a generation of young men.

The Paris Peace Conference that followed ended in the Treaty of Versailles and subsequent agreements that redrew the map of Europe, the Middle East, and much of the rest of the world, replacing the pre-war empires with a bewildering array of new nation states struggling for national identity and political survival.

The newly created nations, and even traditionally stable states, faced a popular demand for political and social change after the carnage of the Great War. Anti-democratic and totalitarian political ideologies that had slowly evolved during the previous century—communism, fascism, and National Socialism—competed openly with democracy for control of the governments of Europe and were not unknown in the United States.

In 1932, the British author Aldous Huxley published his best-selling novel, *Brave New World*. The title of the book became a common term used to describe the growing trends toward totalitarian and dictatorial government. Huxley's novel was set in a futuristic world state where genetically modified citizens lived in an intelligence-based caste system and were conditioned by scientific means to accept a utopian society. Huxley's new world was not specifically fascist or communist, but it was totalitarian, a government that placed all political power in the hands of one person or a class of people, something most Europeans could see taking place around them.

THE COLLAPSE OF THE EMPIRES was followed only ten years later by the collapse of the world's economy. The crash of the American stock market on October 29, 1929, triggered what became known as the Great Depression, an event that would last for a decade and disrupt the lives of millions around the world, including the families of the authors.

The end of the Great War had been followed by a surge in consumer spending resulting from pent-up demand during the war years, relaxed credit standards, huge increases in consumer debt, lagging wages, a widening gap of income disparity between the very rich and the working class, and growing inflation. Most industrialized countries pegged their currency to the gold standard, meaning they could not increase the amount of paper money in circulation without also increasing their reserves of gold. The demands of wartime spending had forced many of the European countries to leave the gold standard during the war, and when it ended, they returned. The Allies had borrowed heavily from the United States and remained deeply in debt.

The stock market crash resulted in a panicked sell-off of assets, which led to a dramatic decline in the value of those assets, followed by a drop in demand for goods and services, a reduction of credit, the disruption of trade, and massive unemployment. Two very different examples of how nations coped with the chaos stand out—Germany and the United States of America—creating the circumstances that led to the Einstein-Szilárd letter and Alexander Sachs's fateful White House visit.

ADOLF HITLER WAS BORN in 1889 in what was then the Austro-Hungarian Empire. His family moved to Bavaria in Germany when he was three. His father, a minor customs bureau official, had a difficult relationship with his son who aspired to become an artist. After both parents died while he was still a teenager, Hitler moved to Vienna to study art but ran out of money and lived on the street or in homeless shelters. It was then that he became attracted to the German nationalist movement and its anti-Semitic overtones.

During the First World War, Hitler served in the German Army and saw action in several major battles on the Western Front. He was wounded at the Battle of the Somme in October 1916 and was gassed in October 1918. He was still recovering when the war ended. By the time he was discharged from the army in 1920, he had already joined and become a full-time organizer for what would become the Nazi Party.

A skilled orator and master manipulator, Hitler became the party's chairman in 1921, speaking to growing audiences about German nationalism, the removal of Jews from Germany, the threat of communism, and his opposition to the governing Weimar Republic.

An admirer of fascist Italy, Hitler sought to emulate Benito Mussolini's 1922 march on Rome a year later when he attempted a similar coup to take over control of the Bavarian government. His attempted putsch was repulsed with the loss of twenty lives. Hitler served a year in jail where he wrote most of his autobiography, *Mein Kampf* (*My Struggle*), which found a ready worldwide audience, selling almost three hundred thousand copies by 1932.

Adolf Hitler 1938. (*Bundesarchiv, Bild 183-H1216-0500-002 / CC-BY-SA*)

Hitler used the world economic crisis and Germany's hyperinflation to rebuild the Nazi Party. By 1930, the Nazis and the communists controlled 40 percent of the seats in the German parliament between them. After the Nazis received more than 30 percent of the vote in the election of 1932, the aging German president, Paul von Hindenburg, reluctantly appointed Hitler as Germany's chancellor when the moderate political parties were unable to come up with a suitable alternative.

On February 27, 1933, the Reichstag, the German Parliament building, mysteriously caught fire. Hitler claimed it was a communist plot to overthrow the government and used the event to suppress the German Communist Party, arresting more than forty thousand of its members. Hitler's control over the nation became complete when the government passed a law combining offices of president and chancellor a day before Hindenburg's death.

Hitler immediately consolidated his power, suppressing and disbanding opposition parties, murdering his political opponents, becoming commander-in-chief of Germany's armed forces, and promoting large-scale reconstruction and rearmament, much of which was funded with assets seized from "enemies of the state," including tens of thousands of Jews. The German people, still resentful of the Treaty of Versailles and hard hit by inflation and unemployment, widely supported Hitler's actions.

The country's half million Jews accounted for just 0.86% of Germany's overall population, but the Nazis claimed the Jews had been responsible for Germany's defeat in the war and for the nation's subsequent economic distress. Beginning in 1933, the German government enacted a series of anti-Jewish laws that restricted their ability to earn a living, gain an education, or work in the civil service. The 1935 Nuremberg Laws stripped them of their citizenship and forbade them to marry non-Jews. Many wealthy or educated Jews, or those who had other means at their disposal, began to leave the country.

Some didn't leave soon enough. On November 10, 1938, Nazi Stormtroopers carried out a coordinated, nationwide attack, against the Jews, that came to be known as Kristallnacht (literally, Crystal Night, but also, Night of Broken Glass). Seven thousand five hundred Jewish stores and businesses were attacked, more than fourteen hundred synagogues and cemeteries were vandalized, and more than thirty thousand Jewish men were arrested and taken to concentration camps.

The German and Hungarian physicists who had collaborated on drafting the Einstein letter were among those who had successfully escaped the Nazi regime. Albert Einstein was a visiting professor in California when Hitler came to power and never returned. Fellow physicist

Leó Szilárd left Germany for the United States in 1938. Hungarian physicists Eugene Wigner and Edward Teller left Germany in 1930 and 1933, respectively.

Germany withdrew from the League of Nations in 1933. Hitler's foreign policy advocated the annexation of Austria, the restoration of Germany's pre-war national borders, rejection of military restrictions on the size of Germany's armed forces imposed by the Treaty of Versailles, the return of the former German colonies in Africa, and the creation of a German zone of influence in Eastern Europe.

Damage to Jewish shop owners in Magdeburg during Kristallnacht, November 10, 1938. (Bundesarchiv, Bild 146-1970-083-42 / CC-BY-SA 3.0)

In March 1936, Hitler reoccupied the demilitarized Rhineland between France and Germany in violation of the Versailles Treaty. The Allies objected, but did nothing. In July of that year, Hitler provided troops and aircraft to support the fascist general Francisco Franco in the Spanish Civil War. Finally, in August—the same month Germany hosted the Summer Olympic Games in Berlin—he ordered the implementation of a four-year plan that would prepare Germany for a total war within four years.

In March 1938, Hitler made good on his pledge to annex Austria. While many in Austria disapproved, Hitler knew he had the backing of the Austrian Nazi Party and millions of German-speaking Austrians. He simply threatened to invade the country if the Austrian government did not capitulate.

Later in March, close on the heels of his Austrian success, Hitler set his sights on the annexation of the German-speaking part of Czechoslovakia known as the Sudetenland. An invasion was ordered to take place in October. Now thoroughly alarmed about further German expansion, Britain and France threatened to curtail oil shipments to Germany and demanded a compromise in which the Sudetenland would be ceded to Germany while Britain and France would guarantee the independence of the remainder of the country. Not surprisingly, the Czech government rejected the agreement.

The Munich Agreement, September 30, 1938. *Left to right*: Chamberlain, French Prime Minister Édouard Daladier, Hitler, Mussolini, and Italian Foreign Minister Count Galleazzo Ciano. (*Bundesarchiv, Bild 183-R69173 / CC-BY-SA 3.0*)

Hitler then hosted a conference in Munich to which the British, French, and Italians were invited but not the Czechs. On September 30, 1938, the Munich Agreement was signed, which allowed the German army to occupy the Sudetenland. Czechoslovakia was informed that it could either fight Nazi Germany alone or agree to the annexation. President Roosevelt informed Hitler that "the government of the United States has no political involvements in Europe, and will assume no obligations in the conduct of the present negotiations."[3] Facing no other choice, the Czech government reluctantly agreed. The British prime minister, Neville Chamberlain, returned to England saying that the agreement represented "peace in our time."[4]

Having taken Austria and Czechoslovakia without firing a shot and after signing a mutual alliance treaty with Italy and a non-aggression pact with the Soviet Union, Hitler now turned his attention to Poland. The plains of Poland provided the lebensraum, or living space for the German people that Hitler had been lusting for since the 1920s. By 1937, he began applying pressure for the return of the port of Danzig and East Prussia, which had been given to Poland at the end of the First World War. In March 1939, as a result of the Munich Agreement and growing concerns about Germany's territorial aspirations, Poland negotiated a military alliance with Britain and France in the hope they would intervene if Poland was threatened by Germany.

At the same time, the Soviet Union was eyeing eastern Poland as a buffer against future German aggression. Secret talks between the German and Soviet foreign ministers in August 1939 resulted in an unlikely agreement between the two competing dictatorships to attack and divide Poland between them. Hitler correctly reasoned that England and France could not come to Poland's defense in time to save it and invaded the country on September 1. An Allied ultimatum demanding that Germany withdraw its troops from Poland was ignored, and Britain and France declared war against Germany two days later on September 3, 1939.

In late February and March 1940, President Roosevelt sent under secretary of state Sumner Wells to Italy, Germany, England, and France during the early "phony war" period of the conflict to determine if a real war could be averted and assess the potential for peace. Wells met with Hitler in the newly completed Reichschancellery and learned first-hand what Europe and, ultimately, the rest of the world were dealing with. "Germany had existed as an empire half a millennium before Columbus discovered the New World," Hitler said. The German people "had every right to demand that their historical position of a thousand years should be restored to them."[5]

IT IS DIFFICULT TO CONCEIVE of two men more different than Adolph Hitler and Franklin D. Roosevelt. The president was born to great wealth and privilege in 1882. His ancestors arrived in New York from Holland in the seventeenth century and prospered as successful merchants and land developers.

As a youth, Roosevelt had accompanied his parents on their frequent trips to Europe. He attended the elite Groton School and Harvard College, where he became editor-in-chief of the school's daily newspaper and graduated with a degree in history. After passing the New York bar exam, he joined a prestigious New York law firm.

In 1905, he married his fifth cousin, Eleanor, the niece of President Theodore Roosevelt, at the White House with the president presiding. With little interest in the law, Franklin Roosevelt entered politics. He was elected to the New York State Senate in 1910 and made a name for himself by opposing the New York City political machine. He supported the progressive Democratic nominee, Woodrow Wilson, in the presidential election of 1912, in spite of the fact that his cousin, Theodore, a Republican, attempted a political comeback by mounting a third-party bid for the office, dividing the Republicans and throwing the election to Wilson.

Once president, Wilson appointed Franklin Roosevelt to the post of assistant secretary of the navy—the same job Theodore had held at the start of the Spanish-American War—where he oversaw the expansion of the American navy during the First World War.

After a failed senatorial race in 1916, the end of the war in 1918, and a severe stroke that left President Wilson incapacitated, Roosevelt

Franklin Roosevelt as assistant secretary of the navy, 1913.
(Library of Congress)

was selected in 1920 by the Democratic presidential nominee, James M. Cox, to run as his vice president. The Democrats were soundly defeated in a year in which the Republican majority in Congress had already failed to ratify the Versailles Peace Treaty or to join the newly created League of Nations.

In 1921, Roosevelt was stricken with poliomyelitis. As a result, he was confined to a wheelchair for the rest of his life. Still only thirty-nine, Roosevelt decided to resume his political career. In 1928 he was elected governor of New York. After the stock market crash in October 1929, Roosevelt was one of the most vocal critics of the Republican administration's inadequate efforts to combat the growing economic crisis.

As governor of New York, Roosevelt was the leading contender for the Democratic nomination for president in 1932. The country was demanding change, and Roosevelt's cheerful message and his use of new technology like the radio resulted in a resounding victory in a wave election. Roosevelt carried all but six of the forty-eight states, forging a coalition of varied political interests. In his acceptance speech, he pledged "a new deal for the American people."[6] Forevermore, his administration would be known as the "New Deal."

With huge majorities in Congress, Roosevelt and his advisors instituted a dizzying array of new legislation during the administration's first one hundred days. Most of it worked, some of it didn't, and some was later rejected by the Supreme Court. In 1935, the passage of the Social Security Act provided economic security for the elderly, the poor, and the sick. Roosevelt insisted that it be funded by payroll taxes, rather than from the general fund.

Roosevelt won another landslide election in 1936, carrying all but two states. Although economic conditions had improved since 1932, more than 20 percent of all Americans were still unemployed. Many more were underemployed. Large numbers of families had lost their homes or family farms and it was not uncommon for several generations of a family to live together. Much of his second term was taken up with fighting the Supreme Court and conservative factions in Congress to save many of the agencies and programs that had been passed in his first term.

Focused on the domestic crisis in the United States, Roosevelt watched dictators come to power in Russia, Italy, Spain, and Germany.

With American public opinion strongly isolationist, he lacked the political support, even within his own party, to intervene in Europe's growing problems. He had made it clear to England and France that the United States would remain neutral if Germany attacked Czechoslovakia; however, American public opinion began to turn against Germany following the Munich Agreement and Kristallnacht, giving Roosevelt the support he needed to undertake a massive rearmament program, which created new jobs and propelled the United States out of the Great Depression.

Roosevelt signs the Social Security Act into law, August 14, 1935.
(*Library of Congress*)

It was against this backdrop that Alexander Sachs visited the White House on October 11, 1939. Late that afternoon, Sachs was finally ushered into the Oval Office by the president's senior aide and gatekeeper, Brigadier General Edwin M. "Pa" Watson. With an understanding of his one-man audience developed over many years, Sachs decided against reading the letter that Einstein had signed or any of the other materials he had brought with him.

Rather, he had prepared his own eight-hundred-word summary, which first emphasized the potential for using nuclear energy for peaceful purposes—power generation and producing isotopes for medical research. Only then did he mention "bombs of hitherto un-envisioned potency and scope."[7] Roosevelt, weary after a long day and the prolonged presentation, told Sachs he found it all very interesting but he considered government intervention to be premature at this stage. Sachs, undeterred and calling on his long personal friendship with the president, was able to arrange an invitation to join Roosevelt at breakfast the following morning.

Robert Jungk, the German-born historian who wrote a book on the German and American efforts to build an atomic bomb, described what happened next. "That night I didn't sleep a wink," Sachs remembered.

> I was staying at the Carlton Hotel [two blocks north of the White House]. I paced restlessly to and fro in my room or tried to sleep sitting in a chair. There was a small park quite close to the hotel. Three or four times, I believe, between eleven in the evening and seven in the morning, I left the hotel, to the porter's amazement, and went across to the park. There I sat on a bench and meditated. What could I say to get the President on our side in this affair, which was already beginning to look practically hopeless? Quite suddenly, like an inspiration, the right idea came to me. I returned to the hotel, took a shower and shortly afterwards called once more at the White House.[8]

"What bright idea have you got now? How much time would you like to explain it?" Roosevelt asked as he greeted Sachs to his breakfast table.

"All I want to do is to tell you a story," Sachs said, and then continued:

> During the Napoleonic wars a young American inventor came to the French Emperor and offered to build a fleet of steamships with the help of which Napoleon could, in spite of the uncertain weather, land in England. 'Ships without sails?' This seemed to the great Corsican so impossible that he sent [Robert] Fulton away. In the opinion of the English historian, Lord Acton, this is an example of how England was saved by the shortsightedness of an adversary. Had Napoleon shown more imagination and humility at that time, the history of the nineteenth century would have taken a very different course.[9]

Sachs finished by reading the last paragraph of his summation in full and aloud. "I think there is no doubt that subatomic energy is available all around us, and that one day man will release and control its almost infinite power. We cannot prevent him from doing so and can only hope that he will not use it exclusively in blowing up his next door neighbor."[10]

The President remained silent for several minutes and then summed up the meeting. "Alex, what you are after is to see that the Nazis don't blow us up?"

"Precisely," Sachs replied.

Roosevelt called in his aide, Pa Watson, and pointed to the documents that Sachs had brought. "Pa, this requires action!"[11]

The president's decision set in motion a secret two-billion-dollar program to develop the atomic bomb and another three-billion-dollar program to build a strategic bomber to carry it. It was a decision that would change the future history of the world.

Chapter Two

AN UNCERTAIN RACE

FOLLOWING HIS BREAKFAST MEETING with Roosevelt, Sachs met privately with Pa Watson to determine what Roosevelt's call for action might mean. Watson proposed creating a small advisory committee to study the current state of uranium research and recommend what the appropriate role of the federal government should be going forward. He suggested Dr. Lyman J. Briggs, the director of the National Bureau of Standards, as chairman of the committee because his agency was in charge of the government's physics research. Two ordnance experts, Army Lieutenant Colonel Keith F. Adamson and Navy Commander Gilbert C. Hoover, were also included.

Alexander Sachs leaving the White House in 1939.
(*Library of Congress*)

To speed the process along, Watson called Briggs from his office and arranged for Sachs to meet with him that same evening. Briggs listened carefully and fully understood the implications of Sachs's warning. He wasted no time in scheduling the first meeting of what became known as the Uranium Committee for October 21, 1939, only ten days away.

Sachs invited the émigré physicists who had been involved in the Einstein letter, and all but Fermi were able to attend. Szilárd made an impassioned plea for government help but met with skepticism from the military members of the committee who felt that radar and other new technologies seemed more promising. Sachs strongly supported the scientists' position, saying, "The issue is too important to wait."[12]

The committee ended up authorizing six thousand dollars to purchase uranium and graphite for Fermi and Szilárd's experiments at Columbia but did not pursue the development of a bomb. The committee also prepared a report for the president, which was delivered on November 1. After reading it, Roosevelt placed it in a file where it sat for the next six months.[13]

In the meantime, new research was casting doubt on the value of natural uranium. "It is very doubtful whether a chain reaction can be established without separating 235 from the rest of the uranium," Briggs wrote to Watson on April 9, 1940.[14] The Uranium Committee met a final time on April 27 with Fermi now in attendance and decided that future decisions should await the results of Fermi's uranium-graphite experiments.

On May 10, the pseudo-war in Europe ended when Germany invaded Belgium, the Netherlands, and Luxembourg and then rolled into France. With a new sense of urgency that followed the British evacuation from Dunkirk and the German occupation of Paris, Roosevelt decided on June 27, 1940, to replace the Uranium Committee with the newly created National Defense Research Committee (NDRC). Vannevar Bush, a major figure in American academic circles, former dean of the engineering department at MIT, and president of the Carnegie Institution, was named as its chair. The NDRC had a much broader mandate than the Uranium Committee. It would explore all types of pressing military research needs—radar, synthetic rubber, and sonar—but it would also pursue isotope separation and graphite experiments. More importantly, the decision meant that atomic research would no longer be dependent on military funding, as it had been under the Uranium Committee. Briggs sent the Uranium Committee's final report to Bush on July 1, asking for $140,000, but with scarce resources available, the NDRC approved only $40,000 of the requested funds.

NDRC/OSRD Chairman Vannevar Bush. (*Library of Congress*)

Meanwhile, separate groups of scientists were working on atomic research at university laboratories around the United States. On February 25, 1941, Dr. Glenn Seaborg at the University of California at Berkeley demonstrated that a fissile element bred in uranium could be chemically separated using a relatively easy and inexpensive process, rather than the difficult and expensive process of physically separating isotopes, creating a long-suspected new element 94. Seaborg's process involved dissolving U-238 in a toxic combination of acid and various chemicals that created submicroscopic amounts of element 94 and then repeating the process over and over again to create larger amounts.

It would not be until the following year that element 94 would receive a name—plutonium—named for the planet Pluto, discovered in 1930 and named after the Greek god of the underworld and the god of the dead.[15] Based on Seaborg's success in producing plutonium, Dr. Ernest Lawrence, Seaborg's laboratory director and a forceful, dynamic man, met with a skeptical Vannevar Bush to encourage a much higher national priority for plutonium research.[16] Lawrence was skeptical about the ability to successfully separate U-235 from natural uranium electromagnetically or by any other means.

On June 22, 1941, Germany invaded Russia with a blitzkrieg of 164 divisions providing even more impetus for increasing and better organizing America's nuclear program. On June 28, Roosevelt issued an executive order that folded the old NDRC into the newly created Office of Scientific Research and Development (OSRD), also led by Bush, and providing it with almost unlimited funding and other resources. James Conant, the president of Harvard, took over NDRC. The former Uranium Advisory Committee became the Uranium Section of the OSRD and was soon renamed the S-1 Section for security purposes.

In accordance with the president's wishes, all policy matters related to the program were restricted to a small group that consisted of Bush as chair, the president, Vice President Henry Wallace, Secretary of War Henry L. Stimson, Army Chief of Staff General George C. Marshall, and James B. Conant, a chemist and president of Harvard University. Bush recommended that the president select the army to administer the atomic program because he wanted to avoid inter-service rivalries and because the army had more experience with building and managing large-scale construction projects.

AT THE SAME TIME, Mark Oliphant, an Australian physicist working at the University of Birmingham in England, and George Paget Thomson, a physicist at Cambridge, were tasked with conducting experiments using uranium. Oliphant delegated the work to two refugee German scientists, Rudolf Peierls and Otto Frisch. The results of their extensive research, completed in July 1941, showed that the amount of pure U-235 needed to set off a powerful chain reaction was much less than had been thought.

Oliphant and Thomson discussed their findings with Sir Henry Tizard, chairman of the Committee for the Scientific Survey of Air Warfare (CSSAW), who then created a special new committee within CSSAW to oversee all of Britain's atomic research. In an effort to disguise the purpose of the committee, they named it the MAUD Committee—a code name rather than an acronym—referring to the Danish physicist

Niels Bohr's former housekeeper. The committee first met on April 10, 1940. The universities funded their own research until government funding finally became available in September.[17]

The committee's work continued over the next year, producing its first report on the use of uranium for a bomb in June 1941. A second report on the use of uranium as a source of power followed. The reports led to the creation of the Tube Alloys program—a meaningless title created to hide Britain's atomic research. Britain's scientists explored various ways of increasing the U-235 found in natural uranium.

In August, Oliphant visited the United States to confer with American scientists about radar and atomic research. He was surprised to learn that Americans were not fully aware of the British research that had previously been reported by the MAUD Committee. Oliphant took it upon himself to bring the Americans up to speed. He met with Ernest Lawrence at Berkeley and then met with Vannevar Bush and James Conant to discuss the MAUD committee report.

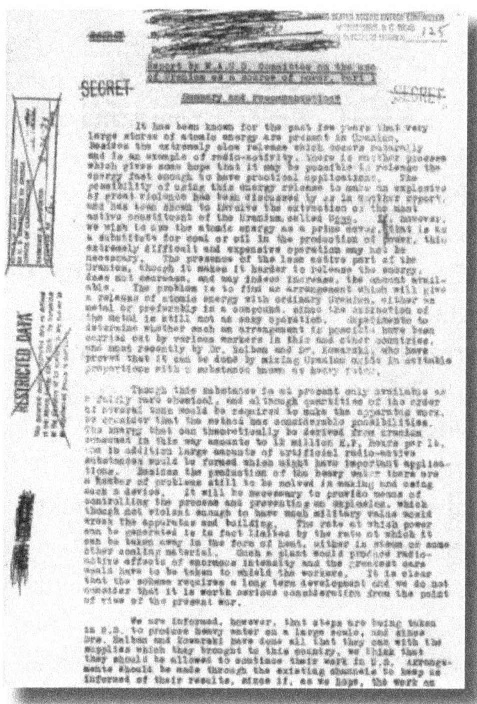

First page of the secret MAUD committee report. *(Library of Congress)*

Bush met with the president and Vice President Wallace on October 9 to summarize the British findings and the committee's estimates of the cost and time it would take to develop an American bomb. He received Roosevelt's permission to explore the cost of building the necessary physical facilities, but not to begin construction on them without his authorization. As historian Richard Rhodes summed up the meeting: "The United States was not yet committed to building an atomic bomb. But it was committed to exploring thoroughly whether or not an atomic bomb could be built. One man, Franklin Roosevelt, decided that commitment—secretly, without consulting Congress or courts. It seemed to be a military decision and he was the Commander-in-Chief."[18]

FROM THERE, EVENTS ESCALATED QUICKLY. Conant was sent to London to open a liaison office with the British. Bush reported back to the president on November 27 to say that the basic findings of the MAUD committee report had been confirmed by American scientists. "If all possible effort is spent, one might . . . expect fission bombs in significant quantity within three or four years."[19] Bush's report, however, dealt only with uranium bombs and did not mention plutonium.

On December 6, 1941, the S-1 Committee met at the prestigious Cosmos Club—located across Lafayette Park from the White House and long known as the location of meetings about sensitive government programs—to lay out assignments for the development and design of the atomic bomb. The following day, the Japanese attacked Pearl Harbor in Hawaii, and Germany declared war on the United States four days later. Now, an even greater sense of urgency drove the government's efforts. On January 19, 1942, Roosevelt returned the committee's report to Bush with a short handwritten note that read: "V. B. OK—returned—I think you had best keep this in your own safe. FDR."[20]

Work was already underway on three different techniques of separating natural uranium to obtain U-235. One subcommittee of the OSRD investigated electromagnetic separation at the University of California. Another team looked into gaseous diffusion technology at Columbia University in New York City. A third group explored thermal diffusion at the Carnegie Institution in Washington.

Roosevelt's note to Vannevar Bush to proceed with the
development of the atomic bomb. January 19, 1942.
(National Archives at College Park, Record Group 227)

Meanwhile, research was being conducted on two different types of nuclear reactors to produce plutonium. At Columbia University, one group of scientists under Harold Urey looked into heavy water reactors (the same technology being pursued by the Germans), while Nobel Laureate Arthur Compton brought the scientists working at Columbia and Princeton together at the Metallurgical Laboratory at the University of Chicago—which came to be known simply as the Met Lab—to study plutonium production using graphite to help "cool" neutrons and maintain a nuclear chain reaction. Because the scientists didn't know the best method to produce a bomb and because the United States could not afford to choose the wrong one, Roosevelt approved a recommendation to proceed with research on all five technologies at the same time on June 17, 1942.

The effort was to be split into two major categories. Scientific research would remain the responsibility of the S-1 Committee and receive thirty-one million dollars for research and development, while the army would receive fifty-four million dollars for construction of atomic facilities. An additional five million dollars was set aside for contingencies hidden as other expenditures in the fiscal year 1943 budget.

With the growing expenditures becoming increasingly difficult to hide, it was not until February 1944 that Secretary of War Stimson and General Marshall met with top congressional leaders of both parties to brief them on the existence and the estimated cost of the atomic program. They were not told how the money would be spent. The fact that they agreed to hide these massive expenditures in the federal budget was largely a mark of their confidence in and respect for Marshall.[21]

Compton's team at the Met Lab included Fermi, Szilárd, and Eugene Wigner, who had first suggested a reactor design in 1941. His design was elegantly simple. It consisted of a cube of graphite into which holes had been drilled to hold slugs of uranium and control rods made of cadmium, which absorbs neutrons to control the chain reaction, similar to the gas and brake pedals of a car. Completed in November 1942 in a squash court beneath the bleachers at the University of Chicago's Stagg Field, the reactor would be called it CP-1 (Chicago Pile-1).

On December 2, 1942, Fermi ordered that the control rods be withdrawn a few inches to speed up the chain reaction. At 3:25 in the afternoon, Fermi and his team achieved the world's first self-sustaining nuclear chain reaction. The tests confirmed that it was possible to produce a sustaining fission reaction using natural uranium. Had they failed, it is possible the Americans would not have developed the graphite reactor and, therefore, the Hanford Site and the B Reactor would have never existed.

THREE DAYS AFTER GIVING the green light to proceed with research on all fronts, Roosevelt entered into another important agreement. He met with Winston Churchill at Hyde Park, his estate on the Hudson, for their second wartime conference. The timing was dire—Churchill would receive word the next day that the British fortress of Tobruk in North Africa had surrendered—but on June 20, their conversation turned to atomic research. Churchill later wrote that he and Roosevelt described to each other the progress their respective scientists had made, and then Churchill made a dramatic proposal. "I strongly urged that we should at once pool all our information, work together on equal terms, and share the results, if any, between us." Roosevelt accepted.[22]

Winston Churchill during the Blitz. *(Library of Congress)*

BACK ON MAY 10, 1940—hours before the German attack through the Low Countries and with Britain's Conservative Party in crisis over the selection of a new leader—King George VI invited Winston Churchill to form a government. The larger-than-life decedent of the Duke of Marlborough had a checkered political career,* but he had shamelessly captivated public opinion since he had first participated in the Battle of Omdurman in the Sudan in 1898 and then served as First Lord of the Admiralty at the beginning of World War I. Britain was finally energized to fight a war it might very well lose.

Britain's leading scientists believed that an atomic bomb was possible, but they wondered if it was practical to develop, given the immense financial, personnel, and facility demands they faced in the

* General John Churchill had been awarded the title by Queen Anne after he led
   the Allies to victory in the Battle of Blenheim during the War of Spanish
   Succession in 1704

early months of the war. However, just as a precaution, the British government arranged to acquire the stocks of uranium ore held by a Belgian mining company in the Congo.

In August 1940—with England under German air attack during the Blitz—Sir Henry Tizard led a British mission to the United States. The Americans had never seen anything like the contents of the black enameled steamer trunk that Tizard had brought with him. It contained information on new military technologies, including radar, anti-submarine warfare, airplane design, and explosives, but he intentionally failed to share the findings of the MAUD Committee with his hosts.

England and the United States had been allies in the First World War but they still shared a mutual distrust of each other's national motives, a dislike for the other's personalities, and very different world views. England had not forgotten that the Americans had entered the First World War late and then had sought to control its outcome, nor had they forgotten that it was the American banking system and protected trade practices that had brought about the Great Depression. For their part, the Americans had no interest in protecting or prolonging the British Empire.

WHILE THE TWO COUNTRIES DISAGREED on many issues, the British and the American atomic research programs shared a singular goal and one overriding fear—that Germany might be ahead of them in what was seen as a race to build the bomb. As events transpired, they were wrong. There was no race—there was not even a real competition. But none of that was known at the time. The Americans invested immense manpower and materials in a race to be the first to get the bomb. No cause could be more urgent!

GERMANY'S ATOMIC RESEARCH PROGRAM, called Uranverein, or "Uranium Club," began in April 1939, soon after Otto Hahn, Lise Meitner, and Fritz Strassmann discovered fission. In September, the program was absorbed by the Heereswaffenamt (German Army Ordnance Office). On the surface, the Germans seemed to have many advantages in acquiring the bomb. They had access to the world's only

Werner Heisenberg in 1933.
(Bundesarchiv Bild 183-R57262 / Unknown / CC-BY-SA 3.0)

heavy-water factory in Norway and to large quantities of uranium ore from the Belgian Congo. They had a world-class chemical industry and world-class physicists, chemists, and engineers.

But they had even more serious disadvantages—many of them self-inflicted. Whereas the Manhattan Project was characterized by a well-coordinated, well-funded effort between government, science, and industry, the very opposite was true in Germany. Too many top German scientists had left Germany, either because they or their family members were Jewish or because they did not support National Socialism. Many of those scientists later came to England or to the United States to work on the Manhattan Project.

Another problem was that the Nazi program was characterized by a systematic disorganization in which government, science, and industry distrusted each other and downplayed each other's importance and motivations. As a result, communication among the various organizations and groups was poor to non-existent.

Yet another problem was that the remaining German physicists did not seem to be much interested in the potential of a bomb. Albert Speer, Hitler's armaments minister, questioned Werner Heisenberg, the chief scientist of the German nuclear program, about how physics could be applied to the development of an atomic bomb. Speer remembered, "He declared, to be sure, that the scientific solution had already been found. . . . But the technical prerequisites for production would take years to develop, two years at the earliest, even provided that the program was given maximum support."[23]

Heisenberg's efforts failed, in part, because of his decision to focus on heavy water (water that contains more than the normal amount of the hydrogen isotope deuterium) as a moderator to control the fission process, rather than the impure graphite available to Germany.

The only known source of such heavy water was the Norsk Hydro heavy water plant in Vermork, Norway. At the time, the facility was producing about three gallons a month to serve the small physics laboratory market in Europe. Both the Germans and the French offered to buy Norsk Hydro's entire supply of about fifty gallons of heavy water, but the Norwegians became suspicious upon learning of the potential future application for the product from the French secret service. The Norwegians gave the heavy water to the French who, after the fall of France, secretly shipped the entire supply to England.

The Germans occupied the facility after the invasion of Norway on April 9, 1940. The Allies repeatedly bombed it, a Norwegian commando attack organized by the British tried to destroy it in February 1943, and employees carried out acts of sabotage, but it continued to operate. On November 16, 1943, an attack by two hundred B-17 bombers finally shut the plant down for good. The heavy water on hand—more than thirteen hundred pounds—was prepared for shipment to Germany, but the ferry carrying the shipment across a lake was sabotaged and sunk along with its cargo.

Finally, and perhaps most importantly, Hitler never embraced the potential of the atomic bomb. Albert Speer—who saw Hitler frequently—later said that the idea of the bomb "quite obviously strained his intellectual capacity. He was also unable to grasp the revolutionary nature of nuclear physics."[24] Hitler was much more interested in ballistic missiles and jet fighter aircraft as a means of winning the war.

Significant work on the German project was halted in June 1942 when the army returned control of the program to the Kaiser Wilhelm Institute in Berlin. The Germans never achieved a successful chain reaction, had not selected a method of enriching uranium, and never seriously considered plutonium as a viable substitute. They were no closer to producing an atomic bomb at the end of the war than they had been at the beginning.

After the institute was partially destroyed by Allied bombing, what remained of the German nuclear program was moved to an underground beer cellar deep under a castle church near Stuttgart, where a primitive nuclear reactor was built. In the last days of the war, Otto Hahn and other scientists conducted what became known as the B8 experiments at the reactor but failed to achieve a chain reaction.

Following the invasion of Italy in September 1943, General Leslie Groves created a special team of military, scientific, and intelligence specialists that advanced through Europe with the Allied armies in an effort to discover enemy scientific developments. Their chief focus was on the German nuclear energy project, but they also investigated chemical and biological weapons and the means to deliver them. Code named Alsos—interestingly, the Greek word for "grove," and thus potentially revealing—the teams searched for personnel, records, material, and sites, evaluated their status, and

Alsos technicians dismantle the German experimental nuclear pile near Stuttgart at the end of the war. *(US Army)*

prevented their capture by the Soviet Union. Between May 1 and June 30, Otto Hahn, Werner Heisenberg, and other German nuclear scientists were captured and interned in a safe house in England where Heisenberg expressed considerable surprise upon learning that the United States had dropped an atomic bomb on Hiroshima.

The leader of the Alsos team, Lieutenant Colonel Boris Pash, later wrote:

> The fact that the German atom bomb was not an immediate threat, was probably the most significant single piece of military intelligence developed throughout the war. Alone, that information was enough to justify Alsos.[25]

But Alsos accomplished much more. It prevented the Russians from capturing the leading German atomic scientists, and it acquired a large volume of high-quality uranium ore, which was soon being processed at Oak Ridge for the first atomic bomb dropped on Hiroshima.

JAPAN ALSO CONDUCTED NUCLEAR RESEARCH aimed at developing a bomb during World War II, but its efforts were even more uncoordinated and unsuccessful than those of the Germans. The most prominent Japanese physicist, Yoshio Nishina, had been a close associate of Niels Bohr and a contemporary of Albert Einstein. In the 1930s, his RIKEN Institute in Tokyo conducted basic research using cyclotrons, which it had purchased from Ernest Lawrence at the University of California in 1932.

Nishina recognized the potential military application of nuclear fission and worried that the Americans might be working on a bomb that could be used against Japan. In 1939, he discussed the issue with Lieutenant-General Takeo Yasuda, the director of Japan's Technical Research Institute, but it was not until April 1941 that War Minister Hideki Tojo ordered the institute to investigate the possibility of atomic weapons. At RIKEN, the army's researchers focused on the thermal diffusion method of separating U-235 but had not been successful by the time the institute was destroyed by Allied bombing raids on Tokyo in March 1945.

Meanwhile, the Imperial Japanese Navy was pursuing its own research, forming a committee to explore the potential of atomic weapons, which met during July 1942 and March 1943. They concluded that while an atomic bomb was feasible, "it would probably be difficult even for the United States to realize the application of atomic power during the war" and switched its emphasis to radar.[26]

Like their other European counterparts, Russian physicists had conducted atomic research at the Cavendish at Cambridge where they focused their attention on the medical and scientific exploration of radium. Hahn and Strassmann's discovery of fission attracted the attention of Soviet scientists, and by the mid-1930s, several research centers in Russia were specializing in nuclear physics.

The largest cyclotron in Europe was located at Leningrad's Radium Institute run by Igor Kurchatov. He and other scientists successfully lobbied the Soviet government to create a commission to study uranium, investigating both isotope separation and the possibility of a chain reaction, but that effort was interrupted by the German invasion of Russia in 1941.

Georgy Flyorov, a Russian physicist serving in the Russian air force, noted that German, British, and American scientists had ceased publishing papers on nuclear science and assumed, correctly, they each had active secret research programs underway. In 1942, he wrote letters to Josef Stalin warning him of the consequences of other countries possessing an atomic bomb and urging him to develop a Russian atomic bomb without delay.

Stalin agreed but entrusted the effort to build a bomb to his Communist Party associates, rather than to the armed forces, assigning responsibility to the Foreign Ministry and the Soviet security services. It took time to acquire the trained personnel—most of whom were by then serving in the armed forces—and to organize the logistics for a large-scale research program. In practice, the party leaders proved to be inept administrators, and the atomic research program languished.

But help was available from another source. The Russian intelligence services had long been successful in establishing spy rings in both Britain and the United States. An American spy for the Soviets, Harry Gold, obtained sensitive atomic information from the British physicist and fellow spy, Klaus Fuchs. By 1945, Soviet intelligence had obtained from them a rough blueprint of the American Trinity device.

In 1945, General Leslie Groves commissioned Princeton University to write a general account of the scientific research and technical development that went into the making of atomic bombs. The report, authored by Henry D. Smyth, chairman of the physics department at Princeton, was published a year later. Its publication, more than the actual dropping of the atomic bombs on Hiroshima and Nagasaki, alerted Russians to both the power of the weapons and the scale of effort necessary to build them. Stalin realized that time was of the essence and greatly ramped up the Soviet effort.[27]

The Soviet Union detonated its first atomic bomb in August 1949, accelerating the Cold War between Russia and the western Allies and setting off an intense internal debate within Russia about the relative importance of espionage compared to the Soviet's own efforts.

BY THE MIDDLE OF 1942, the Americans—unaware that the German atomic effort had been sidetracked, were far outstripping their British counterparts in atomic research. Both efforts continued independently, still exhibiting distrust of each other but united in a common opposition to sharing the atomic secret with their Russian ally.

With regret and resignation, the British finally came to the conclusion that proceeding with their own independent atomic program was untenable in terms of cost and manpower. After many months of negotiations, an agreement was signed during the Quebec Conference in August 1943 between Franklin Roosevelt, Winston Churchill, and Canadian Prime Minister William

Mackenzie King that resulted in the British handing over the results of their own research in return for progress reports on the progress of the Manhattan Project. The leading British atomic scientists—including Chadwick, Oliphant, and Peierls—moved to the United States to work on the Manhattan Project.

Much was still unknown about the ability to actually build an atomic bomb, but a plan and the needed resources were now in place to accomplish it.

THE MANHATTAN PROJECT

BARELY SIX MONTHS AFTER THE attack on Pearl Harbor, President Roosevelt had approved the recommendation that ordered the S-1 Committee to proceed with research on all five nuclear technologies at the same time while directing the army to move forward with construction of all necessary facilities related to atomic research. The American effort to build an atomic bomb now moved ahead quickly.

The Army Corps of Engineers established an office on the eighteenth floor of the 270 Broadway building in Manhattan because it was close to the offices of the engineering firm of Stone and Webster, the army's principal contractor for the project, and to the existing research facilities at Columbia University. It was customary for the corps to name their operating districts after geographic regions, so it drew little attention when the Manhattan District of the Corps of Engineers became official on August 13, 1942. The army's chief of engineers selected Colonel James C. Marshall to lead the effort, but the naturally cautious Marshall had been unwilling to push the project ahead of what he considered other vital military priorities.[*]

Vannevar Bush quickly became dissatisfied with the slow pace of the army's effort and complained to George C. Marshall, the army's chief of staff and a member of the S-1 Committee of the OSRD, who wasted no time in making a change. On September 17, he selected the deputy chief of the corps construction division, Colonel Leslie R. Groves, just forty-six, to lead the Manhattan Project, while keeping

---

[*] Unrelated to Army Chief of Staff George C. Marshall.

Colonel Marshall on in a subordinate position. Six days later, he promoted Groves to brigadier general to give him more stature in dealing with the scientists and the rest of the government bureaucracy.

The son of an army chaplain, Groves had grown up in the army. After graduating from West Point in 1918, he was assigned to the Army Corps of Engineers. He was a dominant, controlling personality, a practical-minded military engineer, brusque, egotistical, and confident. He would later tell his associates, "If I can't do the job, no one man can."[28] He was one of those officers, like Dwight Eisenhower, whose names were rumored to be included in a list General Marshall kept of promising officers. He was named to the War Department's general staff in 1939 and was the officer in charge of building the massive Pentagon building in Washington, DC, but now, he wanted, and expected to receive, a combat command.

Groves learned of General Marshall's decision to select him from Lieutenant General Brehon Somervell, Groves's commanding officer, who cornered him in a corridor of the House Office Building after they had finished testifying before the Military Affairs Committee on the afternoon of September 17.

Taking Groves aside, Somervell said, "The Secretary of War has selected you for a very important assignment."

"Where?" asked Groves.

"Washington."

"I don't want to stay in Washington," Groves replied.

"If you do the job right, it will win the war," Somervell said, carefully choosing his words.

Groves later remembered that he responded with one word: "Oh."[29]

Groves encountered huge obstacles in his new job. One of the most serious was the fierce competition he faced for scarce government resources like money, equipment, personnel, and natural resources. Groves finally had to threaten to go directly to the president to get the War Production Board to assign its highest priority AAA rating to his projects. In turn, Groves promised not to use it unless it was absolutely necessary. He received it.

Major General Leslie Groves. *(US Department of Energy)*

GROVES DEFINITELY BELIEVED in leading from the front. He insisted on a lean organization that allowed him to make "fast, positive decisions. . . . Large staffs lead to inaction and delay," he said.[30] His deputy, Colonel Kenneth Nichols, remembered him as:

> the biggest sonovabitch I've ever met in my life, but also one of the most capable individuals. He had an ego second to none, he had tireless energy. . . . He had absolute confidence in his decision and he was absolutely ruthless in how he approached a problem to get it done. But that was the beauty of working for him—that you never had to worry about the decisions being made or what it meant.[31]

The day after he took charge of the project, Groves was on a train to inspect a fifty-six-thousand-acre site located on the Clinch River in the semi-wilderness of the Appalachian Mountains southwest of Knoxville, Tennessee. Stone and Webster had selected it as the location for the electromagnetic separation plant, the massive gaseous diffusion plant, and the pilot plutonium production reactor and related chemical extraction plant. He visited Compton and Fermi's lab in Chicago on October 3, and immediately moved on to look at Lawrence's laboratory at Berkeley.

Some of the residents at the Clinch River site were given less than two weeks' notice to vacate farms that had been in their families for generations. Officially named the Clinton Engineer Works after a nearby community, the site became better known as Oak Ridge after a nearby mountain ridge located on the site.

While Stone and Webster concentrated on designing and building the production facilities, the nationally known architectural firm of Skidmore, Owens & Merrill designed and built a residential community for thirteen thousand, which grew to seventy-five thousand by the end of the war.[32]

Oak Ridge town site during the war. *(US Department of Energy)*

Of the different isotope separation facilities constructed at Oak Ridge beginning in April 1942, the centrifuge process—similar in concept to a cream separator—was at first thought to be the most promising. Westinghouse was given the contract to build the facility. It estimated it would take fifty thousand centrifuges with three-foot rotors to produce 2.2 pounds of U-235 a day. Early tests achieved only 60 percent of that goal, and frequent equipment failures repeatedly delayed work on the pilot plant. In November 1942, the process was abandoned.[*]

---

[*] Today, this technology is used worldwide and is at the heart of efforts to constrain Iran's nuclear program.

One of the racetracks at the Y-12 electromagnetic isotope separation plant.
(US Department of Energy)

Electromagnetic isotope separation had been developed at the University of Minnesota but was most famously promoted by Ernest Lawrence at the University of California at Berkeley. It worked by using a mass spectrometer to send a stream of electrically charged atoms through a magnetic field. Since U-235 atoms are lighter than natural U-238 atoms, they could be isolated by placing a collecting pocket in its path.* However, it consumed more scarce materials, used more manpower, and cost more to build than the other methods. In spite of those drawbacks, the S-1 Committee decided to go ahead because it was based on proven technology and presented less risk.

Design and construction of the electromagnetic separation plant, designated Y-12, was assigned to Stone and Webster in June 1942, and construction began in February 1943. Giant 184-inch magnets and fourteen-ton vacuum tanks in the shape of a racetrack filled ten buildings. When there was not enough copper available to fabricate the coils for the electromagnetic machines, the army borrowed nearly fifteen thousand tons of silver bullion from its depository at West Point. At peak

---

* Natural uranium contains more than 99 percent U-238 and only .72 percent
  U-235, which is the only naturally occurring isotope that is fissionable.

efficiency, which was rare, Y-12 could separate one hundred grams of U-235 a day, but on most days, it separated only about five grams. The first precious grams of enriched uranium were sent to Los Alamos in March 1944.

By late 1944, Y-12's output of enriched uranium had fallen badly behind schedule because of serious design failures and structural flaws. And then, word arrived from the bomb designers at Los Alamos that almost three times more U-235 than previously anticipated would be needed to produce a gun-type uranium bomb.[33]

The most promising method of isotope separation was gaseous diffusion, but it was also the most challenging. The process was based on the existing knowledge that lighter atoms contained in uranium hexafluoride gas would pass through a porous membrane barrier easier than would heaver atoms, achieving partial separation of the U-235 isotope. By repeating the process over and over again, separating out a little more U-235 at each step and using many separators, U-235 could be produced in industrial quantities but at great cost.

In November 1942, the S-1 Committee granted approval to build a massive six-hundred-stage gaseous diffusion plant and housing for fifteen thousand workers in a flat valley eleven miles south of

K-25 Gaseous Diffusion Plant. *(US Department of Energy)*

Oak Ridge—a place that came to be known as Happy Valley. The plant, four-stories high, a half-mile long, a U-shaped structure consisting of fifty-four contiguous buildings, was dubbed K-25 and cost $512 million.

Work began on the plant in October 1943, which was scheduled to begin operation in April 1944 when Groves decided to limit enrichment at K-25 to 50 percent and use the resulting material to feed Y-12. Even this level of enrichment was not assured because of the problems encountered in finding a suitable barrier material in sufficient quality for the gaseous diffusion process. The decision was part of Groves's new strategy of utilizing a combination of separation methods to produce enough fissionable material for a bomb in the shortest possible time.

A second type of diffusion plant—thermal diffusion—was also built at Oak Ridge. It had been pushed by the navy and was one of the separation methods originally considered by the Uranium Committee, but after the army had been given the responsibility for the Manhattan Project, the navy was frozen out of the process. It continued to conduct research on thermal diffusion using its own funds. In the thermal diffusion method, uranium hexafluoride gas passes through a temperature gradient where the heavier molecules congregate at the colder end of the gradient and the lighter ones concentrate at the warmer end. Since hot gasses tend to rise and cooler ones tend to fall, the process can be used as a means of separation.

Groves became aware of the navy's experiments at the Philadelphia Navy Yard and decided to incorporate the method as another means of feeding enriched uranium to the Y-12 plant. He approved the construction of the $3.5 million S-50 plant in June 1944, with the stipulation that it be completed within ninety days.

The Cleveland-based H. K. Ferguson Company accepted the challenge and finished the S-50 plant in just sixty-nine days. The plant contained 2,142 forty-eight-foot-tall diffusion columns. Inside each column were three concentric tubes. The process demanded an enormous amount of steam, which was available from the adjacent K-25 powerhouse. It flowed downward through the innermost tube made of nickel, while water flowed upward through the outermost tube made of iron. Separation of the uranium hexafluoride gas occurred in the middle tube made of copper.

S-50 Thermal Diffusion Plant (dark building) located
next to the K-25 power plant on the Clinch River
at Oak Ridge. *(US Department of Energy)*

It required the combined production from all three of the separation facilities to provide enough U-235 for the first "Little Boy" atomic bomb that was dropped on Hiroshima. If America were to produce more than one bomb, there had to be another solution. Luckily, there was.

WHEN FERMI ACHIEVED THE FIRST self-sustaining nuclear reaction at CP-1 on December 2, 1942, it was assumed the pilot plant for plutonium production would be constructed near Chicago. It soon became obvious that the potential risk from the facility was not compatible with such a highly populated area, so the pilot plant was relocated to Oak Ridge. It was decided, however, to keep the research and testing facility in Chicago where Arthur Compton had created the Metallurgical Laboratory at the University of Chicago.

Groves began courting the chemical giant DuPont to take charge of the plutonium production plant as soon as he was named to lead the Manhattan Project. He knew that DuPont built its own complex plants and equipment, relied heavily on its own research and development, and had a well-established culture of safety based on its long experience of

Chicago Pile-1, drawn by Melvin A. Miller, the first nuclear
reactor to achieve a self-sustaining chain reaction.
(Argonne National Laboratory)

producing explosives and munitions. On October 30, 1942, Groves contacted Willis Harrington, a DuPont vice president and a member of their executive committee, "to discuss a matter of great military importance to the United States."[34]

Groves must have been persuasive because he met again with Harrington and other senior DuPont executives the very next day in Washington, DC. Groves outlined the plutonium project, its current status, and the need to move on to large-scale production. The DuPont executives were skeptical. They told Groves they had no experience with nuclear physics and felt unqualified to undertake the project. Groves responded that "no one was qualified and that he needed advice badly, and that in view of DuPont's broad experience, he preferred to 'hang his hat' on DuPont's opinion and judgment than to have no opinion at all."[35] Groves later wrote:

> I had decided. . . that we would have to abandon completely all normal, orderly procedures in the development of the production plants. We would go ahead with their design and construction as fast as possible, even though we would have to base our work on the most meager laboratory data.

Nothing like this had ever been attempted before, but . . . we could not afford to wait."[36]

Groves then visited DuPont's headquarters in Wilmington, Delaware, where he met with DuPont's executive committee and its new president, Walter S. Carpenter Jr., who had replaced Lammot du Pont as the company's chairman in 1940. The French historian Pap A. Ndiaye has written that DuPont's senior leadership was also skeptical and expressed serious reservations about joining the enterprise. They were keenly aware of DuPont's reputation as a "merchant of death" after being publicly embarrassed in the mid-1930s hearings of a special US Senate committee that investigated its war profits during the First World War. Groves finally had to appeal to their patriotism, telling them the Germans were working on plutonium, and if "we were successful in time, we could shorten the war and thus save tens of thousands of American casualties."[37]

DuPont chairman Walter S. Carpenter Jr.
(Walter S. Carpenter Jr. photograph, 1948, P.S. du Pont Longwood photograph collection [Accession 1969.002], P72362_1_034, Hagley Museum and Library)

On November 12, 1942, Groves cancelled the giant Y-12 centrifuge project at Oak Ridge. Work on gaseous diffusion, electromagnetic separation, and Fermi's graphite reactor proceeded. Carpenter and DuPont's executive committee agreed to build a full-scale plutonium production plant but suggested it be located as far away as possible from the population centers near Oak Ridge.[38]

At DuPont's request, a site evaluation team was formed consisting of DuPont engineers but led by Warren Lewis of the Massachusetts Institute of Technology to avoid the appearance of its being led by DuPont. It included Crawford Greenwalt, a chemical engineer and one of DuPont's brightest minds, who had been involved with the development of nylon.

They reviewed the research from Columbia, Berkeley, and Chicago regarding the various methods of building a bomb. They were present in Chicago when Fermi achieved the first self-sustaining chain reaction on December 2, 1942. Greenwalt, who would later be the technical liaison between Dupont and the builders of the first plutonium reactors at Hanford, said Fermi "was as cool as a cucumber" when the reaction went critical.[39] The report they sent back convinced DuPont's executive committee to sign a construction contract with the army on December 12, 1942.

DuPont drove a hard bargain with the government. Clearly, it sought to protect itself from any future congressional inquiry. The company refused to accept any profit from the project and only signed the contract with the stipulation that the company would be excluded from acquiring any patent rights to the process. A symbolic fee of one dollar more than expenses was agreed to. DuPont also demanded that the contract stipulate it had been drawn up at the request of the army, not the company, and it would expire within six months of the cessation of hostilities. Finally, DuPont demanded it be indemnified for any damages incurred and that a special twenty-million-dollar claims fund be created to benefit its employees who might experience problems resulting from radiation.[40]

The company also requested the contract be formally approved by the president of the United States. A summary of the company's requests was sent to President Roosevelt by Vannevar Bush on December 16, 1942, and was approved. As an extra precaution, a secret letter was signed by the government, the University of Chicago, and DuPont, spelling out in clear language the state of knowledge, the rationale for building the bomb, and the dangers involved with proceeding with the project.[41] Already well underway, the company signed a final contract with the government on October 6, 1943, effective retroactively.

In spite of its reluctance, DuPont was perfectly suited for its new challenge. Its decentralized, multi-division structure allowed it to add a new department anytime a new product line was developed. Its various divisions were largely autonomous, which allowed for extreme discretion, and even secrecy. DuPont created its new TNX division within its Department of Explosives on December 16, 1942. TNX was a code name for the plutonium project and took its name from a derivative of TNT that had been invented in World War I.

The relationship between DuPont and the scientists at the Met Lab in Chicago was often strained. Many of the scientists shared a suspicious, even hostile, attitude toward the military, and their motivation to participate in the Manhattan Project was based on their strong anti-fascist feelings.[42] When they learned that DuPont would become involved, they staged what Compton called a "near rebellion," believing they were capable of handling the development and construction of facilities on their own.[43] They resented DuPont's involvement and were concerned the company's sole motivation was to make a profit.

For its part, DuPont's corporate culture was much more aligned with that of the military. They resented the physicists who were often difficult to deal with and who focused only on the physics, at the expense of the chemistry, engineering, metallurgy, nuclear medicine, and other disciplines necessary to produce plutonium. The company was torn between an awareness it was indispensable to the success of the project and its concern over the very real corporate risks it was assuming. Crawford Greenwalt later complained that the later accounts of the project depicted the plutonium project as a triumph of the physicists when "it was one of the greatest interdisciplinary efforts ever mounted."[44]

WHILE DUPONT WAS BEING BROUGHT on board to build the plutonium production plant, the physicists at Los Alamos were evaluating different potential bomb designs. The simplest and most predictable form of a nuclear weapon was a gun-type fission bomb in which a uranium-235 bullet was shot down a gun barrel into a set of uranium-235 target rings, creating an uncontrolled critical mass that released an unpredictable but enormous amount of explosive energy. This design became known as the "Little Boy" bomb and it was this type of atomic bomb that was released over Hiroshima on August 6, 1945.

A second bomb design packed a large amount of conventional explosives around a sphere of plutonium. When the explosives were ignited, the resulting force compressed the plutonium sphere into a nuclear explosion. Because of its shape, this design was named "Fat Man." It was this type of bomb, using plutonium produced at Hanford, that was used in the Trinity test of an atomic device in the New Mexico desert on July 16, 1945, and in the bomb dropped on Nagasaki on August 9.

In February 1943, DuPont began construction of an air-cooled pilot plutonium reactor and a chemical separation plant, designated X-10, at Oak Ridge. It consisted of a pile of graphite blocks twenty-four feet long on each side and surrounded by a concrete radiation shield. A chain reaction was achieved on November 4, 1943.

X-10 Pilot Plutonium Reactor at Oak Ridge.
(US Department of Energy)

The companion chemical separation plant consisted of a series of huge underground concrete cells, the first of which sat under the reactor, one story above ground. Aluminum cans containing uranium slugs would drop into a cell containing a caustic and highly toxic bismuth-phosphate solution dissolving the irradiated slugs of uranium as they moved from cell to cell extracting a minute amount of plutonium during the process. Chemical separation techniques proved to be so successful that the first samples of plutonium were sent to Los Alamos in the spring of 1944, heavily influencing the decision to use plutonium rather than uranium in future bomb designs. If the viability of a plutonium bomb had not been successfully demonstrated, many believe the uranium bomb would not have been dropped on Hiroshima. The failure of the Japanese to surrender after the first bomb was dropped confirmed the validity of the decision to have the plutonium bomb in reserve.[45]

GROVES ALSO NEEDED to find a director for the scientists who would ultimately design and build the bomb. That person had to possess unique characteristics. Groves and the scientists came from different worlds. They found Groves overbearing and demanding. He found them theoretical and totally oblivious to the practical problems associated with building huge and complicated construction projects quickly. He needed someone to bridge the gap.

On the recommendation of Arthur Compton, he ultimately chose thirty-eight-year-old Dr. J. Robert Oppenheimer, a charismatic theoretical physicist at the University of California at Berkeley, to head up the bomb design research. Oppenheimer had arrived at Berkeley three years after Lawrence, in 1928, but unlike Lawrence who was an experimentalist, Oppenheimer was a theorist.

Oppenheimer was the son of a wealthy New York textile importer who collected fine art. He entered Harvard at eighteen and graduated summa cum laude in physics in three years. He studied at Christ Church College, Cambridge, and conducted research at Cavendish under Ernest Rutherford. In 1926, he left Cambridge for the University of Göttingen in Germany where he became friends with Werner Heisenberg, Enrico Fermi, and Edward Teller. He received his PhD at twenty-three and accepted a teaching position at the California Institute of Technology. A non-observant Jew, Oppenheimer was an ethical man who believed that man, not God, "must assume direction of his life and destiny."[46]

Already familiar with the design concepts of a bomb, Oppenheimer would be Groves's intermediary with the scientists and direct a new top-secret laboratory that would consolidate, as much as possible, all research on the bomb in one location. The thin, chain-smoking Oppenheimer was "eccentric" by his own admission, had relatively little administrative experience, had not won a Nobel Prize, and had family members who were suspected of being communist sympathizers. In spite of all that, Groves personally issued his security clearance in July 1943 over the objection of the Federal Bureau of Investigation. "I was thoroughly familiar with everything that had been reported about Oppenheimer. . . . I felt that his potential value outweighed any security risk."[47] The two formed a special relationship, understanding the bomb might be the route to future fame for both of them.

J. Robert Oppenheimer in 1944. *(US Department of Energy)*

At first, Oak Ridge was considered for the site of the top-secret atomic weapons research laboratory, but Groves wanted an even more remote location to ensure security. Oppenheimer loved the Southwest from the time he had been forced to move there for health reasons as a young man. He owned a ranch near Albuquerque, New Mexico, and recommended they look in that area. They finally selected fifty-four thousand acres of isolated (the nearest town was sixteen miles away) but stunning beauty in the foothills of the Sangre de Cristo Mountains near Los Alamos, New Mexico, for what would become known as Project Y. The land was acquired from the government and a few private owners beginning in November 1942.[48]

The Los Alamos Ranch School that had previously operated on the site provided almost fifty thousand square feet of housing plus twenty-seven miscellaneous buildings, a public school, an arts and crafts building, a carpentry shop, a small sawmill, barns, garages, sheds, and an ice house. The government enlarged it into a small town of hurriedly built apartment buildings, dormitories, and laboratories.

The Los Alamos site was so secret that only one mailbox, P.O. Box 1663, served as the address for the entire town. The location provided the scientists who worked there with ample opportunity for relaxation, but they spent most of their time at their laboratories, overcoming repeated challenges they faced in designing and developing the bomb. Teams of scientists worked on the two bomb designs at separate laboratories, designated the Gun Site and Site Y, but most residents simply referred to Los Alamos as "The Hill."[49]

GROVES HAD INITIALLY wanted to build the plutonium production reactors at Oak Ridge, but there was a problem. Fermi's original pile fit in a squash court and produced one-half of a kilowatt of energy. The scaled-up X-10 pilot reactor at Oak Ridge produced five hundred kilowatts. The new reactors would each produce at least 250 megawatts of energy.[50]

Los Alamos town with the Sangre de Cristo Mountains in the background. *(US Department of Energy)*

The dangers of an accidental release of radiation demanded that the production reactors be placed in an isolated location. Groves sent thirty-four-year-old Colonel Franklin T. "Fritz" Matthias, his former deputy manager of construction at the Army Corps of Engineers, to look for a site in the West. Like most army officers, Matthias had no background in scientific research. In mid-December 1942, Matthias met with scientists from the Chicago Metallurgical Laboratory and representatives at their offices in Wilmington to establish criteria for the site. Matthias's unauthorized notes of the meeting listed the criteria:

- A rectangle of land about 12 miles by 16 miles;
- Remote setting so that the plants would be at least 20 miles from any town with a population of more than 1,000;
- Abundant water supply of at least 25,000 gallons per minute to cool the reactors;
- Dependable power source that can supply at least 100,000 kilowatts of electricity;
- No main highway or railroad closer than 10 miles to one of the plants;
- Relatively flat terrain;
- Available fuel and concrete aggregate; and
- For security, away from either coast, and at least 200 miles from the Mexico or Canadian border.[51]

Matthias and two DuPont engineers, Gilbert Church and A. E. S. Hall, looked at eleven sites in four states and made a final selection within sixteen days.[52] They discovered what they were looking for on a clear, but cold, day on December 22, 1942, when they flew, drove, and walked over parts of a 670-square mile swath of mostly flat semi-desert shrub steppe located at the great horn of the Columbia River in southeastern Washington State. The site was huge—almost half a million acres*—and sparsely populated with about fifteen hundred people living on scattered farms and ranches

---

* About half the size of the state of Rhode Island.

and in three tiny towns, Hanford, White Bluffs, and Richland. Several hundred of the residents were Native Americans.

The nearest city of any size was Pasco—with a 1940 population of thirty-nine hundred people—located almost fifty miles away to the south. It was a major division hub of the Northern Pacific Railway, a port for barge traffic on the Columbia and Snake Rivers, and the location of two recently completed military facilities, the Pasco Naval Air Station and the army's Pasco Holding and Re-consignment Point, commonly referred to as the Pasco Engineer Depot or simply Big Pasco. Groves later wrote of Pasco: "if an unforeseen disaster should occur, we would be able to evacuate the inhabitants by truck."[53]

The site's sandy soils lay over a base of basalt rock, which created an ideal foundation for large concrete buildings. The almost unlimited availability of cold river water from the Columbia River and vast amounts of electric power from the recently completed Grand Coulee Dam, 175 miles to the north, were also major considerations in reaching their decision. It was winter, and yet the ground was not covered with snow.

Matthias and his team immediately flew back to Washington, DC, where they notified Groves on New Year's Eve that the Hanford Site was "far more favorable in virtually all respects from any other."[54] Groves confirmed their decision when he visited the site on January 16, 1943.

The government named the site the Hanford Engineer Works (HEW) after one of the small towns located there. The title itself suggested this was to be a facility dedicated not to researchers but to engineers. It was created as a manufacturing complex to produce a product—plutonium.

BY THE END OF THE WAR, more than 125,000 scientists, technicians, and support staff lived in the Manhattan Project's three secret cities. In May 2018, Martin Moeller, the senior curator of the "Secret Cities: The Architecture and Planning of the Manhattan Project" exhibition at the National Building Museum in Washington, DC, said of the three communities and the people who lived in them:

There was agreement that they needed to feel at home. They needed to have a community that felt "normal." And so during this time of national emergency, the US government built single-family houses in what we would now consider typical suburban neighborhoods, instead of just jamming all of these people into dormitories and barracks as I would think almost any other country in the world would done for time. That to me, in [and] of itself, is extraordinary.[55]

"A FREE SORT OF PLACE TO LIVE"

THE SITE THAT MATTHIAS and his team chose is located in the Columbia Basin of south-central Washington State. The landscape is characterized by uplifted ridges of basalt rock, separated by broad lowlands, most of it covered in semi-arid shrub-steppe vegetation. The dark volcanic rock that is visible in outcroppings along the ridges is the result of lava flows that erupted from deep fissures in the earth between six and seventeen million years ago. Beginning about fifteen million years ago, the Earth's internal forces squeezed the layers of basalt from north and south—a similar process to squeezing a stack of loose paper from opposite sides—to create a series of east-west trending ridges, three of which— Rattlesnake Mountain, Gable Mountain, and Saddle Mountain—are located on or near the Hanford Site. The lowlands between them are filled with layers of sediment resulting from ancient lake and river deposits, followed later by accumulations of loess, a silt-like sediment formed by wind-blown dust. Today some of these sediments are visible at the White Bluffs located along the river on the eastern boundary of the site.

The area was repeatedly flooded during the Ice Age when a massive ice sheet advanced into what is now northern Washington, Idaho, and Montana. Glacial lakes were created when large ice dams blocked the valleys of the ancient rivers. The largest of these, Montana's Glacial Lake Missoula, was almost two thousand feet deep and contained over five hundred cubic miles of water. Periodically, the ice dams would fail, sending a wall of water and icebergs downstream through eastern

Washington, scouring and reshaping the land and creating what are known as channeled scablands as the flood waters followed the course of least resistance on their way to the sea.

Further downstream, just west of the confluence of the Walla Walla and Columbia Rivers, a narrow opening in the ridges, called the Wallula Gap, so constricted the floodwaters that they backed up to create a temporary lake, named Lake Lewis, that covered the Hanford Site with up to nine hundred feet of water and depositing up to three hundred feet of sediment and even large boulders called erratics—some the size of an automobile—traceable back to Glacial Lake Missoula.[56] The last of the floods occurred at the end of the Ice Age, between thirteen thousand and fifteen thousand years ago.[57] Occasionally, prehistoric animals—most notably, the Columbian mammoth, but also including ancient bison, horses, bears, camels, sloths, and saber-toothed cats—have been discovered in these flood deposits.[58]

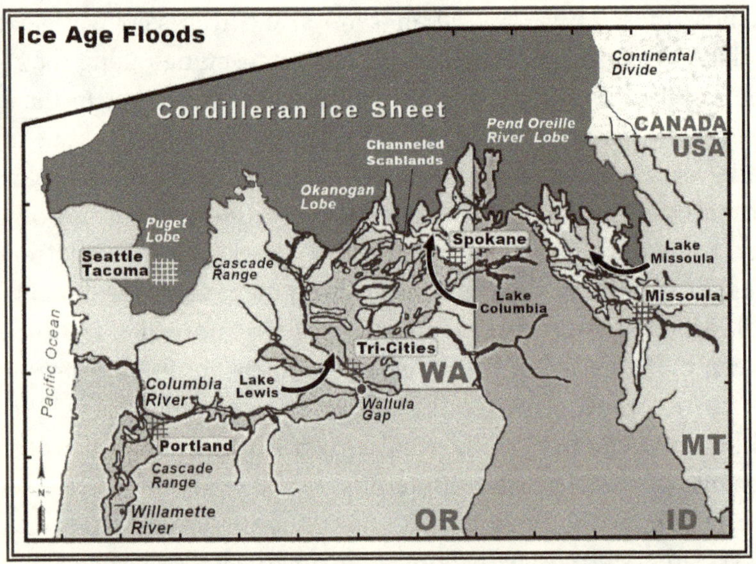

Ice Age floodwaters periodically covered the Hanford Site, backed up behind the Wallula Gap. (*US Geological Survey/Chris Picken*)

The region is a part of one of the largest natural grasslands in North America. It is referred to as a shrub steppe, taking its name from the abundant plant species that grow there and from the Russian word for a vast treeless plain. The most common shrub, or woody plant, is the

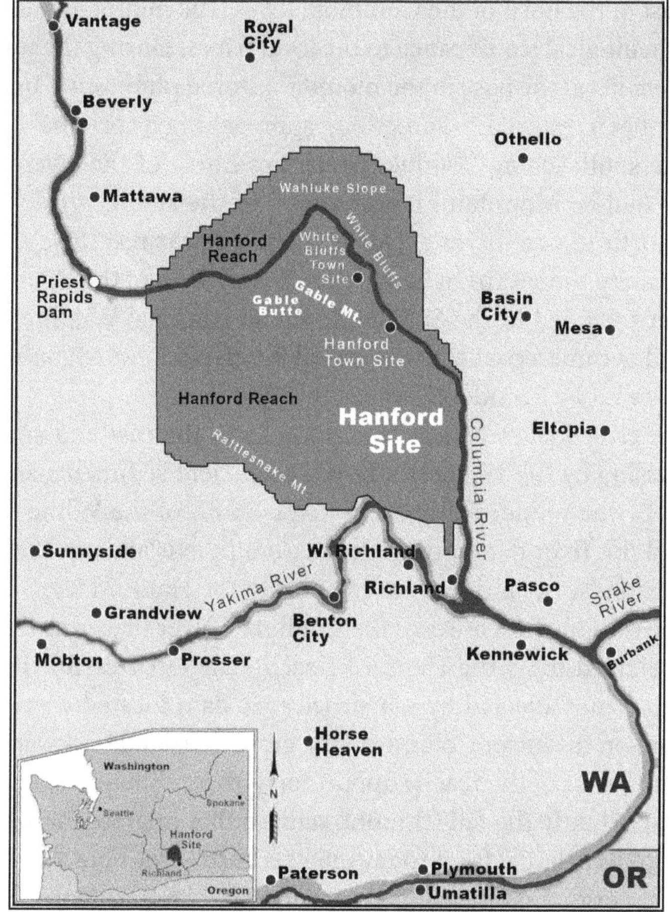

Location of the Hanford Site. *(Chris Picken)*

big sagebrush, growing in communities with grasses such as bluebunch wheatgrass and bluegrass. While arid, these ecosystems receive enough rainfall to support perennial grasses and shrubs, which distinguishes them from deserts.

The most obvious of the ridges located at the Hanford Site is thirty-five-hundred-foot Rattlesnake Mountain, located along the southwest boundary of the site, which the local Indians called Laliik (land above the water)—perhaps a reference tied to a legend when only the top of the ridges rose above the ancient floodwaters.

A second distinguishing geographic feature on the Hanford Site is Gable Mountain, which rises to an elevation of eleven hundred feet southeast of the horn of the Columbia River. The mountain has religious and archeological significance to the local tribes. During the war, underground vaults at the base of the mountain stored plutonium, but the land has now been restored to something approaching its original condition.

The south-facing Wahluke Slope lies north of the river along the flank of Saddle Mountain. It was added to the site to provide a buffer to the north in case of an accident at the nuclear reactors, which were located along the southern bank of the river. Much of the Wahluke Slope was later included in the Saddle Mountain National Wildlife Refuge in 1999 and became a part of the Hanford Reach National Monument when it was created by President Clinton in 2000.

The river makes its southward sweep to the east and south of the horn passing by the White Bluffs, whose ancient sediments are exposed to view by the modern Columbia River. South of the White Bluffs, the land and the river flatten out, creating multiple islands in the river and the flat expanse of land that covers most of the Hanford Site.

The roughly fifty miles of the Columbia River that runs through the site is referred to as the Hanford Reach—the last free-flowing section of the river not affected by a hydroelectric dam located east of Bonneville Dam on the lower Columbia. The gravel bars and backwater sloughs along the banks of the reach support forty-three different species of fish, most importantly the fall Chinook salmon that migrate there each year. It exists in its original form today only because of the objections from the Atomic Energy Commission, environmentalists, and fishermen to the building of a hydroelectric dam there in the 1970s—the AEC claiming higher water levels would raise the water table that lies below the underground tanks where nuclear waste was stored. Later efforts to protect the reach and other parts of the Hanford Site resulted in the creation of the Hanford Reach National Monument.

HUMANS BEGAN ARRIVING in the region sometime around the end of the Ice Age floods. Radiocarbon dating has identified human habitation at the ancient village of Wishram and at Celilo Falls downstream on the Columbia River going back at least thirteen thousand years. In July 1996, the skeletal remains of what became known as Kennewick Man— believed to be ninety-six hundred years old—were found along the bank

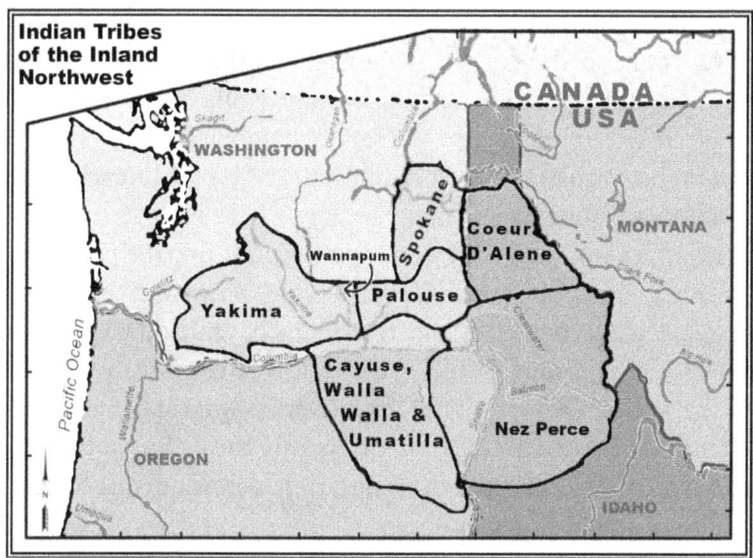

Indian tribes of the Inland Northwest showing the location of the Wanapum living along the Hanford Reach. *(Chris Picken)*

of the Columbia River in Kennewick, representing an important discovery relating to early human habitation of the area.

Before the arrival of the first Euro-American explorers at the beginning of the nineteenth century, thousands of Native Americans belonging to many different tribes lived in the region. When Lewis and Clark transited the area in 1805, they carefully counted the number of winter houses they found along the rivers, estimating how many inhabitants lived in each lodge. They determined that more than 12,500 lived in an area totaling thirty-one thousand square miles. In 1811, David Thompson of the British North West Company, paddled down the length of the Columbia from the north and estimated 13,615 Indians lived along the river.[59]

We now know at least two major smallpox epidemics decimated the native population prior to the overland arrival of the explorers.[60] These may have resulted from contact with Euro-Americans in the Midwest or Southwest, which spread north or west, or from contact with sailors at the mouth of the Columbia or along the Pacific Coast, which spread inland until it reached the Mid-Columbia.

The Mid-Columbia was the place where the mainly Sahaptin-speaking tribes of the region merged—the Yakamas to the north, the Palouse and Nez Perce to the east, and the Walla Walla and Cayuse to the south. A smaller band, the Wanapum—known as the River People—lived along the banks of the Columbia at the Hanford Reach and north to what is now Priest Rapid Dam.

The tribes followed a life of subsistence hunting, fishing, and gathering, living in permanent villages and in numerous fishing camps located along the banks of the rivers. Each year, during the annual salmon migration, they would congregate at the points of land where the Walla Walla, Snake, and Yakima Rivers flowed into the Columbia. Another favorite rendezvous point was along the Columbia River at the salmon spawning grounds at the Hanford Reach where they would fish, trade, and compete in games.

The rhythm of their lives remained relatively unchanged until the modern horse reached the region from Spanish Mexico in the early 1700s. Smohala, a Wanapum religious prophet who lived during the last half of the nineteenth century, claimed that horses did not come from the white man but had been known to Indians long before, perhaps a reference to small wild horses that once lived in the region in prehistoric times. By the time Lewis and Clark arrived in 1805, horses were common all along the Snake and Columbia.

THE FUTURE OF THE VARIOUS TRIBES changed even more dramatically with the arrival of the Euro-American explorers. By 1800, the Pacific Northwest was already clearly within the sights of the great empires of Europe. Their problems were how to gain control and exploit the vast but remote region with its abundant timber and furs and how to keep their rivals at bay.

Spain had claimed the Pacific coast of California as early as 1542, but other priorities in the New World meant California remained an imperial backwater until 1765 when Spain learned Russians were settling in northern California. Spain actively explored the coastline of what is now Canada and Alaska, discovering the availability of vast quantities of fur pelts and establishing a trading post at Nootka Sound on Vancouver Island.

North America on the eve of the Louisiana Purchase.
(C. Mark Smith/Chris Picken)

British claims to the Pacific coast of North America date back to 1579, when the British adventurer, Sir Francis Drake, sailed into San Francisco Bay. In 1788, an American ship captain, Robert Gray of Boston, discovered a large river at approximately 46° latitude but was unable to enter it because of adverse tides and currents. Gray finally succeeded in entering the river in May 1792, establishing the basis for the US claim to the Pacific Northwest.

Later that same year, Lieutenant William Broughton, serving under Royal Navy Captain George Vancouver, entered the Columbia River in his ship, HMS *Chatham*, and rowed up the river in the ship's boats as far as the present-day town of Washougal. His charts, after being published in London, eventually found their way to the new American president, Thomas Jefferson.

Jefferson believed it was America's manifest destiny to control the North American continent from sea to sea. So long as the huge swath of land west of the Mississippi, called the Louisiana Territory, remained a part of the dying Spanish empire, the young United States could bide its time. However, when France acquired it as a result of a European treaty in 1800, Jefferson realized control of Louisiana by a hostile France, or even worse, by a hostile Britain, would threaten the westward expansion of the United States.

Much to Jefferson's surprise, the French emperor Napoleon, in need of cash to finance his ongoing wars with England, offered to sell Louisiana to the United States for only fifteen million dollars. The treaty was quickly signed by Jefferson and ratified by Congress in October 1803.

Jefferson had long been interested in the West. He knew the approximate location of the mouth of the Columbia River from Gray's discovery and Vancouver's charts and drawings. He believed the Scottish fur trader, Alexander Mackenzie—whose journals he had also acquired—had discovered the northern fork of what might be the Columbia River in 1793 after a long exploration across Canada. Jefferson quickly appointed his private secretary, Meriwether Lewis, and Lewis's former military commanding officer, William Clark, to lead an expedition through the Louisiana Territory and on to the Pacific Ocean by way of the Columbia River.

On October 16, 1805, Lewis and Clark and the members of their small Corps of Discovery—including the young Shoshoni woman, Sacajawea, and Clark's black slave, York—arrived at the confluence of the Snake and Columbia Rivers, near the current city of Pasco. They had paddled down the Clearwater and Snake Rivers in unwieldy log canoes after barely surviving an ill-advised winter transit of Montana's Bitterroot Mountains. They were rescued by Nez Perce tribal members who probably spared their lives because of Sacajawea, whose presence in an important role they interpreted as a token of peace. Word of their approach preceded them as they paddled down the Snake, and they were met at the confluence of the Snake and Columbia by hundreds of local Indians who had congregated there to fish and trade during the fall Chinook salmon run.

The following day, Clark and two others paddled in a small Indian canoe nine miles up the Columbia in hopes of finding a new river they had been told about the night before. They stopped at an island located off the northern bank of the river, across from what is now the city of Richland, where they accepted a lunch of boiled salmon from the Indians fishing there. After lunch, they paddled across the river to explore the entrance to the Yakima River, which the local natives called Tapteal. Clark wrote in his journal, "This river is remarkably clear and crowded with salmon in many places. . . . Salmon may be seen to a depth of 15 to 20 feet. . . . The numbers . . . are incredible to say [sic]."[61] It was there that Clark noticed a reach, a part of river between two bends, extending to the north and noted it in his journal—today's Hanford Reach—before continuing down the river where they wintered over at Astoria before returning east in 1806.[62]

The journals of Lewis and Clark and some members of their party offer rich descriptions, physical observations, and maps and drawings of what they encountered. Their journals provide an unparalleled vision of the region, and books based on them remain important reading today.

THE EXPLORERS WERE QUICKLY FOLLOWED into the region by fur traders and missionaries. With Thomas Jefferson's active support, New York investor John Jacob Astor sent parties overland and by sea to establish the first American trading colony on the Pacific Coast at the site of present-day Astoria, Oregon, at the mouth of the Columbia River in April 1811.

Astor's main competitor in the Pacific Northwest fur trade was the British-Canadian North West Company, headquartered in Montreal. One of its partners, David Thompson, set out for the Columbia following Mackenzie's route across a system of rivers and lakes in Canada until he finally came upon the upper tributaries of the Columbia River. He and his party were the first known Euro-Americans to transit the length of the Columbia, landing where Lewis and Clark had arrived six years earlier at the confluence of the Snake and Columbia in the late spring of 1811. There, Thompson tied a British flag to a pole, claiming both the confluence and all territory to the north of it for Great Britain. On July 14, 1811, he arrived at the mouth of the Columbia River, only to discover the partially completed Ft. Astoria – already occupied by the Americans.

Britain and the United States went to war again in 1812. Astor's small trading post was no match for the power of the Royal Navy and the Americans, waiting in vain for supplies to come from New York,

Ft. Nez Perce, later Ft. Walla Walla, in 1853 with Twin Sisters and Wallula Gap in background. *(Colored lithography by John Mix Stanley, 1814-1872) Plate 42 of US House, 36th Congress, 1st Session. "Reports of Explorations and Surveys for Pacific Railroad, Vol. 12, Bk. 1" [H.Ex.Doc.56])*

agreed to sell the post to the North West Company in 1813. The North West Company was then acquired by the Hudson's Bay Company in 1821.

Following the War of 1812, the Pacific Northwest region remained in joint occupancy by the United States and Great Britain from 1818 and 1846, when the northern boundary of the United States was finally determined.* In 1818, the North West Company established a trading post at the mouth of the Walla Walla River. Named Fort Nez Perce (later changed to Ft. Walla Walla), it operated until 1857, when some of its buildings were moved inland to the new Ft. Walla Walla, an American military post built following the end of the Cayuse Indian War.

Joint occupancy of the region was characterized by the British exploitation of the local fur trade and later by the creation of a system of corporate farms tied to their local trading posts, as well as by their inability to effectively colonize the region with immigrants

---

* The current states of Washington, Oregon, and Idaho, plus a small portion of northwest Montana.

from Britain or eastern Canada. Americans, on the other hand, increasingly moved into the region, arriving either by sea or over the Oregon Trail.

Roman Catholic missionaries began arriving in 1826, following the French-Canadian trappers who were employed by the fur companies. They established a series of missions near important tribal villages and were well-established by the time the first Protestant missionaries began to arrive in the mid-1830s.

Perhaps the most famous of those were the Methodist missionaries, Marcus and Narcissa Whitman, who established a mission among the Cayuse Indians and local fur trappers and farmers who worked for the Hudson's Bay trading post and lived in the Walla Walla Valley. The mission became an important stop on the Oregon Trail during the 1840s.

After an initial welcome by the local natives, distrust and disillusionment built up on both sides. In 1847, a devastating outbreak of measles occurred among the Cayuse, killing nearly half of the tribe. The Whitmans were blamed for the disaster, and they and eleven others at their mission were massacred. Forty-seven other mission residents were taken hostage. News of the event so shocked the American public that Congress moved to create the Oregon Territory in 1848 and launched the Cayuse Indian War, which lasted from 1847 to 1855. The passage of the Donation Land Claim Act by Congress in 1850, allowed those who agreed to settle in the Oregon Territory for four years to receive 320 acres of free land, leading to more conflict between the settlers and the local tribes.

In 1855, a series of treaties were imposed on the tribes following their defeat at the hands of the US Army, opening up the land for settlement and establishing a system of Indian reservations throughout the Northwest. The small Wanapum band that lived along the banks of the Hanford Reach did not participate in war and, therefore, was not a signatory to the treaties that followed, leaving it unrecognized by the federal government. The American Civil War briefly slowed down the pace of settlement in the region, but it quickly revived as towns like Portland, The Dalles, and even tiny Wallula, located near the mouth of the Walla Walla, became important steamboat and rail stops on the Columbia River.

THE NORTHERN PACIFIC RAILWAY received its land grant from Congress in 1864 during the Civil War. By 1872 its rails had reached Bismarck, North Dakota, but had ended there when the railroad went into bankruptcy, a casualty of a major financial scandal and stock market crash in 1872. Henry Villard, a German-born, Portland-based entrepreneur who already held a monopoly on rail and steamboat transportation on the lower Columbia, had only one potential competitor—the Northern Pacific Railway. Using his European financial connections, he outbid his competitors and acquired the railroad in a hostile takeover.

Villard's goal was to change the western terminus of the Northern Pacific from Puget Sound to Portland. To achieve that goal, he restarted construction on the west bank of the Snake River at a depot-construction camp called Ainsworth, located only a mile from where Lewis and Clark and David Thompson had landed at the river's mouth. From there, he built a railroad bridge across the Snake River, allowing the line to connect to Villard's other rail holdings at Wallula, on the east bank of the Columbia. From there, the Northern Pacific later extended its route north to Spokane and, ultimately, west across Stampede Pass to Tacoma.

The Northern Pacific railroad bridge over the Snake River
and the town of Ainsworth in 1894.
(Franklin County Historical Museum)

Ainsworth proved to be prone to spring flooding and was insufficient in size to accommodate the railroad's needs, so the Northern Pacific created a new rail hub and a larger town site four miles away. The railroad's chief engineer, Virgil Bogue, named Pasco after a high desert region in Eastern Peru he had known. The railroad advertised extensively to attract settlers and immigrants to the region, extolling the area's temperate climate, long growing season, available water, and the means to ship their crops to the East. By 1940, Pasco was the largest city in the Mid-Columbia region with a population of nearly four thousand.[63]

IN ADDITION TO PROVIDING the land grant for the Northern Pacific Railway, the federal government played other important roles in the development of the Mid-Columbia region. While the Homestead Act of 1862 allowed farmers to claim land for agriculture, the Newlands Reclamation Act of 1902 allowed them to access federal funding for irrigation. In places like the arid Hanford Reach, irrigation was the only thing that made farming possible.

In 1933, President Roosevelt authorized the construction of the massive Grand Coulee Dam—the second dam to be built on the Columbia River after Bonneville. It was completed in 1942, just after the beginning of World War II. Due to wartime considerations, its output was dedicated primarily to generating power for the growing aluminum and other war industries in the Pacific Northwest and to the Hanford Site.

After the war, Grand Coulee provided electricity for the Columbia Basin Project, the largest water reclamation project in the United States. It provided irrigation water to more than 670,000 acres in an area stretching from Pasco to the north, more than one hundred miles, to Ephrata and beyond. However, those living on the west side of the river at what would eventually become the Hanford Site were not included.

SOME OF THOSE EARLY SETTLERS established ranches and small farms along the Hanford Reach. The location was remote, the climate severe, and irrigation water difficult to obtain. Efforts to dam the nearby Yakima River and provide irrigation to the area began as early as 1892, but were frustrated by a lack of funding and poor construction methods. The early settlers had used the land to graze cattle and sheep, but a series of severe winters and droughts reduced the herds. Then, the settlers had tried to grow apples but found it difficult to compete with other areas of the state. A significant drought began in 1920, and the local economy became even worse with the arrival of the Great Depression in 1929.

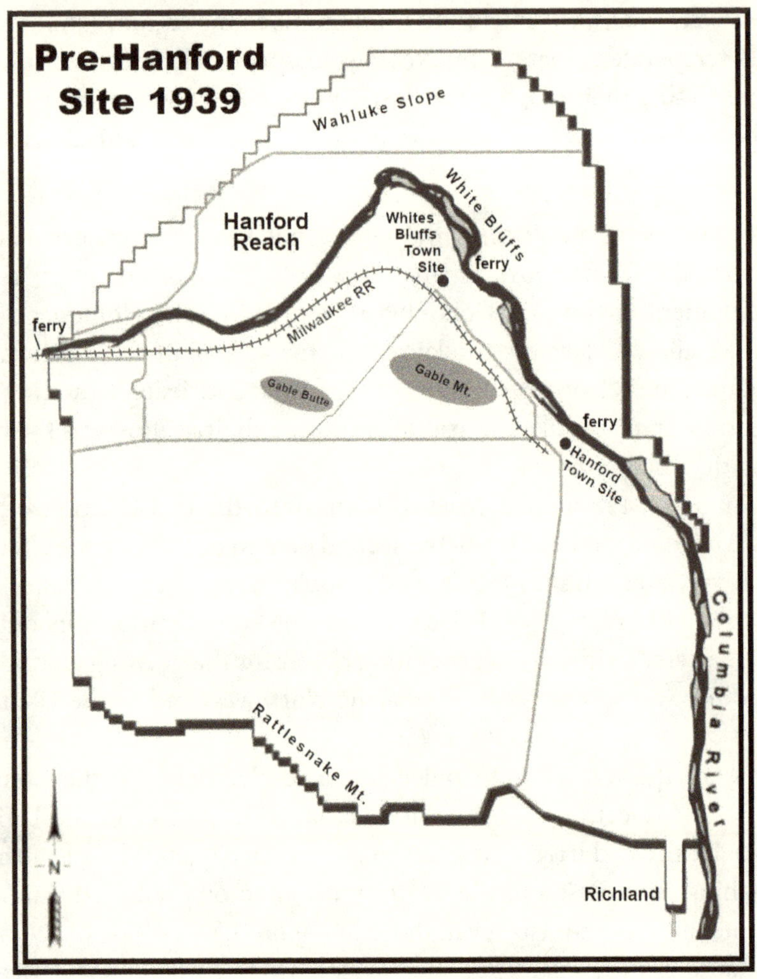

Hanford Site in 1939. (*Chris Picken*)

When the Hanford Site was selected by Colonel Matthias and his team in late 1942, most of the land was still being used to graze sheep, but around the three small towns of Hanford, White Bluffs, and Richland—with their dusty, unpaved streets and false-front buildings—there were irrigated orchards, vineyards, fields of asparagus, alfalfa, and hay, and even two thriving fields of peppermint that had been planted to support the war effort.

There had long been a fording spot across the river near the town of White Bluffs. It was a favorite fishing and camping spot of the local Wanapum tribe and, later, a favored route for travelers taking the north-south wagon road to the gold fields of the upper Columbia and British Columbia. It was also the final stopping point for the small river steamboats before encountering the Priest Rapids. A settlement was established on the east bank of the Columbia River at the river crossing in 1861 and a horse-drawn ferry soon followed. In 1894, the town moved to higher ground on the west side of the river following a devastating flood. Because of the ferry, the residents were drawn more to Yakima and even Wenatchee than to Pasco and Kennewick to the south. The town grew rapidly in the late nineteenth century but came upon hard times when commodity prices fell after the end of World War I.[64]

The town of Hanford was platted in 1907 as a real estate venture that purchased thirty-two thousand acres of land west of the White Bluffs town site with the intent of irrigating it with water pumped from the Columbia River and distributed through a network of irrigation canals. Several companies failed trying to complete the project. In 1908, the Hanford Irrigation and Power Company built a concrete pump house, now one of the few remaining pre-Hanford buildings, and began to extend power and irrigation canals to White Bluffs and Hanford. Unfortunately, settlers still had to rely on a hodgepodge of wells, pumps, and other methods of irrigation, as the desert claimed the water in the unlined irrigation canals faster than it could reach its intended customers. In Hanford, many lots remaining from the boom times remained unsold. A branch line of the Chicago Milwaukee St. Paul and Pacific Railroad (known as Sagebrush Annie) finally reached the two small communities in 1913, making it possible for the local farmers to ship their fruit and crops overnight to Seattle.

Richland, the third of the small towns, was located thirty miles to the south, near the mouth of the Yakima River, and separated by twenty miles of shrub steppe from White Bluffs and Hanford. The first cattle ranchers arrived in the 1860s. The town was platted in 1905 by W. R. Amon and his son, Howard, who had bought out two previous homesteads, naming the town for one of them, Nelson Rich, whose last name suggested a promise of future success. It was incorporated as a city in 1910. Lacking railroad access, its residents were more naturally drawn to nearby Pasco and Kennewick for

Hanford street scene, 1938.
(US Department of Energy)

access to transportation, shopping, and entertainment. Bridges built over the estuary of the Yakima between Richland and Kennewick would periodically wash out during the spring floods, further isolating the community. The town remained without a railroad until the army arrived in 1943.

Groves's land acquisition specialists began arriving in Pasco almost immediately after the Hanford Site had been approved. Because of the severe limitations of office and living space in Pasco during the war, they had to operate out of the basement of the Liberty Theater in downtown Pasco and live in people's garages. By the end of January 1943, the government had acquired almost 430,000 acres from approximately two thousand owners for a cost of approximately $5.1 million.

On March 6, 1943, all the residents of White Bluffs and Hanford received eviction notices from the government notifying them that they had thirty days to leave their land and their crops—the only form of livelihood for most—behind. It was particularly hard on those who had limited resources or were too old to start over. The residents of Richland were given a little longer because of their location at the southern end of the site. For a time, the Wanapum were allowed access to their fishing sites, but even that was soon terminated. Lloyd Wiehl, whose parents operated the White Bluffs ferry, said that the order "came like a bombshell . . . we didn't have any place to go."[65]

Some owners were anxious to sell. Others were not. They resented being told that their land was not very productive and being offered less than what they considered fair market value. The small towns were described as "lean" by the acquisition specialists, but many owners agreed with one resident who remembered them as "a wonderfully free sort of place to live."[66] Another displaced farmer, Edith Hansen, recalled, "They didn't give us much money and more or less insulted us."[67]

Some owners held out for higher prices or went to court to block the acquisition. There was no way to appeal to the court of public opinion since the whole process was top secret and local newspaper editors had been visited by stern-faced army officers who told them not to report anything having to do with Hanford, and that included reporting on litigation between the landowners and the government.[68]

CHAPTER FIVE

HANFORD AND THE B REACTOR

DuPont broke ground at the Hanford Site in March 1943, only two months after Colonel Matthias and his team had selected it and while many of the property owners were still living in their homes and the sale of their properties was being negotiated. Most of the residents—willingly or unwillingly—moved on, but some remained and went to work for DuPont. Some, whose properties were out of the way of immediate construction, were allowed to remain a little longer to harvest their crops.

The town sites of White Bluffs and Hanford were almost totally demolished. Today, only the remnants of three pre-Hanford structures remain. Fortunately, the White Bluffs bank building has been almost fully restored and is one of the stops on the DOE's popular pre-Hanford tour. Richland was more fortunate, but even there the government retained only twenty-four of the more than one hundred existing structures as being suitable for housing or other purposes.

DuPont faced three different needs—each equally important and immediate—as the massive construction project began. The first was finding a staging area for the delivery of workers and material arriving at the project site. Pasco, with its size, small airport, and the fact that it was a major hub for the Northern Pacific Railroad, served that need.

Second, they needed housing and other facilities for the thousands of workers who were arriving monthly. DuPont selected the former Hanford town site, which was still in the process of being demolished, as the location of Hanford Camp where as many as forty-five thousand construction workers could be housed and fed.

Attracting enough workers was a challenge, but keeping them was eminently more difficult. DuPont interviewed more than 262,000 candidates and hired more than 94,300 of them to obtain the maximum work force of 45,000, even negotiating draft deferments to get specific workers they wanted. The War Production Board dictated whom and where DuPont could recruit.[69] Because of the competition from the shipyards and aircraft manufacturing plants on the West Coast, the board directed DuPont to focus on the Southeast and Midwest, regions of the country still recovering from the Great Depression.

Hiring advertisement for Hanford construction workers.
(*Milwaukee Sentinel*, June 6, 1944)

Because of Groves's emphasis on security, recruitment ads mentioned only an unspecified "war construction project" in southeastern Washington, offering "attractive scale of wages" and living facilities.[70] The wages were indeed attractive. Unskilled workers could make as much as eight dollars a day, more than twice what they would typically have made in other parts of the country. Skilled workers made as much as fifteen dollars a day.

At first, arriving workers lived in tents while semi-permanent barracks and other buildings were being built by Hanford Camp. Eventually, the camp contained 131 barracks housing 24,892 men, 64 barracks housing 4,347 women, 880 smaller hutments housing 9,834 men, and 3,639 trailer lots, as well as the necessary mess halls, recreation facilities, commercial services, warehouses, and storage facilities required to serve them.[71]

The fact that women, mostly single, were also housed there caused its own problems. Prostitution and unauthorized relationships were not unknown. Essential African American workers were housed at the camp in segregated barracks, and all aspects of their life there were similarly segregated. Non-essential black and Hispanic workers were required to live in already-crowded Pasco.[72]

Hanford Camp, 1944. Columbia River in upper right.
(US Department of Energy, Hanford Collection)

Residents of Hanford Camp were provided with large portions of unrationed food and various forms of entertainment that included beer halls, movies, dances, and performances by touring Hollywood stars, all also strictly segregated. Workers received excellent healthcare. DuPont maintained an amazingly effective worker safety record. From the start of construction in March 1943 until mid-February 1945, there were only 613 major injuries reported by the more than ninety-four thousand workers hired.[73]

DuPont's third need was to build the necessary facilities for administration, services, and support activities and to build permanent housing for those workers and their families who would be engaged in those activities. Richland, on the southern edge of the site, was selected because it was considered far enough away from the production reactors to provide an adequate margin of safety for those living and working there.

Given the small size of the nearby communities and other wartime demands, there was already an acute housing shortage in the area by the time DuPont arrived. Some white workers found housing in Pasco or Kennewick or in small farming communities like Prosser and Sunnyside, as much as forty miles away, but that was not an option for non-white workers.

From the very beginning, Richland was different from any of the other atomic cities and certainly different from any other community in the Mid-Columbia. It was built from the ground up and from the very beginning was identified by DuPont and the army as a "village." Construction began in early 1943. A year later, it was home to fifteen thousand people, making it—virtually overnight—the largest city in the Mid-Columbia region.[74]

In those class-conscious times, Richland Village was designed not for construction workers, who it was felt did not want or need single-family housing, but for the middle-class operators, engineers, and administrators and their families who did. Roger Williams, a key DuPont manager, summed up Richland's prospective residents in April 1943 as "a distinctly higher type than that encountered in the usual war emergency project."[75]

However, Groves and DuPont saw Richland Village in very different ways. Groves, his eyes always on the cost of the program and on speed, wanted only the "bare essentials" provided—he had even argued, unsuccessfully, against providing hot plates in the houses that had been built at Oak Ridge—while DuPont, with its eye on the need to attract and retain skilled employees wanted to make the village as appealing as possible. The result was a compromise. While the residential streets and sidewalks (if they existed at all) were narrow—Groves had opposed workers having their own private automobiles—and fireplaces, garages, and most porches were eliminated, the houses were built with high-quality building materials and had adequate yards in well-designed residential neighborhoods.

The prominent Spokane architect G. Albin Pehrson was retained and told to create a planned community virtually overnight. Nine styles of stick-built homes—each designated by a letter and known thereafter as alphabet homes—were built between 1943 and 1945. Construction of the stick-built homes could not keep up with the demand, and they were soon joined by several styles of smaller, less desirable, prefabricated houses, which were manufactured in Portland and barged to the Tri-Cities. Single residents lived in dormitories located near the headquarters complex in the center of the village.

Richland Village in 1945 (note prefab housing with white roofs).
(Hanford History Project, Washington State University Tri-Cities)

Residents paid no local sales or property taxes within the village. DuPont provided them with all essential public services, good schools, a hospital, even free fuel for their coal-fired furnaces, and grass seed to put in a lawn. And, unlike the primary contractors at Oak Ridge or Los Alamos, DuPont was able to keep the army from enclosing the town with a fence.

Richland Village was unique in other ways as well. Since most of the residents were in their twenties or early thirties, there was much interaction and socializing among them, resulting in the town having one of the highest birth rates in the nation. The daughter of one wartime family remembered, "At one point, every woman who lived on two-block-long Falley Street was pregnant, leading residents to call the street 'fertile Falley.'"[76] Another resident later remembered:

> We were all young when we first hired in there.
> There weren't any old people to speak of in the town, and
> everybody was in the same boat. We all came in there
> with . . . the job that they wanted us to do and we all had
> our families there and everybody got along.[77]

While DuPont and the army limited each other's ability to dictate daily life in the village, neither felt a need to consult with its residents regarding important decisions. Richland residents had no political power and no representation. The army kept a close watch over them. It had a key to every house in town. Mail was censored, phone calls were monitored, and security agents were alert to any loose talk or unusual activity. Even the Richland telephone directory was classified. Military police and the FBI also maintained a presence. Workers were told their work was vital to the war effort, but they were prohibited from talking about it, even with their families. Those who were caught breaking those rules were discharged immediately.

What the residents of the village *did* have was an optimistic, active, and outgoing community spirit. They were not quite sure what they were involved in, but they were proud of the role they were playing in the nation's defense. Many of them had come from other DuPont facilities and most had at least some college education. They saw themselves as living in a classless community and living out a unique experience. They developed a singular self-image. As historian John Findlay put it, "The experience of moving to the town and living there in the 1940s made them feel like pioneers." They quickly styled themselves as "the Atomic City of the West."[78]

From the start, Hanford unions and their workers took intense pride in the role they were playing to keep the nation safe. Back in 1944, all fifty-one thousand Hanford workers contributed a day's pay to purchase a B-17 bomber for the war effort. The bomber, named "Day's Pay" as a result of a local contest, was presented to the Army Air Corps in a ceremony held at the Camp Hanford airstrip on July 23, 1944. Colonel Matthias had called it "the most effective single morale building [event] during the job."[79]

Hanford workers who donated a day's pay to purchase a B-17 bomber welcome the plane and its crew to the now-abandoned Hanford Field for its christening ceremony on July 23, 1944. *(National Archives at College Park, DuPont Collection)*

Their neighbors in nearby communities often saw them differently. They were jealous of their relative wealth and status. One Pasco resident was quoted as saying that "Richlanders are like seagulls. They're protected by Uncle Sam, they get everything for free, and they crap wherever they want."[80]

WORKERS HAD HIGH MORALE but suffered from the difficult working conditions and housing shortages, the isolation of the site, the intense security, and a lack of understanding of the importance of their work, all of which led to the high rates of worker turnover. Construction workers pulled double shifts six days a week and often on Sundays. In their off-hours, there was little for them to do except drink and sleep. Some complained about the conditions, but after living through the Great Depression, most workers were making more money than they had ever seen in their lives.

One recruiting booklet described Hanford as being "a little on the rugged side," but many workers were not prepared for what they actually encountered there. One recalled, "It was so darned bleak. If I'd had the price of a ticket I wouldn't have stayed."[81] With the loose earth disturbed by all of the construction activity, vast clouds of dust and dirt were created in even moderate winds. Sometimes the visibility was less than fifty feet. These dust storms came to be known as "termination winds" because new workers and their families, when first confronted with them, often terminated their contracts and returned home. Groves issued orders that new arriving workers be housed and fed immediately after their arrival in an effort to keep them from turning around and leaving on the same train.

The area's isolation was also a particular problem for many. Shopping and services were virtually non-existent in Richland—the government had never intended it to become a permanent city. The nearest shopping and restaurants were in Pasco, twelve miles away, accessed only by driving over the notoriously dangerous and narrow Green Bridge over the Columbia River, which connected Pasco to Kennewick. Kennewick itself was not always easy to access because of the tenuous road that crossed the estuary of the Yakima River to the Richland Y that was prone to flooding during periods of high water.

Hanford security poster. (*David Harvey,* History of the Hanford Site 1943-1990, [*Richland, WA: Pacific Northwest National Laboratory, 2000], 14)*

Groves's primary focus was on the security of the Manhattan Project. All aspects of the program were tightly compartmentalized so that virtually no one—except Groves himself—had a full picture of the scope and details of the project. That carried over to the acquisition and development of the Hanford Site. Displaced property owners were told they could not even tell their sons or daughters serving in the military that they had been forced to move. Local newspapers were prohibited by federal law from reporting on any activity at the site or any news resulting from it, including publishing public court documents involving the lawsuits resulting from property acquisition as they commonly did with other legal proceedings. Thefts occurring at HEW were not prosecuted in local courts because Matthias was unwilling to disclose the nature of what had been stolen.

Because of the shortage of skilled workers, DuPont resorted to recruiting large numbers of African Americans from southern states. DuPont felt the pay at Hanford would appeal to southern laborers who made less than white workers in other regions of the country. Of the forty-five thousand workers on the job in mid-June 1944, more than fifty-four hundred were African American. As an important division hub on the Northern Pacific Railway, Pasco was already home to black train crew members, such as cooks and porters. Historian Robert Bauman writes that state and local government officials saw the government's hiring of blacks as a "temporary expedient" and notes that Pasco officials demanded that black workers who lived in Pasco be transported to the

Black workers at Hanford. *(US Department of Energy)*

Hanford Site on separate buses and that DuPont pay to transport them back to their home states after their work at Hanford ended.[82]

In addition to the black residents of Pasco, several hundred Chinese and Japanese families lived in Pasco and Kennewick. The Chinese had helped build the Northern Pacific Railway, and some had remained. The small number of Japanese were mostly involved in farming or, like their Chinese counterparts, in retail trade and services.

On February 19, 1942, President Roosevelt signed Executive Order 9066, which authorized the internment of Japanese Americans living on or near the West Coast of the United States. In his previous job, General Groves had been responsible for building the many internment camps where the Japanese lived for the remainder of the war. The Columbia River was the dividing line between areas affected and not affected by the order. Japanese Americans living in Kennewick were sent to internment camps. Their friends and relatives across the river in Pasco were not, although most first-generation Japanese and some second-generation males living there were incarcerated.

THE ENTITIES, PERSONALITIES, AND MOTIVATIONS that were brought together to build the HEW were unique. The overriding goal of acquiring the bomb before the Germans did gave Groves and his team what amounted to a blank check approved by the president of the United States. Impossible today, HEW received no congressional oversight. It required no multiple agency approvals, no state or local governmental interference, and no environmental reviews. While Senator Harry Truman, chairman of the watchdog Senate Special Committee to Investigate the National Defense Program, was generally aware of the project, the full nature of the Manhattan Project was not disclosed to him until after Franklin Roosevelt's death when he assumed the presidency.

Groves delegated responsibility for HEW to Colonel Franklin T. Matthias, his local officer in charge, giving him full authority to make any decisions he felt were necessary. Matthias was also the person responsible for coordinating with the prime contractor, DuPont, and was the lead troubleshooter responsible for dealing with state and local governments, suppliers, organized labor, and commanders of other nearby military installations who sometimes outranked him. When those officers sometimes failed to grasp the priority and national importance of the secret project under way at Hanford, they were quickly reminded by higher authority. When an investigator for Senator Truman's Special Committee arrived unannounced at a Hanford gate, he was refused entry. Matthias called Groves who immediately contacted Secretary of War Henry Stimson, who called Senator Truman and told him to back off.

Franklin T. Matthias.
(US Department of Energy)

Matthias closely followed Groves's streamlined approach to management. His communications were "almost 100 percent oral," and he held no regularly scheduled meetings.[83] His relationship with Groves was equally informal. He later wrote, "I just told my people to talk to Groves whenever he contacted them, and to write down everything he said—and then come and tell me about it."[84]

Matthias generally received high marks for his working relationships with state and local government officials and with organized labor. The local Building Trades Council in Pasco set aside jurisdictional boundaries and gave Matthias a no-strike pledge during the duration of the war. The four longest work stoppages at Hanford lasted a total of twenty-eight hours.[85]

THE DUPONT COMPANY WAS equally unique. While the army's simplified organization chart for the Manhattan Project could fit on a standard sheet of paper, DuPont's organization chart for Hanford was twenty-four feet long.[86] The company had originated and used the critical path method of project planning since at least 1940. It understood that once it became involved in the Manhattan Project, the program's success or failure would affect the future of the company. Therefore, DuPont assigned its best people to the project.

HEW was by far the largest and most complicated project that DuPont had ever undertaken. Much of the design and engineering had never before been attempted at that scale. Between March 1943 and the end of the war, the company built three nuclear reactors, two chemical separation plants, and 554 other buildings, as well as Hanford Camp housing forty-five thousand people and Richland Village housing for almost sixteen thousand. The fleet of buses needed to carry the workers between their housing and their jobs was reported to be larger than the city of Chicago's at the time.[87]

Crawford Greenwalt had been part of the original DuPont team that had reviewed the plutonium production program for Groves. He had been present when CP-1 reactor went critical in Chicago. It was his responsibility to translate the scientific information from the physicists at the Met Lab in Chicago to the DuPont engineers and chemists who were actually building the reactors and chemical separation facilities at Hanford. Sometimes the information flowed in reverse with Greenwalt having to explain to the scientists why something couldn't be built the way they wanted and requiring them to come up with a new solution. He was so successful at his job that he later became president and CEO of DuPont after the war.

Matthias and his local DuPont counterpart, Field Project Manager G. P. ("Gil") Church, who had been a member of the original site selection committee, established a close personal and working relationship. Matthias would later write, "We two 34-year-olds promptly established a working, team relationship that pervaded our developing

DuPont Field Manager G. P. "Gil" Church with General Leslie Groves in 1944.
(US Department of Energy)

organizations, dedicated to the single objective of fast and efficient construction of the project."[88]

In addition to the reactors, chemical separation plants, and more than five hundred other buildings, DuPont also built a massive water treatment plant capable of supplying enough domestic water for 1.3 million people, 386 miles of new roads, 158 miles of railroad track (it had already acquired the "Sagebrush Annie" branch line of the Milwaukee Road, which served White Bluffs and Hanford), more than fifty miles of electrical transmission lines, four substations, and railroad, automobile, and electrical maintenance facilities. Hundreds of miles of fencing were installed. Construction consumed forty thousand tons of structural steel and 780,000 cubic yards of concrete. Virtually everything had to be built from scratch. The estimated cost of the wartime construction was $230 million.[89]

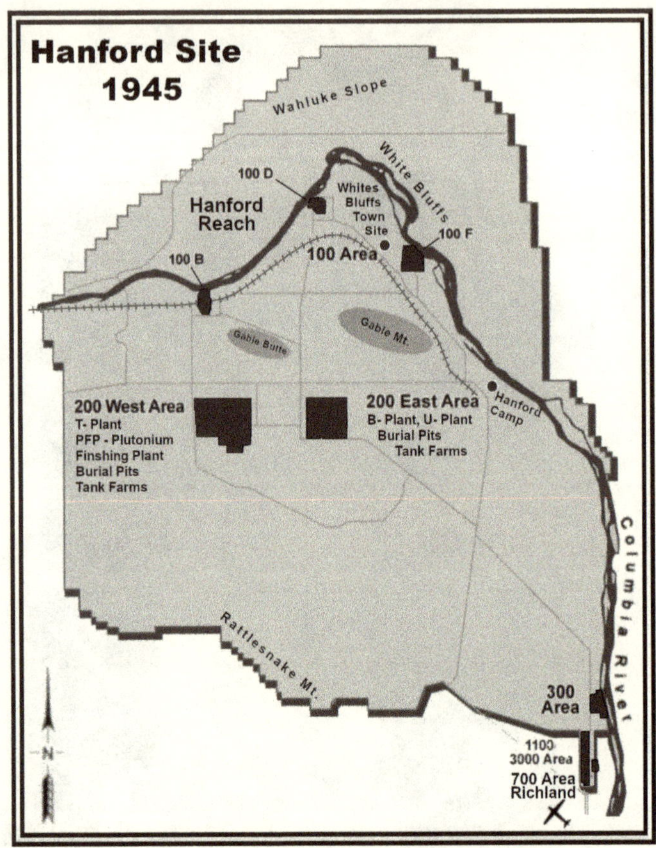

The Hanford Site in 1945. *(Chris Picken)*

FOR SAFETY REASONS, the production reactors were built near the horn of the Columbia River, several miles apart from each other. Preliminary construction on the first reactor, designated 105-B, began on June 10, 1943, just a month before the invasion of Sicily and before the blueprints for it had even been finalized.[90] Excavation of the site began in October, and it was completed and ready for operation in eleven months, although work on the related water, electric, rail, and other infrastructure continued.[91]

During construction, it was not unusual for workers to receive hand-written notes or sketches to guide them through that day's work. Many of the specialized tools needed to build the project hadn't been invented, so skilled craftsmen often designed and built

Workers load uranium slugs into the face of the B Reactor.
(US Department of Energy)

them as they were needed. Since computers were not yet available, calculations were made using slide rules or a pencil and paper. By late 1943, twenty-five thousand people were working at the Hanford Site, along with a few remaining farmers who were still bringing in their crops and trying to stay out of their way.

The reactor's design had been created by Eugene Wigner, one of the Hungarian physicists who had worked on the Einstein letter, working with Compton, Szilárd, Fermi, and the rest of the plutonium researchers at the Met Lab in Chicago. The reactor's core, thirty-six by twenty-eight feet, lay on its side and consisted of a pile of more than seventy-five thousand stacked graphite blocks thirty-six feet tall, penetrated through its entire length by 2,004 aluminum tubes. Two hundred tons of natural uranium slugs—each eight inches long, an inch and an half in diameter, and weighing eight pounds—would fill the tubes.[92] The slugs were encased—canned was the term of art—in aluminum, a necessity to prevent radioactive contamination of the cooling water and to prevent water from contacting the uranium slug. The canning process needed to be perfect—no gaps or spaces of any kind—to ensure proper heat transfer from the uranium to the water. Earlier problems in perfecting the process had been discovered, but fortunately, they were solved in time for the initial operation. The natural uranium slugs were only slightly radioactive and could be handled by operators with relative ease with no radiological control requirements needed to assure safety. However, once the slugs had been irradiated, they became highly radioactive.[93]

The irradiated slugs of uranium were pushed out the back of the graphite pile as new slugs of uranium were inserted into the front. The thermally hot, and now highly radioactive slugs, fell into a twenty-foot-deep pool of water located behind the pile where they were held for sixty-days while the most intense radiation decayed

B Reactor in operation 1944. Note large water treatment plant on left.
(Hanford History Project, Washington State University Tri-Cities)

away. Then they were transported in shielded rail cars to one of two chemical separation plants located near the center of the Hanford Site.[94]

The chain reaction was controlled during normal operation by the operator withdrawing or inserting one or more of the nine horizontal control rods. To assure the safe shutdown of the reactor, there were two more safety systems at the top of the reactor. The first was a series of vertical safety rods that could be dropped quickly into the reactor while the second was a hopper of boron balls that could also be dropped into the reactor. Boron was used because it captures neutrons, stopping the chain reaction.

Unlike the X-10 pilot reactor at Oak Ridge, which was air cooled, the production reactors at Hanford were cooled with water pumped out of the Columbia River and treated in massive water treatment plants located next to each reactor. The water was then pumped through the process tubes, which contained the slugs of uranium at a rate of twenty-seven thousand gallons a minute—enough to meet the needs of a city of four hundred thousand people.[95] This increased over the years as the power of the reactor increased. After passing through the reactor, the water was discharged into a retention basin where it was held for several hours to allow short-lived nuclides to decay before being released back into the river. *

Huge chemical separation facilities were located about four miles away from the reactors and screened from them by Gable Mountain in the central plateau of the Hanford Site known as the 200 Area. The buildings were known as "Queen Marys" because of their size—860 feet long, sixty-five feet wide, and eighty feet high.[96] By the end of 1943, only the shells of the giant buildings had been constructed. There was no rush to complete them as long as the reactors were not operating and producing plutonium.

DuPont had never designed a chemical plant in which all the processing work had to be done remotely. Although there were many unknowns, different separation methods were evaluated and

---

* A nuclide is a distinct kind of atom or nucleus characterized by a specific
    number of protons and neutrons

then reduced to two in early 1943. In June, the bismuth phosphate process was selected, and research intensified as researchers tried to better understand its properties and characteristics.[97] Since both the process and the discovery of plutonium were new, almost nothing was known about the physical aspects of the compounds being used that would chemically transform the irradiated uranium into a liquid state. After the processing, an overhead crane remotely syphoned the resulting solution through a series of large concrete cells lined with stainless steel where it was subjected to specific chemical treatments and centrifugation, separating the plutonium from the uranium and other unwanted products before leaving the plant as plutonium nitrate paste, which was then shipped to Los Alamos.

The process created significant quantities of highly radioactive liquid waste products that were stored indefinitely in sixty-four specially designed single-shell, underground tanks. To protect the safety of the workers, a whole new field of environmental and biological research was created, including radiation monitoring programs, routine blood tests, and a requirement that those workers employed in highly radioactive and contaminated areas leave a

The 221-T chemical separation plant under construction in 1944.
(US Department of Energy)

urine sample on their door steps once a month for analysis. While permissible personnel exposure standards today are more restrictive than they were in 1943, Hanford's safety record was extraordinary.

The health and safety of the workers was a prime consideration, especially with respect to radiation. Led by medical physicist Herbert M. Parker, an extensive health physics program was established at Hanford Laboratories. Everyone entering the protected areas was given a film badge to wear, and many were also provided with additional radiation monitoring devices known as pocket ionization chambers, or pencils. Numerous safety measures were also incorporated into the design of the reactors and chemical processing plants, and operations were controlled to minimize exposure to radiation. To ensure safety and account for unknown factors, the permissible radiation exposure limits used at Hanford were one-tenth of those recommended by the National Council on Radiation Protection at the time.[98]

The first of the separation plants, 221-T, was completed in early December 1944. On February 3, 1945, the first precious batch of plutonium produced at Hanford was personally transported by Matthias and a security guard by car along the Columbia River to Portland in a plain wooden box about fourteen inches square. Inside the box was a leak-proof stainless steel flask containing 3.5 ounces of plutonium slurry. At Portland, they boarded a train to Los Angeles, where Matthias turned it over to a courier from Los Alamos.[99]

The 300 Area, located along the river just north of Richland, contained equipment fabrication shops, repair and maintenance buildings, and research and development facilities that were used to develop and fabricate the aluminum jackets for the solid slugs of uranium. The 1100 Area was located in North Richland in an area now operated by the Port of Benton. It contained rail and truck repair shops, warehouses, and other similar facilities. The 700 Area was located in downtown Richland and contained the headquarters buildings for the site, dormitories, the hospital, laundry, and other support facilities.

WORK ON THE B REACTOR was finally finished by August 19, 1944, less than two years after Fermi and his team had achieved the world's first chain reaction in Chicago and about thirteen months after the start of construction at Hanford. Enrico Fermi personally supervised the first loading of uranium slugs into the reactor on September 18, a month before the US invasion of the Philippines. DuPont's Crawford Greenwalt was there. He had witnessed the first chain reaction in Chicago. So was Leona Marshall Libby, then twenty-five and the only female member of Fermi's team, who remembered that "some of those who had worked so hard for so many months" smelled "pleasantly of a drink or two of good whiskey."[100]

Fermi directed the removal of the control rods, as he and the others watched the power level of the reactor climb to nine million watts—a fraction of the reactor's 250-million-watt-design capacity—stall and then slowly die. The same thing happened the following day. Was it possible something that had cost so much and consumed so many valuable resources didn't work?

Something was poisoning the nuclear reaction. Fermi, Libby, and others quickly determined the cause was an isotope of the element xenon, a byproduct of nuclear fission, which was able to capture enough neutrons to slow and then stop the reaction, although the reactor could be restarted about twelve hours later after xenon decayed. This effect, known as poisoning, had not been detected at the Oak Ridge pilot plant because of its much smaller size (1 megawatt compared to 250 megawatts).

The problem was resolved quickly because DuPont's conservative engineers had earlier made a decision to build the reactor core to accommodate a larger number of uranium slugs than its designers had thought necessary. As a result, Fermi and DuPont's operators were able to load additional slugs of uranium into the pile, overcoming the effect of the xenon and sustaining the reaction.[101]

The problem was a perfect example of the earlier conflicts that had occurred between the physicists and the engineers. DuPont had no background in nuclear physics and generally deferred to the physicists at the Met Lab. Wigner's design was elegantly economical. He had originally designed the reactor core to contain 1,504 tubes. DuPont's corporate culture systematically incorporated margins of safety that

B Reactor Control Room. *(US Department of Energy)*

sometimes slowed down construction but often prevented later problems. The scientists in Chicago had vigorously protested when DuPont decided to use the corners of the pile to increase the number of tubes to 2,004. During startup, Fermi and his team had loaded only the original number of tubes. When the additional 500 tubes were loaded, the reactor climbed to full capacity and stayed there.[102] DuPont's decision saved the government from having to rebuild the first three reactors at huge additional cost and the loss of critical time that, most likely, would have resulted in the decision to invade Japan.

The first test of irradiated uranium fuel was made in November, and full production began in December while the Battle of the Bulge still raged in the Ardennes Forest. This provided the first fuel to be processed in T Plant in early 1945, which produced the plutonium nitrate delivered to Los Alamos in early February 1945. When D and F Reactors came on line in early 1945, it became immediately clear that Hanford could produce plutonium at a rate necessary to sustain nuclear weapons production, which later led to the decision to expand Hanford's production capabilities in the Cold War.[103]

IN THE CLOSING MONTHS OF 1944, it became obvious to the decision-makers that the United States would be able to produce, and probably use, an atomic bomb during the war. With the war in Europe winding down following the defeat of the German armies after the

Battle of the Bulge, what had previously been somewhat theoretical, ethical, and geopolitical decisions regarding the use of the bomb now became very real. Scientists, many of whom were refugees from Nazi-occupied Europe, had assumed the bomb would be used against Germany. Now, some of them began to have second thoughts about using the bomb against others.

Russian armies had invaded Eastern Europe and showed no sign of withdrawing after the war was over. If the device worked, could the Allies use the implied threat of the bomb to force better behavior on the part of the Russians? And what about the Japanese? Fierce battles in the Philippines and on Saipan and Okinawa showed that the Japanese would fight to the last man, and those battles were just a taste of what the Allies could expect with an invasion of Japan, scheduled to begin on November 1.

Could the bomb end the war and prevent what would almost certainly be unacceptable levels of Allied casualties? Tokyo and other Japanese cities were already being systematically destroyed by American fire bombing, and the number of targets suitable for the atomic bomb was running out without any appreciable decrease in the resolve of the Japanese government to fight on. There could be no answers to these questions unless the bomb—particularly the plutonium "Fat Man" bomb—worked. There had to be a test to find out.

President Roosevelt died on April 12, and his vice president, Harry Truman, who had not yet been informed of the details of the atomic bomb project, became president of the United States.

As the new president was briefed on the Manhattan Project and the proposed use of the bomb, his advisors struggled over the ethical and practical questions over sharing the secret of the bomb with the Soviet Union. Secretary of War Stimson and Groves briefed the new president on the status of the atomic bomb program on April 27, and the decision was made to generally inform the Soviets about the existence of the bomb if the upcoming testing of the device was successful.[104]

Unbeknown to the Americans, the Russian premier, Joseph Stalin—as a result of a Russian spy network working inside the program—already knew almost as much about the bomb as Truman

Full-size model of the "Fat Man" plutonium bomb.
(US Department of Energy)

did. One such spy, Theodore Hall, had worked on the development of the bombs at Los Alamos and provided the Russians with the specifications of the bomb dropped on Nagasaki. Another, Klaus Fuchs, was a physicist who had joined the German communist party before fleeing to Great Britain in 1933 and worked on the British atomic research program. In 1943, he was one of the British scientists who moved to the United States to work on the Manhattan Project. Fuchs's particular benefit was the fact he worked at Los Alamos and was therefore able to interpret and understand the information he was stealing.

On May 1, German radio announced Adolf Hitler's suicide amid the ruins of Berlin, and Germany surrendered six days later. The war now shifted to the Pacific.

No one doubted the "Little Boy" U-235 bomb would work. Indeed, the world's only uranium bomb was already on its way to the Pacific, and Groves had already convened a committee to recommend Japanese cities as its targets. But it had taken all the weapons-grade uranium that the massive separation facilities at Oak Ridge could produce to scrape together enough uranium for this one device. If there was going to be a second atomic bomb anytime soon, the plutonium "Fat Man" bomb had to work. The future of the war and its aftermath rested on the success of a full-scale test of the device, code-named "Trinity."

By July 1945, enough plutonium was available from the reactors at Hanford to conduct a test of the plutonium device, nicknamed "The Gadget" by the scientists who worked on it. The test site chosen was at an Army Air Corp bombing range in Alamogordo, New Mexico, 230 miles south of Los Alamos.

On July 12, Groves visited Hanford, along with Vannevar Bush and James Conant, the chairmen of the Office of Scientific Research and Development and the National Defense Research Committee, respectively, on their way to the test site. Sensing that a test was imminent, Matthias asked Groves if he could come along.

"Hey, I'd like to go down with you and see the test."

Groves pleaded innocence and replied, "What ?"

Vannevar Bush, James Conant, and General Groves visit Hanford on July 12, 1945, on their way to the Trinity test in New Mexico. Colonel Matthias, *right*, wanted to go along. *(Visitors to Hanford Engineering Works, 1958, DuPont Company Product Information photographs (Accession 1972.341], 1972341_3940, Hagley Museum and Library)*

Then he relented and told Matthias the real reason he couldn't go. "I'm not going to let you or Nichols go because you are running production. If we lost you it would be a lot worse for the program than if I got killed."[105]

Indeed, Groves had been asked to limit his guest list to ten. They included himself, Oppenheimer, Bush, Conant, and Sir James Chadwick visiting from England, some other physicists, and Groves's personal aide.

Anxiety was high as the day of the test approached. There were numerous problems. A preliminary test using tons of conventional explosives had failed. The necessary components were late in arriving at the test site. Groves had ordered a massive steel containment vessel called "Jumbo" at a cost of twelve million dollars to contain the explosion and allow the rare plutonium to be recovered in case the device failed to detonate properly. In the end, it was deemed unnecessary. Even the weather had failed to cooperate as thunderstorms pummeled the test site until hours before the test. Groves became irritated when Fermi offered to take bets among those present on whether the test would ignite the atmosphere and destroy the planet.[106]

On 5:29 a.m. on July 16, 1945, the first explosion of a nuclear device took place, ushering in the atomic age. Physicist Norris Bradbury, who would replace Oppenheimer as director of the Los Alamos lab, wrote: "Most experiences in life can be comprehended by prior experiences, but the atom bomb did not fit into any preconception possessed by anyone."[107]

The pressure to conduct the test as planned on July 16, 1945, had been immense. President Truman had delayed the start of the Potsdam Conference—the last meeting of the Allied leaders during World War II—until July 17 to learn the results of the test before telling Stalin about the bomb, and then only if it had been a success.

Evidence of the Trinity test showed up at an unexpected source. Nineteen hundred miles away in Rochester, New York, Kodak began to receive a flood of complaints that film produced in two of its Midwest plants was experiencing unexplained spotting and fogging. Julian H. Webb, a physicist in Kodak's research department,

Trinity test, July 16, 1945. *(Los Alamos National Laboratory)*

determined that the spots on the film were caused not by radium or any other naturally occurring radioactive material but by "a new type radioactive contaminant not hitherto encountered." What was the source of this unknown radioactive material? It is highly unlikely that Webb had knowledge of the Trinity test when he was conducting his research in 1945, but a report he wrote for *Popular Mechanics* magazine in 1949 made the connection abundantly clear. "The most likely explanation of the source of this radioactive contaminant appears to be that it consisted of wind-borne radioactive fission products derived from the atom-bomb detonation in New Mexico on July 16, 1945."[108]

One who *did* know about the Trinity test was becoming increasing concerned about the use of the bomb against innocent civilians. Leó Szilárd had probably thought more about the consequences of the atomic bomb than anyone else. Groves had never trusted his activism and at one point had considered interning him as a security risk. Concerned about actually using the bomb against civilians, Szilárd, Nobel laureate James Franck, and others who had worked at the Met Lab in Chicago wrote a report which accurately predicted the postwar arms race and recommended a series of international controls that might prevent it. It was signed by 155 scientists and released on June 11, 1945. With the war in the Pacific rapidly reaching its climax and the invasion of Japan pending, the report was largely ignored.

CHAPTER SIX

WAR AND PEACE

IT WAS ONE THING to develop the massive facilities needed to build the atomic bomb; it was completely another matter to find the means of delivering it to a target.

The solution was the Boeing B-29 Superfortress, a four-engine, high-altitude, state-of-the-art, heavy bomber. Like the bomb itself, the B-29 was an engineering marvel, featuring such new innovations as a pressurized cabin, dual-wheeled tricycle landing gear, and an analog computer-controlled system to direct the fire from its four remote machine-gun turrets that could be operated by a single gunner. At a cost of more than three billion dollars for design and production, it was the single most expensive weapons project of World War II, exceeding the cost of the Manhattan Project by between $1 billion and $1.7 billion.[109]

The B-29 was also one of the largest aircraft developed up to that time. With a flight crew of eleven, it measured ninety-nine feet in length, had a wingspan of 141 feet, and had a tail as tall as a three-story building. It was designed to have a maximum speed of 357 mph, a cruising speed of 290 mph, a range of 3,250 miles, and a bomb load of up to 20,000 pounds.[110]

The Seattle-based Boeing Airplane Company began work on the design in 1938 at a time when a war in Europe appeared likely. The US Army Air Corps had no funding for the project, so Boeing continued the development as a private venture.

In December 1939—two months after the creation of the Uranium Committee—the air corps issued a formal specification for what it called a "super bomber," capable of delivering twenty thousand pounds of bombs to a target located 2,667 miles away at a speed of four hundred miles per hour. Because of its previous work on the design and the overwhelming success of its earlier B-17 bomber, the company received an order for two flying prototypes in August 1940. A further 250 planes were ordered in May 1941, and this order was expanded to 500 planes in January 1942 after the Japanese attack on Pearl Harbor. The first prototype made its maiden flight from Seattle's Boeing Field on September 21, 1942.

Early prototype of the Boeing B-29 Superfortress. *(US Air Force)*

The plane soon encountered serious developmental problems because of its state-of-the-art design. Several of the prototype models crashed, one killing its entire crew. After Pearl Harbor and the German and Italian declarations of war, the pressure placed on Boeing to produce the B-29 was similar to the pressure placed on the Manhattan Project to produce the bomb. Four huge assembly plants were built in Seattle; Wichita, Kansas; Marietta, Georgia; and Omaha, Nebraska to produce the plane. Early models of the B-29 suffered chronic engine problems, and an entirely new engine had to be designed and manufactured. Change orders came so often that planes were flown from the production plants to modification depots for extensive rebuilds to incorporate the latest changes before being put in service. By the end of 1943,

Boeing had delivered nearly one hundred B-29s to the air corps, but only fifteen of them were airworthy. Facing similar deadlines to the Manhattan Project, 150 of the planes were modified during a five-week period between March 10 and April 15, 1944.

With the war in Europe winding down and air fields in England, Italy, and North Africa already crowded with Allied bombers, it was decided to use the B-29 primarily against Japan. Long-range operations began from bases in mainland China against the Japanese home islands in June 1944. That same month, US forces invaded Tinian in the Mariana Islands, Saipan, and Guam, which were secured by August at great cost of life and of warships lost or damaged by Japanese kamikaze attacks.

US Navy Seabee construction battalions immediately began to build airbases suitable for handling the B-29 on the newly captured islands, eventually building five major air fields in the newly captured Northern Mariana Islands, each capable of handling 180 B-29s.

The massive firebombing of Japan's major cities—built primarily of wood—including the Japanese capital of Tokyo, began in February 1945 at the same time Frank Matthias was delivering the first plutonium from Hanford to Los Alamos. Before long, the only cities that remained on the target list were either historically significant or were unsuitable for incendiary bombs for one reason or another.

The American invasion of the Philippines, which had begun in October 1944, turned into a lengthy series of bloody battles that continued until the final Japanese surrender on September 2, 1945. The Battle of Leyte Gulf broke the back of Japanese naval power in the Pacific, but the Japanese army was a difficult and relentless foe, often fighting to the last man before committing suicide rather than being captured.

Capturing Saipan was even bloodier. The invading Marines suffered thirteen thousand casualties, of which three thousand died. Almost the entire Japanese garrison of the island—almost twenty-nine thousand troops—died while twenty-two thousand Japanese civilians jumped off cliffs and into the sea rather than surrender.[111]

The battle for Okinawa lasted from April 1 to June 21, 1945. It was the largest and bloodiest battle of the Pacific, with more than one hundred thousand casualties suffered by the Japanese military. Nearly 150,000 Okinawans were killed, committed suicide, or went missing—about half of the pre-war population of the island. Allied casualties were more than seventy-five thousand.[112] At the height of the battle, on April 12, 1945, President Franklin Roosevelt died after twelve years in office. Six days earlier, he had named Douglas MacArthur to command all ground forces in the Pacific.

The experience of fighting the Japanese in the Philippines, in Saipan, and on Okinawa gave pause to the planners of Operation OLYMPIC, the planned Allied invasion of Kyushu—the southernmost of the Japanese home islands scheduled to begin in November—and later to Operation DOWNFALL, the invasion of the remainder of Japanese home islands. The invasion was scheduled to involve more than six million US and Allied troops, many of them transferred from Europe after Germany's surrender. They would face more than 4.3 million regular military and 31 million conscripted Japanese defenders. Allied intelligence estimated that Allied casualties in the first ninety days of the battle would exceed 113,000, more than a thousand a day.[113] In addition to casualties suffered by the invading troops, it was later learned that the Japanese planned to kill all their Allied prisoners when the invasion commenced.

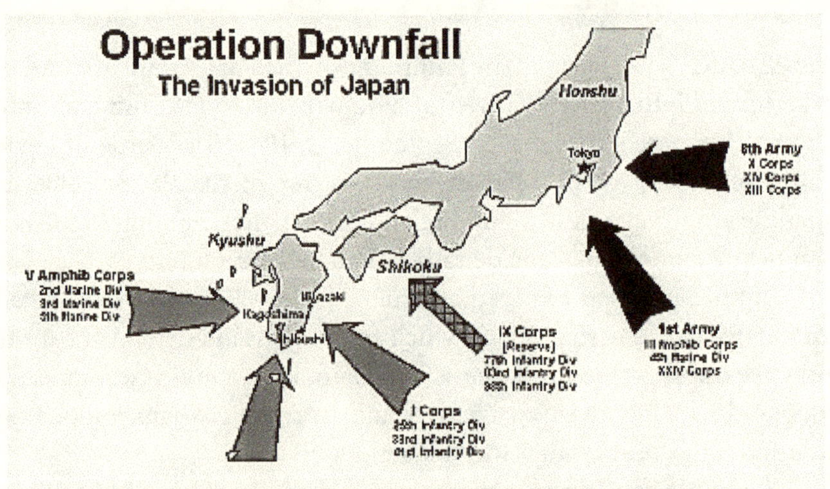

Operation DOWNFALL, the scheduled invasion of Japan.
(US Army Corps of Engineers)

The Joint Chiefs of Staff in Washington began to seriously question whether the American public would accept these levels of casualties. An alternative strategy, favored by the navy, consisted of a combination of aerial bombardment and blockade aimed at starving the Japanese into submission. That approach was tempered by the fact that Allied bombers had already virtually leveled every major city with no apparent impact on the willingness of the Japanese to fight on.

Back in May, a special Interim Committee had been created to advise President Harry Truman on the future uses of nuclear energy. Chaired by Secretary of War Henry Stimson, it consisted of former senator and Truman confidant—and soon to be his secretary of state—James F. Byrnes; Ralph A. Bard, the under secretary of the navy; Assistant Secretary of State William L. Clayton; Vannevar Bush; Karl T. Compton; James B. Conant; and George L. Harrison, a special assistant to Stimson and president of the New York Life Insurance Company. Serving under it was a scientific panel, consisting of Arthur Compton, Enrico Fermi, Ernest Lawrence, and J. Robert Oppenheimer, which provided advice both on the physical impact of the bomb as well as on its military and political consequences.

On June 1, the committee met with Stimson absent and Byrnes leading the discussion. According to the minutes of the meeting recorded, "*Mr. Byrnes recommended,* and the Committee *agreed,* the Secretary of War should be advised that . . . the present view of the Committee was that the bomb should be used against Japan as soon as possible; that it be used on a war plant surrounded by workers homes; and that it be used without warning."[114] Byrnes shared the committee's recommendation with Truman later that same day.

WITH THE WAR IN EUROPE OVER and a new president facing an uncertain postwar world, events now moved quickly. On June 28, General Douglas MacArthur announced that Luzon had been liberated. On July 16, the Trinity test in New Mexico proved the feasibility of the plutonium bomb. On July 25, President Truman approved the dropping of the atomic bomb on Hiroshima, and if that did not bring peace, the dropping of a second bomb on Nagasaki.

The "Little Boy" bomb arrived on Tinian aboard the cruiser USS *Indianapolis* on July 26. Additional components and two "Fat Man" assemblies were flown to Tinian on specially modified B-29s. A joint targeting committee had already considered potential targets and recommended Kokura, Hiroshima, Niigata, and Kyoto. Secretary of War Stimson, who would make the final decision, had intervened, announcing that he would not approve the bombing of Kyoto, Japan's ancient capital, on the grounds of its historical and religious significance. Nagasaki was added as the substitute.

Enola Gay, the B-29 that dropped the first atomic bomb on Hiroshima, sits on the runway at Tinian.
(*US Air Force*)

On August 6, 1945, the *Enola Gay*, a B-29 of the 393rd Bombardment Squadron, took off from Tinian's North Field and set course for Hiroshima, the headquarters of the Japanese Second Army and an important port. "Little Boy" was dropped at 8:15 a.m. and detonated at an altitude of 1,750 feet. With a blast estimated to be the equivalent of thirteen thousand tons of TNT, the bomb destroyed almost everything in a 4.7-square-mile radius. Japanese officials later determined that 69 percent of Hiroshima's buildings were destroyed and between seventy thousand and eighty thousand people died—twenty thousand of whom were Japanese combatants and another twenty thousand were Korean slave laborers. Thirty percent of the population of the city was killed immediately, while another seventy thousand were injured.[115]

In keeping with the intense security surrounding the Manhattan Project, MacArthur was still operating under the assumption that he would be leading the invasion of Kyushu in a few weeks when he saw the headline in *Stars and Stripes* on August 6 that said: "ATOM BOMB DROPPED." He told his staff, "That's far beyond anything you can imagine."[116]

Three days later, on August 9, a "Fat Man" bomb, using plutonium manufactured at Hanford, was dropped on Nagasaki. The city of Kokura had been the primary target but was obscured by cloud cover, forcing the B-29 to divert to Nagasaki, the secondary target. The bomb was dropped over the city's industrial valley and resulted in a blast equivalent to twenty-one kilotons of TNT, roughly the same as the Trinity test explosion. A major portion of the city was shielded by hills, but the bomb still destroyed about half of it, killing approximately thirty-five thousand civilians and injuring another sixty thousand.[117]

More "Fat Man" bomb assemblies were already arriving at US airbases in the Marianas when Emperor Hirohito announced his nation's surrender on August 15, 1945. Even then, it had been a near thing. A

Nagasaki, Japan. August 9, 1945.
(National Archives at College Park, NAID 535795)

team of Japanese army fanatics had stormed the grounds of the Imperial Palace in an effort to stop the broadcast.

Hanford's role in producing the atomic bomb was announced to a stunned local community on August 6, 1945, in identical two-page extra editions of the weekly *Richland Villager* and *Pasco Herald* newspapers. Four-inch, bold headlines proclaimed, "IT'S ATOMIC BOMBS." It is estimated that less than 1 percent of the Hanford work force knew what they had been working on.[118] DuPont's role was revealed three days later in another headline reading, "AT LAST WE CAN SAY THAT NAME, DuPONT."[119]

Front page of the *Richland Villager*, August 6, 1945.
(Hanford History Project, Washington State University Tri-Cities)

DuPont had broken ground on the 640-square-mile Hanford Engineering Works in March of 1943. Twenty-nine months later, the company had produced and delivered the plutonium used for the Trinity test and for the "Fat Man" bomb that speeded up the end of World War II.

The very first nuclear chain reaction occurred on December 2, 1942, at CP-1 in Chicago. The first plutonium production reactor, 105-B, became critical on September 26, 1944, slightly more than one year and ten months later. During that time, DuPont had organized, designed, constructed, and operated a vast plutonium production facility—a remarkable achievement then, and virtually impossible today.

THE GOVERNMENT HAD KNOWN from the beginning that DuPont would withdraw from the Manhattan Project immediately following the end of hostilities, but that fact was not generally known to the residents of Richland Village. Still controlled by the army and with a very limited commercial infrastructure, its residents were rightly concerned about the city's uncertain future. The June 6, 1946, announcement that General Electric would take over from DuPont as Hanford's prime contractor was greeted with great relief. The message from GE's president, Charles Wilson, was reassuring and hinted at new uses for the Hanford Site:

> The General Electric Company was engaged in atomic research for peace-time application before the war. With this background, we are convinced that the quickest possible development of the non-military application, not only is the most constructive solution to the problem which atomic energy presents to the world, but our greatest opportunity for more jobs and more goods for more people in the future.[120]

WHEN IT FIRST NEGOTIATED its construction contract with the government, DuPont stipulated it would be paid only a dollar more than the actual cost associated with the project. When it signed the contract with the army on December 12, 1942, DuPont estimated it would take three years to complete the work. All three of the first production reactors were in operation by February 1945, slightly more than two years after DuPont had started work. When the governments' auditors were closing out the contract, they determined that DuPont's token reimbursement of one dollar should be reduced by thirty-two cents, a proportional cut reflecting the reduced time it had worked on the contract.

A somewhat tongue-in-cheek reference to the government's action was buried in a story in the *Pasco Herald* regarding DuPont's immense contribution to the war effort. However small, the reference to the government's action did not go unnoticed by the paper's readers.

Late in the week of August 12, 1946, a clerk in the mailroom at E. I. du Pont de Nemours Company corporate headquarters in Wilmington, Delaware, received a small package. It was addressed to Walter S. Carpenter Jr., president, and contained a short letter and thirty-two cents. The letter was signed by Mel Swanson, president of the Pasco Kiwanis Club, and thirty-one other members. It read:

> Dear Mr. Carpenter:
>
> At the last regular meeting of the Pasco Kiwanis Club a resolution was passed which reads as follows:
>
> "An article in a local newspaper states that the DuPont Company received only One Dollar profit from the operations at the Hanford plant and that an expense item of thirty-two cants [*sic*] was not allowed by an accountant, leaving a balance of sixty-eight cents. Thirty-two members of this club ere [*sic*] contributing one cent each to make up the difference and also placing their signatures to this letter."
>
> We are very proud to be so closely situated to the Hanford project, and all of us feel very sincerely that we have had a part in this magnificent enterprise. We also hope that the Lord will see fit to direct the future efforts and achievements of this product into the right channel for the good of all mankind.
>
> - - /s/ Mel Swanson[121]

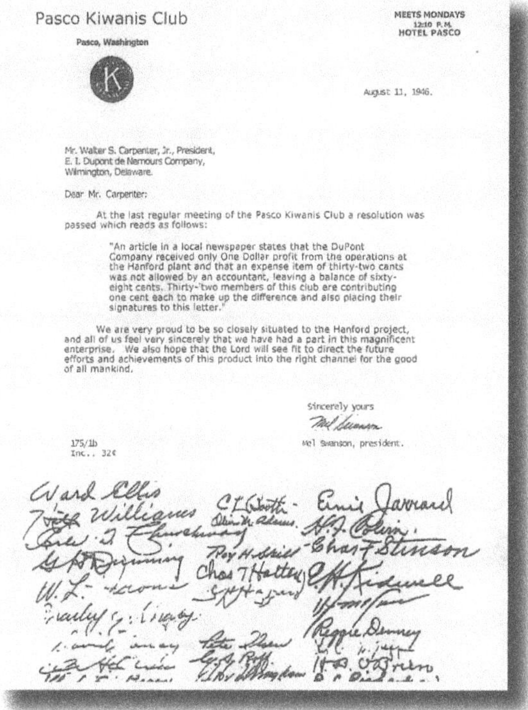

Pasco Kiwanis letter to DuPont president Walter S. Carpenter.
(E.I. du Pont de Nemours & Company records
[Accession 0500:II], Box 830, Hagley Museum and Library)

It is unknown if Mel Swanson and his fellow Kiwanians received a direct response from Carpenter, although he later used the letter as an example of the cooperation his company had received from the communities surrounding Hanford, saying in a speech that he had placed both the letter and money in the DuPont archives.[122]

In his memoirs, Groves commented on the matter, writing:

> This resulted in a disallowance by government auditors, since the entire time of the contract had not run out. Consequently, DuPont was asked to return thirty-three cents to the United States. Fortunately, the officers of DuPont had retained their sense of humor throughout their many years of association with the government, and were able to derive considerable amusement from this ruling."[123]

CHAPTER SEVEN

A NEW THREAT ARISES

ON September 2, 1945, General Douglas MacArthur directed the representatives of the Japanese Empire to sign the Instrument of Surrender on the veranda deck of the battleship USS *Missouri* anchored in Tokyo Bay, surrounded and overflown by the assembled military might of the Allies. Overhead flew the American flag that had flown over the nation's capital on December 7, 1941.* For their part, each of the Japanese representatives considered the surrender document a humiliation so devastating that they would rather have committed suicide than sign it. They had signed it only at the express order of their emperor.

The atomic bomb had ended the war, but would it ensure peace?

THE END OF THE WAR left the United States and the Soviet Union, each suspicious of the other, to pursue their postwar goals. The Americans had suffered remarkably few casualties—fewer than three hundred thousand had died. They were geographically distant from the war and had experienced no fighting on their own land, with the exception of Pearl Harbor and some early fighting in the Aleutian Islands in Alaska. They emerged from the war with a thriving economy, the strongest military in the world, and in sole possession of the bomb.

---

* MacArthur also had on hand the pennant that had flown from Commodore Matthew Perry's flagship in 1854 when his fleet had arrived in Tokyo Bay to open up trade with Japan.

The Russians enjoyed no such advantages. Much of their land, cities, and towns had been ravaged. As many as twenty-seven million Russians had died in the war. Most of their industrial base had been relocated east of the Ural Mountains. They were rightfully proud to have survived what they called the "Great Patriotic War."

The Soviets did have one advantage. They were the only one of the three great powers whose wartime leader, Josef Stalin, survived the war. Roosevelt had died in April 1945 and been replaced by Vice President Harry Truman. Three months later, Prime Minister Winston Churchill's government fell, and he was replaced by Clement Atlee. When the three leaders met at the last major conference of the war in Potsdam, on the outskirts of Berlin, Stalin knew exactly what he wanted in the postwar period, while the United States and Britain were much less sure of their goals.

The three Allied leaders (*seated from left*: Clement Atlee, Harry Truman, and Josef Stalin), met at Potsdam between July 17 and August 2, 1945, to chart the future course of the war. (*National Archives at College Park, Army Signal Corps Collection*)

Stalin most wanted security for himself, for his regime, for his country, and for his communist ideology. He wanted the return of the territories he had lost to the Germans during the war, the return of the territories he had seized as a result of the 1939 non-aggression pact with Hitler, and territorial concessions along its southern border with Iran and Turkey, including access to the Mediterranean Sea, a traditional Russian goal. Beyond that, he wanted a belt of friendly buffer states in Eastern Europe to provide safety in the case of a future invasion, another of Russia's traditional goals. The latter appeared easily attainable since Russian armies controlled those states, as well as much of Germany.

The Americans also wanted security, but they were uncertain about how to secure it. The nation's long-standing isolationism was no longer realistic. It could not achieve its geopolitical and economic goals by remaining apart from the rest of the world. The war had forced the United States to form alliances with nations it distrusted because it had been unable to defeat Germany and Japan alone. Roosevelt hoped to secure Allied support in shaping the postwar settlement, because without it, there could be no lasting peace. He believed the fledgling United Nations could be that vehicle *if* it could be sold to the American people.

Europe during the Cold War. (*Chris Picken*)

British postwar objectives were even simpler—to survive at all costs—even if it meant reluctantly subordinating themselves to the Americans and weakening the British Empire. In October 1944, Churchill had even been willing to negotiate with Stalin to create separate spheres of influence in Eastern Europe and the Mediterranean. As a practical fact, the Russians controlled or influenced those disputed nations in any event. They installed subservient governments in the nations they occupied and effectively moved their border several hundred miles to the west.

The most disputed country was Germany itself. The Russians controlled the eastern half of the country while the Allies controlled the western half in three separate zones. When the Soviets created a German puppet state, the Allies were forced to create an opposing Federal Republic of Germany, allied with the West.

The Allies' experience in Germany and Eastern Europe provided little incentive to include Russia in the occupation of Japan, even though the Russians at Potsdam had agreed to declare war on Japan three months after the German surrender. It had earlier been thought that Russia's assistance would be necessary to defeat Japan, but that was before the United States knew it possessed a practical atomic bomb. Another area of concern in Asia was the former Japanese colony of Korea, where US and Russian forces faced each other across a divided peninsula.

Meanwhile, the knowledge that the Americans had the atomic bomb only intensified the paranoia and distrust of the Soviet leadership. Would the Americans use the bomb to extract postwar concessions from the Russians? Stalin certainly thought so, declaring that "A-bomb blackmail is American policy."[124]

Because the Allied-Russian relationship had begun to unravel before the end of the Second World War, it is difficult to say precisely when the Cold War began, although 1947 is the year generally used. On February 22, 1946, the State Department received an eight-thousand-word telegram from George Kennon, America's chargé d'affaires in Moscow, which recommended a policy of containment toward the Soviet Union. The contents of what became to be known as the "Long Telegram" became US policy toward the Soviet Union for decades to come.

One month later, on March 12, 1946, President Truman announced to Congress that he was implementing what became known as the

Truman Doctrine, a policy of providing political, military, and economic assistance to all democratic nations—particularly Turkey and Greece—that were being threatened by external or internal authoritarian forces, a thinly disguised reference to the Soviet Union. "We must assist free peoples to work out their own destinies in their own way," he said.[125]

The war left Europe near economic collapse. Many countries, including France and Italy, had active communist, second-front political parties, which might gain control of their governments. On April 3, 1948, Truman signed into law the European Recovery Plan in which the United States provided more than sixteen billion dollars (more than $167 billion in 2018 dollars) of economic assistance to the war-torn economies of Europe. Although they were eligible to receive assistance, Stalin prohibited the countries under Soviet control to participate in the program. Instead he erected a virtual—and sometimes, as in Berlin, an actual—wall that divided East from West.

Beginning on June 24, 1948, the Russians attempted to block Allied access to their zones of occupation in Germany. It was the first major confrontation of the Cold War in which Allied and Russian troops faced off against each other. The blockade was broken by a massive Allied

Hungry West Berliners watch a Douglas C-54 transport plane land during the Berlin Airlift in 1948. *(US Air Force)*

airlift that provided food and fuel to the occupants of the western zones until May 1949.

While the relationship between the western Allies and the Russians was becoming more adversarial, it changed entirely on August 29, 1949, when Stalin announced that the Soviets had successfully tested its own atomic bomb. The implications for the Truman administration were daunting. Would it have to permanently station troops in Europe? Would it have to build more atomic bombs and improve its delivery capabilities to stay ahead of the Russians? Would it now proceed with the development of a thermonuclear or hydrogen super bomb, as proposed by one of the original Hungarian refugees, Edward Teller? In the end, President Truman approved all three courses of action.

Almost simultaneously, the Chinese communist leader, Mao Zedong, announced the creation of the People's Republic of China, following his defeat of the Chinese Nationalist armies under Chiang Kai-shek. Now much of Asia, as well as Europe, was under communist control.

General Douglas MacArthur (*center*) observes the naval
shelling of Inchon on September 15, 1950.
(*National Archives at College Park, Record Group 111*)

About the same time, two major espionage cases erupted—one in England and one in the United States—that exposed the degree of penetration by Soviet spies into the workings of the two governments. Members of the Republican Congress blamed the Truman Administration, and particularly its state department, for losing China.

Finally, if the Americans needed any more proof of what they believed was a worldwide conspiracy to expand communism, it came on the early morning of June 25, 1950, when General Douglas MacArthur, still commander of US ground forces in the Pacific, was awakened in Tokyo and informed that the North Koreans were invading South Korea in great force. There was little or nothing he could do to stop it. Most US forces had been withdrawn from the peninsula after the Japanese surrender, and only token forces were stationed in Japan.

When word of the invasion reached President Truman, he took aggressive action to secure help from the United Nations, calling up reserves, and sending reinforcements to the region as fast as possible. Unfortunately, by the time they arrived, the Americans and their South Korean Allies were holding on by their teeth to a small perimeter around the southern port city of Pusan at the very tip of the Korean peninsula.

The dire situation was relieved when MacArthur overcame the objections of the navy and the Joint Chiefs of Staff to conduct a risky end-around invasion at Inchon, halfway up the west side of the Korean Peninsula near the original dividing line of the 38th parallel. MacArthur asked for and received permission to invade North Korea. By November 1950, his forces were nearing the Yalu River, which divided North Korea and China, when three hundred thousand Chinese troops crossed the border and forced the Allies to retreat south during the height of the Korean winter.

At this point, historian Arthur Herman writes that MacArthur developed a four-part strategy for winning the war. The first step involved dropping twenty to thirty atomic bombs to take out Chinese airbases and supply installations in Manchuria. The second was to lay a radioactive belt of nuclear-contaminated material across the northern neck of the peninsula separating North Korea from China and sealing one off from the other. The third was to move half a million Nationalist Chinese forces from Taiwan to North Korea. Finally, a reinforced Eighth Army would again invade North Korea from the south.[126] It is not clear if he ever submitted the plan to Washington DC, where it would have been rejected out of hand, but it was not the first time the use of tactical atomic weapons on the battlefield had been discussed, and MacArthur's strategy had its supporters in Congress.

Ultimately, the war ground down to a stalemate near the original dividing line of the 38th parallel where an armistice—still in effect—was finally signed on July 27, 1953, six months after Dwight Eisenhower became president of the United States.

While the Korean War and, later, the Cuban Missile Crisis and the American intervention in Vietnam were the defining events of the Cold War, the period also brought many changes to the Hanford Site and to the Tri-Cities community and with them, new opportunities and challenges.

CHAPTER EIGHT

NEW CHALLENGES AND MISSIONS

IN ACCORDANCE WITH its wartime agreement with the army, DuPont relinquished control of the Hanford Engineer Works in September 1946. It was replaced by the General Electric Company, an iconic manufacturing and research conglomerate that had an interest in the potential of nuclear power generation. As the new lead contractor, GE would be responsible for operating both the Hanford Site and Richland Village. The huge construction camp at Hanford was in the process of being demolished.

Following President Truman's signing of the Atomic Energy Act, the army's role was replaced by the new civilian Atomic Energy Commission (AEC) on January 1, 1947. It was a time of great uncertainty for Hanford workers, their families, and the growing number of others in the Tri-City community that relied on Hanford for their livelihood. Fortunately, the transitions from the Manhattan Project to the AEC and from DuPont to General Electric both went smoothly.

Just as the early atomic scientists had warned against the potential of Germany developing the bomb, postwar decision-makers believed they faced a similar threat from the Soviet Union, particularly after it had developed its own atomic bomb. As the emerging realities of the Cold War became better understood, America's military planners realized that plutonium production would have to be increased, not cut back, and a massive postwar expansion of HEW began. Hanford had a new lease on life.

North Richland trailer camp c. 1950. *(US Department of Energy)*

However, there were growing concerns about the existing production reactors. They had been running at full production since coming on line near the end of the war. Now, they began to be affected by what was known as graphite creep in which the graphite blocks that constituted the piles began to expand and threaten the tight tolerances of the tubes as a result of the constant exposure to heat and radiation. The B Reactor was shut down and placed in standby status.

In 1947, AEC and General Electric began planning for new production reactors. Two were finished during this period, designated DR (for D replacement) and H, located further east along the Columbia River. The new reactors would be similar to the wartime reactors. Innovative new designs would have to wait for another time. The wartime reactors were modified to eliminate the various problems associated with the swelling of the graphite piles. The effort represented the largest peacetime construction project in American history and cost more than the entire wartime effort to build the HEW. Housing and related facilities for up to fifteen thousand construction workers and their families were created in North Richland and called Camp Hanford.[127] Some called it the largest trailer park in the world.

The first of the postwar reactors was completed in 1949, just after the Russians announced they had successfully tested their atomic bomb and the North Atlantic Treaty Organization (NATO) had been created. General Electric also completed the Plutonium Finishing Plant, which made it possible to convert the plutonium-nitrate paste into plutonium metal formed into units the size and shape of a hockey puck. These were then shipped to Los Alamos and then Rocky Flats, Colorado, where the nuclear devices were assembled. The plant operated until 1989.[128]

A second postwar expansion of HEW followed the revelation that Russia possessed the bomb and the start of the Korean War in June 1950. A sixth production reactor, designated as C Reactor, and an improved chemical separation plant, called REDOX, were completed in 1952. The REDOX separation process was a significant improvement over the previous process, which wasted large amounts of valuable uranium. General Electric also began to build a number of research facilities in the 300 Area, which became known as the Hanford Laboratories.

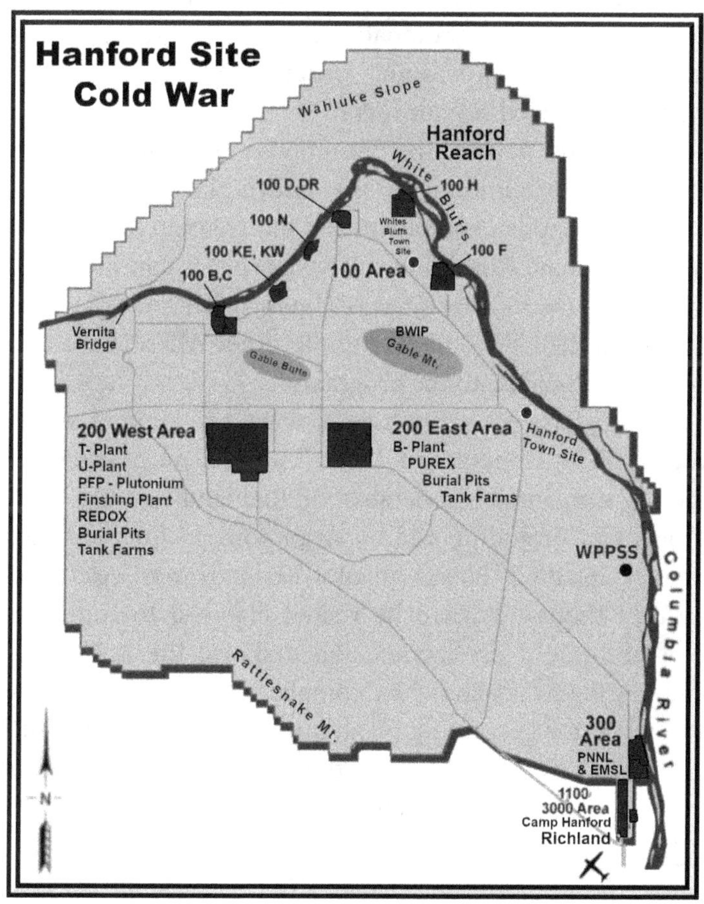

Hanford Site during the Cold War. (*Chris Picken*)

A third expansion occurred during the Eisenhower administration. With a huge lead in the number of nuclear devices and multiple methods of delivering them, the government adopted a policy called "mutually assured destruction" (MAD), in which only the United States had the ability to respond to a first strike launched against it by unleashing a massive response that would destroy the Soviet Union as a nation and negate any advantage it had by unleashing a first strike. While the Cold War was contested in obvious and not-so-obvious ways around the world for decades, the MAD policy kept the world from nuclear war, even during the 1962 Cuban Missile Crisis.

Two new second-generation production reactors, designated K West and K East, were completed in 1955. A final chemical separation plant, named PUREX after the plutonium-uranium extraction process it used, also became operational in 1956. It featured a continuous flow extraction process that was able to separate both plutonium and uranium from irradiated reactor fuel.

During this period, the Eisenhower administration announced its Atoms for Peace initiative at the United Nations in December 1953. The initiative supplied equipment and information to schools, hospitals, and research institutions and allowed private, commercial, and non-defense programs to be located at Hanford. The Atomic Energy Act of 1954 allowed the US to cooperate with other Allies in the development of their own peaceful atomic programs.

Funding for the last production reactor to be built at Hanford was appropriated by Congress in 1958. The dual-purpose N Reactor was justified as a major job generator for Richland and the Tri-Cities and as a means of providing additional plutonium for the Cold War. On September 26, 1963, President John Kennedy was welcomed by more than thirty thousand when he visited Hanford to commemorate the start of plutonium production and dedicate the associated Hanford Generating Plant, which, when completed, would transfer steam from the reactor to the generating plant, producing electricity, which went to the Bonneville Power Administration's power grid.* Two months later, Kennedy would be assassinated in Dallas, Texas.

---

* Following the creation of the Tennessee Valley Authority in 1933, the federal government was expressly prohibited from producing electricity.

President John F. Kennedy dedicating the Hanford Generating Plant associated with the N Reactor on September 26, 1963.
(US Department of Energy, Hanford Collection)

THE RESIDENTS OF RICHLAND—like the others involved in the Manhattan Project—existed in a kind of limbo following the end of the war. The town's population declined to less than thirteen thousand in 1946 but began to grow rapidly again during the Cold War expansion. Almost twenty-three thousand lived there by 1950. An additional fifteen thousand construction workers and their families were housed in Camp Hanford, a huge community of travel trailers and hutments located in North Richland, not to be confused with the World War II–era Hanford Camp located at the former Hanford town site.

Like DuPont and the army before them, General Electric and the AEC continued to view Hanford and the community as a means of maximizing their production of plutonium at Hanford. Its citizens could not vote or run for local office because those elected positions did not exist. Almost everyone who lived there had come from somewhere else. There was little local history or culture. The past had been razed to create the present. So they created their own community narrative. Residents already shared a unique experience of seeing themselves as pioneers on the western frontier. In promotional materials,

Richland became "The Atomic City of the West." The annual Atomic Frontier Days celebration included a rodeo, and residents dressed up in western clothing. In 1945, the team name of the local high school became the Bombers with a mushroom cloud as their logo. That feeling of pride continued through the Cold War and beyond, becoming part of the bedrock of the Hanford culture.

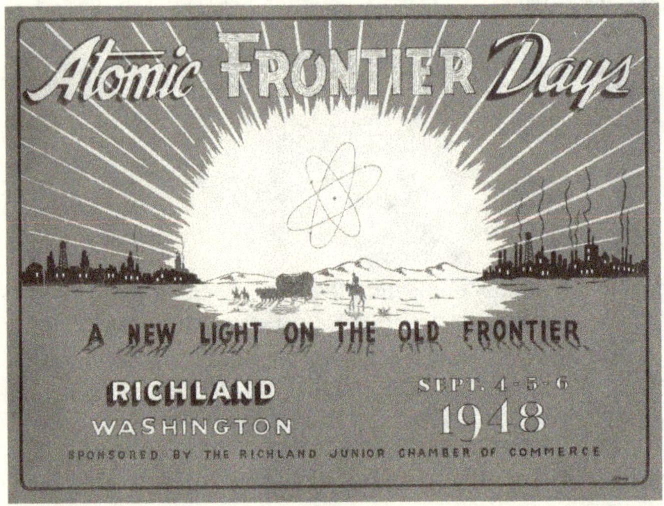

Brochure cover from the first Atomic Frontier Days celebration.
(Hanford History Project, Washington State University Tri-Cities)

By the late 1940s, with the city rapidly growing as a result of the Hanford expansion, the government finally realized that Richland was there to stay and began developing a land use plan and planning for new commercial development. They created the Richland Community Council as a bridge to the residents, but it was subservient to the government's wishes because most of its members worked for either GE or the AEC.

IN THE 1950s, the growing but still small business community and other groups began to press for self-government, setting off a battle that would continue for most of the decade. Residents were split between those who supported "disposal and incorporation"—the sale of government-owned houses and businesses and incorporation—and those who wanted to continue their comfortable, and financially attractive, dependence on the federal government.

Without direct representation at the local government level, the community became adept at establishing effective relationships with its representatives and senators in Washington, DC, who took up their cause with the AEC in Washington. The effort came to a head in 1958 when Richland residents voted to incorporate the city for a second time—it had first been incorporated in 1910 and remained a fourth-class city until the army acquired the town in 1943.

The incorporation efforts were led by local business leaders but none more effectively than Sam Volpentest, fifty-three in 1957 and the son of Italian immigrants who had located in Seattle before the turn of the century. Volpentest had entered the work force at age eight, and by 1943, he had spent twenty-five years as a wholesale grocery salesman in downtown Seattle. The customers on his route included speakeasies, Italian grocery stores, and clubs that had first-hand knowledge of his tenacity, persistence, and close association with Democratic politicians gained from his years serving as president of the Italian Club in Seattle.

In 1949, he answered a blind ad placed in the *Seattle Times* by the Atomic Energy Commission that was planning to expand the meagre commercial opportunities in Richland. Sam's goal was to buy a grocery store, but when that was promised to others, he settled for a tavern and owned several more by the mid-1950s.

He was joined in his efforts by the owners of the influential *Tri-City Herald*, Glenn Lee and Robert F. "Bob" Philip. They believed government control stifled community growth and, therefore, their potential business profits. Volpentest enlisted his long-time friends, Albert Rosellini, who had been elected as Washington's governor in 1960, and the state's senior US senator, Warren G. Magnuson, a former Seattle prosecutor and congressman, to help him in his efforts. Washington's other influential senator, Henry M. "Scoop" Jackson, took an active interest in Hanford and Richland and already believed the AEC should divest itself of its atomic cities. After a decision by the AEC to allow residents and business owners to buy their buildings and a vote by the residents to incorporate on July 15, 1958, Richland finally was on its own.

Richland thrived under its newly independent status but remained heavily dependent on Hanford and the federal government. It also remained physically isolated—it lacked major highway access, as well as passenger rail and airline service. It gained national recognition after Volpentest organized a campaign to win *Look* magazine's All-America City award in 1961. He also used his political connections to secure funding and convince the AEC to allow the construction of a highway across the Hanford Site and a new state-funded bridge at Vernita, significantly cutting the time it took to drive to Seattle and Spokane.

Sam Volpentest (*left*) points with pride to a newly erected All-America City sign in 1961 as Richland mayor Joyce R. Kelly and city manager Murrey Fuller look on. (*Richland Public Library*)

Volpentest and others spearheaded efforts to obtain funding and land for a new Joint Center for Graduate Study in North Richland where Hanford workers could pursue post-graduate degrees. The center would become a branch campus of Washington State University in 1990 and begin accepting freshman and sophomore students in 2007.

By the mid-1960s, it became obvious the Tri-Cities' dependence on Hanford was not sustainable. In his State of the Union message of January 8, 1964, President Lyndon Johnson—hoping to limit southern opposition to his proposed Civil Rights bill—promised to cut government spending. One place that could be cut was the plutonium production at Hanford because the nation now had a considerable stockpile of the element. In spite of heavy lobbying to delay the inevitable, each of the first eight reactors was shut down between 1964 and 1971. Only the new N Reactor was granted a reprieve until 1987.

Two weeks following the president's announcement, General Electric announced it would be leaving Hanford as the prime contractor. The immediate, and not surprising, impact of the two announcements was a deep and protracted local recession. Many residents moved away, and local businesses closed their doors. Sam Volpentest later remembered, "Hell, it wasn't a crisis; it was an out-and-out catastrophe."[129] He later told a reporter, "I was broke. I *couldn't* leave."[130]

Civic leaders used their political clout to help them "get a leg up on other industries and other programs we thought we could get in here," Sam Volpentest remembered.[131] With the considerable help of Senator Jackson, they successfully lobbied the AEC to adopt a "segmentation and diversification" strategy to replace GE with six or seven specialized contractors who would each be responsible for a portion of the Hanford work. Each winning bidder was required to submit another sealed bid

The new campus of Pacific Northwest Laboratory under construction in 1966.
(Pacific Northwest National Laboratory)

outlining what it was prepared to invest in the community to diversify its economy. New contracts began to be awarded in August 1965. The winners were some of America's major corporations, including United Nuclear, Douglas Aircraft, and eventually, to Atlantic Richfield. Some were more successful with their non-Hanford diversification efforts than others. Perhaps the largest and longest-lasting contribution came from the Columbus, Ohio–based Battelle Memorial Institute, which took over GE's Hanford Laboratories, announcing it would spend twelve million dollars acquiring a 275-acre site and building a new campus complex in North Richland on a portion of the former postwar Camp Hanford construction site. That complex was the start of what would become Pacific Northwest National Laboratory (PNNL), still managed today by the Columbus-based Battelle Memorial Institute on behalf of the US Department of Energy.

Each of the original and postwar reactors was in the process of being deactivated during the decades of the 1960s and 1970s with devastating impacts to the Tri-Cities economy. Community leaders made repeated attempts to find new missions and programs at Hanford to replace the reactors and stabilize the local economy.

The first opportunity presented itself in January 1965. The 200 BeV Accelerator was commonly referred by the press as an "atom smasher," but in reality it was a purely scientific research tool capable of accelerating subatomic particles to high energy to better understand the makeup of the atom, which was necessary to conduct advanced research studies in nuclear and particle physics. PNNL officials learned that the AEC was looking for a location for the facility. It seemed like a perfect match for Hanford because of its economic impact. It would cost between $275 and $300 million and employ 2,250 people, including many highly paid scientists. By September, the AEC had received 126 proposals from forty-six states. On March 22, 1966, AEC narrowed its recommendation down to six sites, but Hanford was not among them. In the end, congressional politics decided the matter. The project went to Batavia, Illinois, located in congressional district of Melvin Price, the ranking member of the Joint Committee on Atomic Energy.

It was often said that the Fast Flux Test Facility (FFTF) was a consolation prize for losing the 200 BeV Accelerator. Although it was a part of the nation's breeder reactor program, FFTF was not technically itself a breeder reactor. It was a sodium-cooled, fast-neutron research reactor used to test advanced nuclear fuels, materials, components, nuclear power plant operations and maintenance protocols, and reactor safety designs. AEC officials quietly responded to Senator Henry Jackson's request that it be located at Hanford. The program was authorized by Congress in July 1967 at a cost of $87.5 million plus contingencies.

Almost immediately, the designers of the prototype reactor at PNNL ran into opposition from AEC officials in Washington, DC, who wanted to change the original design. Failing to reach agreement on the reactor design, AEC brought in Westinghouse to take over the project in 1970. President Richard Nixon attended the groundbreaking for the reactor in 1971.

By November 1973, more than one thousand construction workers were on the job, creating a new boom in the Tri-Cities economy, but by the mid-1970s, FFTF was in deep trouble, several hundred million over budget, and behind schedule. It was finally completed in April 1982 at an announced cost of $647 million. When President Carter decided to abandon the breeder reactor program, FFTF remained in operation, testing advanced nuclear fuels, materials, and components, but without a mission.

Fast Flux Test Facility under construction in the 1970s.
(US Department of Energy)

In 1993, DOE decided to deactivate the reactor and, in 1997, ordered FFTF be placed on cold standby condition, pending a decision as to whether the reactor could be incorporated into the US government's tritium production program or for medical or fusion research. While the Tri-Cities community rallied in support of FFTF, none of the efforts to find a new mission was successful, and the sodium coolant was drained from the core in 2005.

FFTF SPAWNED SEVERAL other large projects at Hanford. In 1977, the government began a crash program with Westinghouse to build a $105 million Fusion Materials Irradiation Test (FMIT) facility at Hanford. The FMIT was a large engineering installation designed to help move the theory of nuclear fusion out of the laboratory into the practical process of producing electricity. But before any decision could be made to build a fusion test reactor, materials had to be developed that could withstand the intensive bombardment of neutrons released in the fusion process, and that was the purpose of the FMIT. Unfortunately, DOE favored a slower pace of development and the program didn't survive President Reagan's budget cuts of the early 1980s.

Completed in 1983, a mammoth 170,000-square-foot, $550-million Fuels and Materials Examination Facility (FMEF) was built near the FFTF in the Hanford 400 Area to develop fuel fabrication processes, equipment, and handling systems for the FFTF and the broader breeder reactor program. Like FFTF, the FMEF was left without a mission when the breeder reactor program was cancelled, and the building sits unused and largely vacant today.

PASSED BY CONGRESS in 1982, the Nuclear Waste Policy Act (NWPA) directed the secretary of energy to develop guidelines for the selection of two permanent, underground nuclear waste repositories, which would be selected by the president after a full environmental impact statement had been completed. Tri-City Nuclear Industrial Council (TCNIC) and local community leaders immediately proposed Hanford as the location for one of the sites, with Sam Volpentest testifying before the AEC in 1974 that Hanford was the perfect place to bury nuclear waste. "What is being proposed is the culmination of more than 30 years of research at

Sam Volpentest testifying before Congress in support of the BWIP waste repository at Hanford. *(C. Mark Smith)*

Hanford. We in the Tri-Cities are not worried about living with the end product."[132]

Investigation of a potential nuclear waste repository at Hanford began in 1976 with the groundbreaking for the Basalt Waste Isolation Project (BWIP) under Gable Mountain where an underground basalt rock formation had been chosen as one of three finalists for the national underground repository. A test facility was bored into the mountain, and plans were underway to drill a 2,500-foot hole beneath the 200 Area. A drill bit was purchased but never used. Between 1976 and enactment of the Nuclear Waste Policy Act (NWPA) in 1982, up to 1,200 employees were engaged at one time or another in construction or in evaluating the geologic and hydrologic suitability of the BWIP site.

By the mid-1980s, public attitudes about nuclear waste were changing. Increasingly, state officials and environmental groups were arguing against storing nuclear waste at Hanford. This fundamentally changed the equation about where the nation's nuclear waste would be buried. In 1987, only nineteen months after President Reagan approved BWIP at Hanford, a salt formation in Texas, and a site at Yucca Mountain located near the Nevada test site as potential underground repository sites, the public and political outcry against locating the repository in either Texas or Washington became so strong that Congress passed the infamous "Screw Nevada Bill," which designated Yucca Mountain in Nevada as the nation's only nuclear waste depository to be evaluated for suitability as a waste storage site for high-level nuclear waste.

In 2009, after DOE spent billions studying and preparing the Nevada site, the Obama administration decided to close down the Yucca Mountain site. The Nuclear Regulatory Commission (NRC) agreed and refused to approve a use permit. That decision was successfully challenged in federal court by one of the authors and two other Tri-Cities residents who were joined by the states of Washington and South Carolina, as well as other parties.* In August 2013, the litigants obtained a ruling by the US Court of Appeals ordering the NRC to "approve or reject the Energy Department's application for [the] never-completed waste storage site at Nevada's Yucca Mountain."[133] The NRC has yet to take action regarding a permit.

No vision of Hanford's future has so captivated community leaders, or held them for a longer time, than the vision of a massive nuclear energy park supplying electric power for the growing west. The potential unleashed by the dual-purpose N Reactor led community leaders to embrace a vision that would solve the uncertainty of Hanford forever. They were not alone. In 1968, AEC chairman Glenn Seaborg was in Richland to mark the tenth anniversary of the city's incorporation. Hanford had recently been selected as the home of the FFTF, and it was thought that the reactors producing vast amounts of electric power were sure to follow. At a gala dinner, Seaborg spoke enthusiastically about creating a "nuclear-powered industrial complex," or "nuplex," where a variety of nuclear reactors producing electricity, conducting research, advancing nuclear medicine, and producing other nuclear benefits would be clustered together.[134]

In 1970, TCNIC, along with the city of Richland, sponsored a fifty-thousand-dollar study by Douglas Laboratories to determine if Hanford would be a suitable site for a nuclear energy park. The study concluded that the Hanford Site offered "unique merit" as a future location for nuclear power plants.

The mechanism for achieving that goal already existed. In 1957, the Washington State Legislature authorized the creation of a state-

---

* One of the authors of this book, Robert L. Ferguson, was one of the three private citizens who successfully sued the Obama administration and the Nuclear Regulatory Commission to reverse their decision on the Yucca Mountain nuclear repository

chartered municipal corporation called the Washington Public Power Supply System (WPPSS)—allowing small public utility districts and municipalities to combine their money and resources to build "a system of works, plants and facilities for the generation and transmission of electricity to provide a dependable source of power supply for the participants."[135]

In 1962, WPPSS decided to enter into a complicated agreement to finance, construct, and operate the steam-generating plant associated with the N Reactor at Hanford. Having gained confidence from its earlier project and bolstered by a Bonneville Power Administration (BPA) report calling for new nuclear power plants, WPPSS took the lead in developing more nuclear capacity in Washington State. The construction of a new nuclear plant to be built at Hanford was approved in May 1972. That same month, the agency began to plan two more nuclear plants, one at Hanford and another in Grays Harbor County in southwestern Washington. They were expected to be completed in 1980 and 1981 at a cost of between $581 million and $633 million, respectively. Its board of directors, consisting of well-meaning but unsophisticated members of local utility boards, was unprepared for what would come next. Nevertheless, WPPSS announced in 1974 it planned to build two more nuclear power plants.

The original estimated cost of the five plants had been $4.1 billion. By 1976, it had risen to $6.6 billion. By 1979, it had grown to $11.9

Uncompleted WPPSS nuclear power plants at Hanford in 1985.
(US Department of Energy)

billion. After a new cost estimate of $23.8 billion had been received in May 1981, it was found that it would take an additional $4.3 billion to finish the first three plants and a further $8.9 billion would be needed to finish the last two plants, which were still only 25 and 16 percent completed. WPPSS—now derisively known as "Whoops"—was already the nation's largest issuer of tax-exempt bonds.

Meanwhile, on March 28, 1979, a partial meltdown occurred at one of nuclear reactors operated by Metropolitan Edison at Three Mile Island, on the Susquehanna River near Harrisburg, Pennsylvania. It was the worst commercial nuclear disaster in American history and served to validate the public's growing suspicion of nuclear power. Although there were no injuries and no release of radiation, the accident served to highlight the efforts of a growing number of anti-nuclear activists and environmentalists who had already turned against nuclear power. There were even calls to take the word "nuclear" out of the name of the Tri-City Nuclear Industrial Council, causing Sam Volpentest, its powerful recruiter to say, "Hell no. . . . We're not going to drop it. We're stubborn. We've got nothing to fear from nuclear energy."[136]

In spite of that bravado, construction schedules for the WPPSS nuclear plants lagged and drove costs to three and four times the original estimates. Inflation and design changes plagued each of the projects. Both human-caused accidents and freaks of nature, such as the May 18, 1980, volcanic eruptions of Mount St. Helens, created delays. So did the high cost of labor, frequent job turnover, low worker productivity, and jurisdictional disputes among unions. Added to these problems was the fact that the Pacific Northwest's increasingly sluggish economy reduced the demand for power, just at the time when the cost of that power was going up.

Efforts to improve the management of WPPSS led to a national search for a new managing director and led to the hiring of Robert L. "Bob" Ferguson. Ferguson was an experienced manager with close ties to Senator Henry M. Jackson and had worked at the B Reactor, previously managed the FFTF program, and served as assistant secretary of the Department of Energy's nuclear reactor program, but he arrived on the scene too late to affect the final outcome. The stress of managing the collapsing WPPSS system took its toll on Ferguson's health. He underwent quadruple bypass heart surgery in March 1982,

Managing director Robert L. Ferguson (wearing vest, right) speaks at a contentious WPPSS board meeting in 1981. (Robert L. Ferguson)

but his early return to work prevented his full recovery and led to his resignation.

In June 1982, the workforce that had numbered 6,300 in April dropped to 2,100 and then down to 1,000 in September. In August 1983, WPPSS was forced to default on $2.25 billion of its bonds in August 1983. At the time, it was the largest municipal bond default in United States history. Ferguson spent the next five years as a fact witness during the litigation that followed the WPPSS default in addition to having to hire a security detail to protect him when he travelled.[137]

The Tri-Cities community continued to be emotionally and economically joined at the hip to Hanford's up-and-down fortunes. In the 1950s and 1960s, more Hanford workers had located in Pasco and, particularly, in Kennewick, meaning that what happened at Hanford affected all the Tri-Cities.

The 1960s had seen the major recession caused by the cutbacks at Hanford and slow closure of the production reactors. The 1970s had been much better. Thousands were employed building the first of the WPPSS nuclear power plants, FFTF, and BWIP. The N Reactor received a welcome stay of execution. The area's population grew by more than forty-two thousand, with the city of Kennewick nearly doubling in size because of commercial growth fueled by a new regional mall.

Transportation access was improved. With more growth came more economic diversification. Agribusiness, always a staple, remained strong, while research and development, led by Pacific Northwest Laboratory and new technology companies tied to Hanford, grew. Tourism related to the region's growing wine industry became a significant growth factor.

The 1980s were a different story. The nation experienced a short, but severe, recession at the start of the decade. Hanford contractors began to reduce their work forces in the late 1970s. A costly labor strike shut down work at WPPSS and other projects for five months. Not surprisingly, companies that TCNIC was trying to attract to Hanford were concerned about the local labor climate. In 1981 and again in 1982, work on two of the three WPPSS nuclear reactors being built at Hanford slowed down and then stopped altogether as the Supply System self-imploded. Unemployment rose to 15.5 percent in July 1982, compared with 11.6 percent for Washington and 9.8 percent for the rest of the nation. The WPPSS collapse and the severe recession that followed, when combined with mounting public concerns about nuclear power after the Three Mile Island and 1986 Chernobyl disaster in Ukraine that released large amounts of radioactivity into the atmosphere over much of Western USSR and Europe, meant the Tri-Cities needed to change its economic focus.

By the mid-1980s, the severity of the recent recession and the pressure it placed on city budgets and corporate profits led many in the Tri-Cities to search for greater efficiencies and reductions in costs. Many believed both could be achieved through various forms of consolidation. Beginning in 1984, there were two controversial attempts to achieve consolidation among Richland, Kennewick, and Pasco. Both failed, largely over issues related to the consolidation of the three school districts but also as a result of parochialism stemming from long-standing cultural and competitive relationships of the three cities.

With population growth came more diversification in the local business community that was unhappy with TCNIC's top-down approach to economic development, particularly in the face of a deep recession. It demanded more inclusion, and in 1985 a group of community leaders led by Bob Ferguson and Kelso Gillenwater, the publisher of the *Tri-City Herald*, led an effort to rebrand TCNIC by removing the word "nuclear" from its name and expanding its board membership, rebranding itself as TRIDEC, the Tri-City Industrial Development Council. Ferguson became its first president.

Meanwhile, the Cold War that had sustained Hanford since the end of World War II was coming to a close. The Soviet Union had engaged in an expensive arms race with the United States, which the ailing Soviet economy could not sustain. Ultimately, it agreed to a series of arms control treaties that limited the number, range, and size of nuclear weapons, reducing the threat of mutually assured destruction and the underlying premise upon which both nation's nuclear arsenals had been created in the first place—including Hanford and the B Reactor.

A revolving door of elderly Soviet leaders proved unresponsive to the needs to their people. By 1989, it had engaged in—and lost—a costly occupation of Afghanistan, the wall dividing East from West Berlin came down, and series of mostly peaceful revolutions in the puppet buffer states of Eastern Europe changed the balance of power in Europe. A new, reform-minded Soviet leader, Mikhail Gorbachev, met American president, Ronald Reagan, to discuss an ease of tensions between the two nations. Most Americans thought the Soviet Union would continue in some form, but in 1991, after an attempted coup, it collapsed with many of its former provinces becoming independent nations.

Soviet General Secretary Mikhail Gorbachev and President Ronald Reagan sign the Intermediate-Range Nuclear Forces Treaty in 1987. *(Ronald Reagan Library)*

THE COLD WAR YEARS also saw an evolution in the government's administration of nuclear policy. In 1974, the Atomic Energy Commission was replaced by the Nuclear Regulatory Commission, which was tasked with regulating the growing nuclear power industry, and the new Energy Research and Development Administration (ERDA), which was tasked to manage the nuclear weapon, naval reactor, and energy development programs.

In 1973, the major petroleum-producing countries of the Middle East began to cut production and raise the prices of the oil they produced in retribution against countries they perceived to have helped Israel during the recent Yom Kippur War. As a major oil importer from the Middle East, the United States under the Carter administration found itself embroiled in a major oil crisis, which helped lead to its defeat in the next presidential election. On August 4, 1977, President Carter signed a law that consolidated the nation's energy policy by creating a new Department of Energy, which replaced a number of federal agencies, including ERDA and the Federal Power Administration.

THE END OF THE COLD WAR and evolving national nuclear policy raised new questions about the future of Hanford and, by extension, the future of the Tri-Cities. The growing anti-nuclear sentiment, statewide and across the nation, would provide the answer.

CHAPTER NINE

HANFORD CLEANUP AND BEYOND

ON JULY 1, 1984, thirty-six year-old Mike Lawrence, became DOE's manager of Hanford Operations, the youngest site manager in the agency's history. Son of a Washington, DC, police officer, Lawrence attended the University of Maryland where he majored in physics. Upon graduation, he joined the AEC's production division, which was responsible for the reactors and production facilities that provided the material for America's atomic weapons. After President Nixon signed the National Environmental Policy Act (NEPA) in 1970, Lawrence began developing environmental impact statements that were required under the act. He worked on nuclear non-proliferation issues during the Carter administration and was involved in the search for a national underground nuclear waste repository, which included a proposed site at Hanford.

When the US Environmental Protection Agency (EPA) was created by executive order in late 1970 after NEPA became law, the AEC contended that it was regulated only by the Atomic Energy Act and that state and other federal laws did not apply to it. That changed in 1984 when a federal court rejected that contention.

In 1976, the Washington State Legislature passed a law regulating the management of hazardous wastes located within the state. After the 1984 federal court ruling, it didn't take long for Lawrence to realize the Hanford Site was in substantial non-compliance with both EPA and state regulations and they had the statutory authority to force DOE's compliance. However, many within DOE and Hanford Site contractors still operated under the corporate culture and cloak of secrecy left over from the AEC and the Cold War. They resisted all efforts at regulation.

Plutonium production at Hanford ended in 1988 in a time of growing opposition to nuclear energy and with high levels of distrust about what had occurred at Hanford over the past forty-five years. Lawrence felt DOE's secrecy caused the agency to lose credibility and only the opening up the site and releasing previously classified documents to the public would change that.

The political landscape had also changed. The state's legendary Democratic US senators, Warren Magnuson and Scoop Jackson—who had supported Hanford and provided Sam Volpentest with much of his political clout—were gone, replaced by Republicans who were generally supportive but maintained their distance. Volpentest and Bob Ferguson overcame their early suspicions to create a close working relationship with Senator Slade Gorton, who had replaced Magnuson. Moreover, the national Democratic Party and the state's leading Democratic politicians—like Senator Brock Adams who replaced Gorton—were openly hostile to Hanford.

Then, on April 26, 1986, a graphite moderated reactor similar to Hanford's dual-purpose N Reactor, exploded at Chernobyl in Ukraine, releasing radiation across much of Europe. While the two reactors shared some similar characteristics, the design problem that caused the Chernobyl was not one of them, but that made little difference to an alarmed public. Unable to travel to Ukraine, the national press flocked to Hanford. DOE headquarters told Lawrence he couldn't talk to them. "That's crazy," he said. "There will be articles written, they can be based on fact or fiction; we've got to talk with them."[138] Reluctantly, Lawrence was given permission to take reporters on a tour of the N Reactor.

In 1986, Washington voters, spurred by anti-nuclear sentiment and hostile environmental groups, were overwhelmingly successful in placing Referendum 40—which authorized the state's governor to veto any attempt to store outside nuclear waste at Hanford—on the November 4 ballot. A day earlier, thousands of Hanford supporters, dependent on Hanford for their jobs, fought back. Almost two thousand jammed the Cable Bridge over the Columbia between Kennewick and Pasco to protest anti-nuclear sentiment in the state. Mike Lawrence attended the event. "I'm just here to support what they're doing,"

Thousands of pro-nuclear supporters rally in Kennewick to protest a statewide referendum that allowed the state to ban the storage of outside nuclear waste at Hanford, November 3, 1986.
(Hanford History Project – Washington State University Tri-Cities)

he said.[139] In spite of the pro-nuclear sentiment in the Tri-Cities, the measure easily passed statewide. Meanwhile a new report, written by a high-level task force sponsored by the governors of Washington and Oregon, suggested that Hanford could be cleaned up in thirty years, given adequate federal funding.

On his own authority but with the knowledge of DOE headquarters, Lawrence began a community education campaign, holding community meetings and releasing previously classified material detailing the history of Hanford operations, including repeated leaks and emissions going back to the start of the Manhattan Project. Probably the most dramatic disclosure detailed a deliberate 1949 experiment that released 5,500 curies of iodine 131 and other fission waste products into the atmosphere in a two-hundred-mile-by-forty-mile plume that reached from Spokane, Washington, to The Dalles in Oregon.

The purpose of the release was to help detect Soviet nuclear weapon production, but for national security reasons, no warning to the public was given.[140] Details of the release were still classified, but the Washington and Oregon congressional delegations received a classified briefing that dispelled their concerns that the test involved human experimentation.[141] However, Hanford's detractors immediately took full advantage of the disclosures.

With the end of plutonium production at Hanford, the collapse of WPPSS, the termination of the BWIP underground waste repository program, and the decision to shut down the Fast Flux Test Facility (FFTF) research reactor in 1992, it was clear that Hanford's primary focus was going to have to shift from the production of plutonium to civilian nuclear programs and to the management of the remaining nuclear wastes that had been produced over the past forty years.

Canisters of spent nuclear fuel sit under water in Hanford's K Basin awaiting removal in 2002. (*Joshua Trujillo*, Seattle Post-Intelligencer)

The majority of the waste then consisted of approximately fifty-three million gallons of high-level liquid waste—the results of the chemical separation processes that produced plutonium—stored in 177 aging underground tanks in the 200 Area located in the center of the Hanford Site. Additional non-high-level waste, called transuranic, or TRU, waste, containing elements heavier than uranium, was disposed of in cribs, similar to septic fields, where tightly packed soil restricted the movement of the waste into the groundwater. Large, water-filled basins located in the K-East and K-West Reactors and at the N Reactor contained spent reactor fuel. Low activity waste—items like shoe covers and gloves—were stored in drums and buried in trenches. Finally, DOE later estimated that as many as 444 billion gallons of contaminated liquids had been disposed of or had leaked from the underground tanks into the soil during the years of operation, creating groundwater contamination that was slowly moving toward the Columbia River.[142] Additionally, many buildings were contaminated, including the various reactors, chemical separation plants, the Plutonium Finishing Plant, and research reactors and buildings located in the 300 Area.[143] In addition, large amounts of plutonium were being stored onsite.

DOE's Richland office began negotiations with the state of Washington and regional Environmental Protection Agency officials to enter into agreement that would regulate the cleanup of the Hanford Site. The detailed negotiations were technical and difficult and went on for several years, but it became clear to all that it would be better to reach an agreement than to risk unknown consequences in court.

The Hanford Federal Facility Agreement and Consent Order—the Tri-Party Agreement (TPA)—was signed on May 15, 1989, at a formal signing ceremony in Richland. The agreement set the stage for a goal of cleaning up the Hanford Site by 2018 at a total cost of fifty-seven billion dollars, even though the negotiators didn't yet know the extent of the contamination or the technology they would use to eliminate it. At the time, none of those who signed the agreement could have guessed that the life-cycle costs to complete the cleanup of the Hanford Site would grow to an estimated range of between $323 billion and $677 billion in 2019 dollars or that cleanup could possibly take one hundred years to complete.

While DOE headquarters had agreed to the terms and conditions of the TPA, President George H. W. Bush's new energy secretary, Admiral James Watkins, was only vaguely aware of the TPA, and neither he nor the new administration's Office of Management and Budget had been briefed on the estimated price tag of the eventual cleanup effort. Lawrence nearly lost his job. Fortunately, the public and national press reacted favorably to the announcement of the agreement, and Watkins was quickly able to claim credit for it.[144]

Left to right: Washington State Department of Ecology director and future governor Christine Gregoire, EPA regional administrator Robie Russell, Mike Lawrence, and Washington governor Booth Gardner celebrate the signing of the Tri-Party Agreement in Richland on May 15, 1989. *(US Department of Energy)*

By June, DOE had reversed itself and announced a "fundamental change in priorities" and a $19.5 billion five-year plan to clean up the agency's nuclear sites, promising to change its internal culture and past "dysfunctional" activities and corporate posture.[145] The decision would validate Hanford's efforts to regain credibility and signal a dramatic change for Hanford and the Tri-Cities.

The TPA resulted in a number of unanticipated consequences. First and foremost, the decision to clean up the Hanford Site would funnel billions of federal dollars into the Tri-City economy. By 1990, Hanford's environmental management budget was at $1.2 billion, an all-time high.

Second, no future DOE site manager would ever enjoy the decision-making freedom that Lawrence had exercised. Going forward, major decisions would be made at DOE headquarters in Washington, DC, ensuring that they would be more bureaucratic and, as a result, much more political.

A third consequence was that long-term cleanup efforts would become much more technically difficult and expensive than had been anticipated. A fourth consequence was a result of the third—slipping timelines and ever-increasing costs.

Fifth, the TPA created a new set of community stakeholders, including environmentalists, Indian tribes, and other federal agencies such as the Fish and Wildlife Service and the National Park Service, perhaps making oversight more democratic and accountable but further complicating and delaying the decision-making process.

Finally, while it was always understood the cleanup would be a costly, long-term environmental and management problem, it was and remains a major *political* problem, requiring huge appropriations of funds over multiple decades while having to compete with the changing priorities of successive Congresses and presidential administrations.

HANFORD CLEANUP WAS JUST ONE of the issues facing Lawrence when he arrived in the Tri-Cities. He and his staff soon realized that there were too many contractors at Hanford and that a great deal of money could be saved if DOE reduced the current nine contractors to four, which was done in 1987. Lawrence resigned in July 1990 and energy secretary James Watkins appointed a new hard-nosed manager of the Richland Operations office to replace him.

THE NEW CONTRACTORS FACED daunting challenges. The first was the need to change the culture of the Hanford workforce—and many at DOE headquarters in Washington, DC—from production to cleanup. Many of the workers were newly hired and largely untrained for their new roles. Worker safety was an increasingly difficult problem plagued by inadequate safeguards and training. Contractors suffered from a lack of leadership and technical knowledge.

As early as 1986, some in the Tri-Cities had a vision for a new facility where they could train Hanford workers to become more proficient in dealing with potential emergencies resulting from the transportation of hazardous materials. They called their idea the Volpentest Hazardous Materials Management and Emergency Response Training Facility—HAMMER for short.

The thirty-million-dollar Volpentest HAMMER Training Facility at Hanford opened in 1997. *(HAMMER)*

Mike Lawrence was supportive but had many other issues to deal with. Members of his staff, however, worked with a growing coalition of local advocates and finally attracted Sam Volpentest's attention. His reaction was typical. "I'm looking for billions while you guys are looking for a few million," he said.[146] With the support of Westinghouse, a strong coalition of local supporters, national trade unions, and Washington's congressional delegation, the concept took shape over the next several years. It was Volpentest's last major project, and in 1997, the thirty-million-dollar, eighty-eight-acre Volpentest HAMMER Training Facility was officially dedicated.

With better training and growing environmental remediation budgets from DOE, the pace of cleanup began to pick up in the 1990s. The last remaining vestiges of Hanford's plutonium production closed. The N Reactor was shut down in 1987 and finally decommissioned in July 1991, a casualty of the end of the Cold War. DOE announced its final plan for disposing of the other production reactors in 1993, and the PUREX separation plant was deactivated—fifteen months ahead of schedule—in 1997. A Waste Receiving and Processing Facility began processing solid waste that had been contaminated with plutonium. Massive water treatment facilities began to effectively address the groundwater contamination. More than two thousand tons of irradiated fuel was removed from water-filled basins and placed in dry storage in a former chemical separation plant prior to eventually being sent to a permanent underground repository. In 2005, $1.9 billion of anti-recessionary funding was made available for labor-intensive work along the Columbia River. Hundreds of buildings were demolished, and thousands of acres of contaminated soil replaced. In 2009, 2,300 canisters of plutonium were shipped offsite to a DOE facility at Savannah River, South Carolina.

Yet, for all this success, the major unresolved Hanford cleanup mission continued to be what to do with what was now fifty-six million gallons of nuclear waste stored in aging and increasingly leaking, underground tanks. Under the terms of the TPA, DOE had agreed to remove the waste from the underground tanks and separate it into high- and low-level waste. The high-level waste would be combined with other materials and vitrified under intense heat to form molten glass, which would then be poured into steel canisters where it would harden and be buried at the underground nuclear waste repository.

In December 1998, construction began on a facility called the Waste Treatment Plant (WTP), located at Hanford's Central Plateau near the chemical separation facilities, burial pits, tank farms, and a huge open pit that would eventually contain more than one hundred reactor compartments from decommissioned US Navy nuclear submarines and surface warships awaiting inspection from Russian satellites passing overhead.

Bill Clinton won the presidency in 1992, ushering in the first Democratic administration in a dozen years. In March 1993, the signatories of the TPA agreed to a six-month delay in the start of construction of the WTP while evolving technical problems were resolved. Pumping the waste out of the aging single-shell tanks had also became a much bigger, costlier, and longer-term problem than had been anticipated. DOE estimated the eventual cost of Hanford cleanup alone could exceed the original fifty-seven-billion-dollar estimate.

By 1994, about five million dollars a day was being spent on the cleanup effort at Hanford with very little return on investment. In November, Spokane's *Spokesman-Review* newspaper ran a special report that referred to Hanford funding as a "river of public money that waters the south-central Washington economy."[147] By then, the Hanford budget had grown to $1.88 billion a year. The eighteen thousand Hanford workers were earning an average salary of forty-five thousand dollars a year. Even Sam Volpentest was impressed. "The green stuff is just raining down from heaven. All the stuff that's in the ground at Hanford I think of as a gold mine. The whole world has to be cleaned up, and this is where it could all start."[148]

Richard "Doc" Hastings was elected to Congress in the 1994 "Gingrich Revolution," from Washington's Fourth Congressional District, which included the Hanford Site. He knew adequate long-term funding would be one of the most difficult issues he would face. "The federal government created this problem. It's their responsibility to clean it up, but in a responsible way," he maintained.[149] Rather than compete with each other for DOE funding, Hastings and other members of Congress from DOE sites convinced Speaker of the House Newt Gingrich in 1995 to create the Nuclear Cleanup Caucus, allowing them to lobby for DOE appropriations together.

By 1996, the processes for treating both high- and low-level tank waste were still unresolved. Two years later, with costs still rising, DOE hit upon a strategy of privatizing the waste treatment process by entering into a contract with British Nuclear Fuels Ltd. (BNFL) to finance and build the WTP and to vitrify the waste for eventual disposal by DOE. The company estimated the actual cost of building the WTP and vitrifying an initial seven million gallons of tank waste would be $6.9 billion. The processed waste would then be sold back to DOE for long-term underground storage. BNFL estimated it would begin vitrifying waste by 2006 or 2007 and the waste from eleven of Hanford's 177 tanks would be vitrified by 2018. Thirty percent of design work, regulatory permits, and financing would be obtained within three years.

Because of the amount to time and attention it was taking, Bob Ferguson, former managing director of WPPSS and now president of the Tri-City Industrial Development Council (TRIDEC), and others began to see the management of the tank waste issue as separate from the management of the rest of the Hanford Site. They lobbied Congressman Doc Hastings to create a second DOE project office at Hanford that would focus its attention solely on the tank waste problem. Hastings got language creating the new Office of River Protection inserted into the 1999 National Defense Authorization Act. The addition of a second Hanford project office effectively increased the amount of funding authorized by

Congress for Hanford cleanup, but no one was prepared for just how much would be required.

In April 2000, BNFL submitted a new cost estimate, prepared by its subcontractor, Bechtel, and based on 100 percent private financing, of $15.2 billion. Shocked at the cost, DOE immediately terminated BNFL's contract. Mike Lawrence, who had returned as BNFL's local manager in 1999 but had resigned before the contract termination in a dispute over BNFL's refusal to renegotiate with DOE, told the *Tri-City Herald*, "We seriously underestimated the costs. It was the best (estimate) we had, but we were wrong. We have enough information now to know that this is a price that DOE cannot afford."[150] DOE went looking for a new contractor.

The Hanford Waste Treatment Plant under construction in 2005.
(US Department of Energy)

In December 2000, a consortium consisting of Bechtel National and Washington Group International had revised their cost estimate and was awarded a ten-year, four-billion-dollar contract to design and construct facilities to vitrify Hanford's tank waste. Bechtel was a different kind of contractor. Its concept was to build the WTP and leave.

Bechtel finally began construction on the WTP in July 2002, estimating that 10 percent of the tank waste might be processed by 2013, five years sooner than the previous estimate. The estimated cost of building the plant alone had grown from $3.9 billion to $5.8 billion. Like the earlier estimates, this one also turned out to be wildly optimistic—

proving once again the truth of one of Bob Ferguson's oft-repeated axioms: "When you stop work on a project, it doubles its cost."[151] By 2004, eighteen hundred workers were building the plant, but Bechtel's design-build construction concept led to frequent delays as construction outpaced design.

Then, on July 19, 2004, DOE stopped work on the plant to address new seismic concerns, increasing costs and technical difficulties. Bechtel laid off almost a third of the thirty-eight hundred workers, and a new senior-level management team was appointed to oversee the project.* The estimated cost of the facility had now soared to $11.5 billion in 2006, then $12.2 billion in 2007, and then $13.4 billion. Hastings worked with congressional appropriators to approve a flat-line annual funding level of $690 million a year. Work resumed in September 2007, but the estimated completion date had slipped to 2019 with full operation estimated to begin in 2022. The facility was 60 percent complete in 2011 when DOE notified the state regulators that it might not be able to meet several court-mandated milestones on time. Construction slowed down again while a panel of experts reviewed technical issues at the project.

Hanford's B tank farm under construction during World War II.
(Hanford History)Project – Washington State University Tri-Cities)

---

* Bob Ferguson notes that Sam Volpentest—the ultimate Hanford promoter—when nearing the end of his life in 2005, prophesized that the WTP would never be completed because of the ever-increasing cost.

Unquestionably, the construction of the WTP presented an incredibly difficult undertaking. Much of the design and equipment had never been used before. It was made more difficult by the myriad-chemical composition of the tank waste that was to be vitrified. Over the years, five different chemical separation processes had been used at Hanford, complicating the maintenance of the storage tanks, as well as the waste streams to the WTP. The first separation plants were unable to recover valuable uranium. The PUREX and REDOX plants solved that problem, but issues remained about what to do with the cesium and strontium in the tanks themselves, encapsulating them and storing them separately.[152]

In 2016, a federal court order imposed a deadline that required DOE to start producing glass by 2023, with full operation of the WTP delayed until 2036 because of further technical difficulties. The delays raised the estimated cost of the WTP from $12.2 billion to more than $17 billion, leading to mutual recriminations between DOE and Bechtel over its management practices and resulting in the agency awarding its contractor only 48 percent of what it could have earned in 2017. That same year, Congress ordered an analysis of alternative options for treating the waste. It would be conducted by a panel of experts from DOE's national laboratories and reviewed by a committee of the National Academy of Sciences.

In February 2019—thirty years after the signing of the TPA and the release of DOE's five-year plan that estimated Hanford cleanup would cost $57 billion and be completed by 2018—DOE released a new report providing the first new estimates of the cost of Hanford cleanup since 2016. The estimated cost of treating and disposing of just the tank waste increased from $53.5 billion in 2016 to between $221.4 and $518.3 billion in 2019. DOE now estimated that the total cost of cleaning up the Hanford Site had tripled from $107.7 billion in 2016 to at least $323.2 billion in 2019. The upper range of the estimate soared to $677 billion. Even DOE's lower estimate would require Congress to increase the level of its appropriations from $2.4 billion to nearly $9 billion a year and extend the estimated time needed to clean up the site out to 2079.[153]

Doc Hastings, who had retired from Congress in 2015, responded to the report by saying, "I think we have to be realistic about what we can reasonably expect Congress to appropriate every year, particularly in times like this when discretionary spending is being squeezed by mandatory spending requirements. I think at some point Congress is going to come back to DOE and tell them, 'You have to find some less expensive way of doing this.'"[154]

The dramatic cost increases and slipping timeframes had been suspected for some time by the regulators but not confirmed until the release of DOE's 2019 report, prompting growing concerns about the viability of some planned components of the WTP and accelerating the search for other solutions. One possible solution is to change the way DOE contracts are awarded, requiring that new contracts describe a start, middle, and end to cleanup projects, rather than viewing them as ending many decades in the future. Another approach would require that more of the annual appropriations are spent on actual cleanup, rather than on overhead. TRIDEC, the regional economic development organization, estimated that almost half of the annual funding for Hanford cleanup is spent keeping the aging facilities at Hanford in a "minimum safe" condition.

The WTP had been designed to treat all the high-level radioactive waste in Hanford's underground tanks but not all the low-level waste. Another proposed solution is to change the way that tank waste is classified and treated in the first place. The United States is the only country in the world that defines all waste resulting from the chemical processing of irradiated nuclear fuels as high-level waste as opposed to classifying it based on its radiological properties. In 2017, a national coalition of local governments located near DOE sites began calling on DOE to consider changing its definition of high-level waste, arguing that 90 percent of the fifty-six million gallons of waste stored in Hanford underground tanks could be managed as low-level waste after being pretreated and removing cesium from the waste stream. Proponents contend that the remaining low-level waste—most of the current tank waste—could be combined with a concrete-like grout substance and sent to existing permitted facilities in other states. After removing as much of the waste as possible, the tanks themselves could be filled with grout and then remain in the ground permanently. The remaining high-level waste would still need to be vitrified and buried in a deep underground repository like Yucca Mountain, Nevada.

In 2018, DOE conducted a demonstration project called the Test Bed Initiative (TBI) in which three gallons of low-level waste were treated commercially and shipped out of state for final disposal. In 2019, DOE began a larger demonstration project that would have treated two thousand gallons of low-level waste before it was shut down by Washington State regulators who required a new permit.

Spurred on by the higher cost estimates of treating and disposing of the tank waste at Hanford and other sites, DOE announced on June 5, 2019, that it would allow what had previously been considered high level waste to be reclassified on a case-by-case basis. The new policy allows DOE to expand its potential disposal options based on the

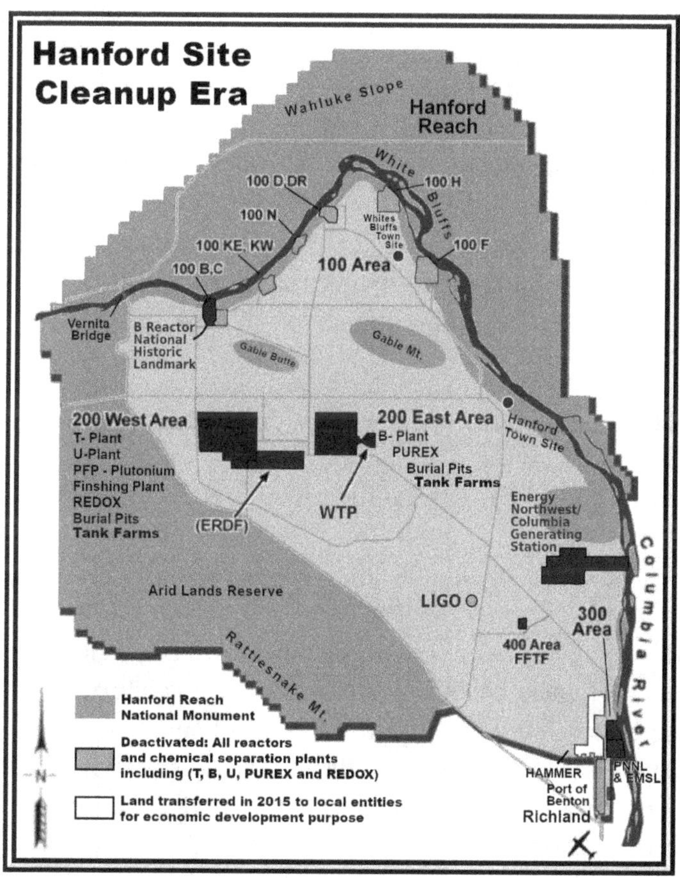

The Hanford Site in the modern cleanup period, showing the Hanford Reach National Monument and deactivated facilities. (Chris Picken)

composition of the waste, using existing licensed disposal sites and limiting the time and cost of storing the waste at DOE sites. This is particularly important because DOE is decades away from opening a deep underground depository like Yucca Mountain.[155]

Skeptics, including state regulators and environmental groups, have argued against changing the legal definition of tank waste, using any technology other than costly vitrification to treat tank waste, or taking any action that would result in the long-term storage of tank waste at Hanford, setting up the possibility of a costly and time-consuming legal confrontation between the states and the federal government in federal court. An added complication is that court-ordered deadlines are not enforceable if Congress declines or fails to appropriate the necessary funding to achieve them. It is now apparent that the court-imposed 2023 deadlines under the TPA will not be met, and community leaders are speaking out, urging the parties to support these new technologies.[156]

As this is being written, it is increasingly clear that the rising cost of treating all the waste at the WTP is unacceptable but that politics, government inertia, and over-regulation are all impeding future progress. The current history of Hanford remains as extraordinary as its past. How the story will ultimately end is unknown.

THE EFFORTS TO CLEAN UP the Hanford Site, while frustrating in their cost and complexity, had resulted in major changes to the Tri-Cities economy. The double-digit unemployment that had plagued the Tri-Cities during the 1980s as a result of a national recession and the WPPSS debacle finally fell below 8 percent. The Tri-Cities metro area had grown by only fourteen thousand between 1980 and 1990—Richland's population had actually declined by 1,263 residents—but the community had also become more diverse. These efforts needed to be expanded in order to recognize the growth of small business, tourism, and research and development, rather than rely solely on Hanford. So, while DOE and its regulators were struggling with the issues related to cleaning up the site, community leaders like Bob Ferguson and Sam Volpentest continued their efforts to find new missions and projects that would bring diversification and new jobs to the community. One such project was already at hand.

The collapse of WPPSS had led to few positive outcomes, but one of them was the completed WNP-2 nuclear power plant, the only WPPSS reactor to be finished. Construction had begun in 1977 on the $465 million reactor located on the Hanford Site about ten miles north of Richland. By the time it began operation in 1984, it had cost $3.2 billion. By that time, the stress of trying to save WPPSS had resulted in a major heart attack, open heart surgery, and the resignation of Bob Ferguson, then only forty-nine, who had been recruited to try to save the troubled agency. A year later, he was serving as chairman of the Richland-based UNC Nuclear Industries and president of the TCNIC, the region's local economic development agency.

WNP-2, renamed the Columbia Generating Station, was operated by WPPSS's renamed successor entity, Energy Northwest, a joint operating agency formed in 1957 by Washington State to supply at-cost power for Northwest utilities. Its 1,207-megawatt output is enough to power the city of Seattle and is equivalent to about 10 percent of all the electricity generated in Washington and 4 percent of

Columbia Generating Station. *(Energy Northwest)*

all electricity in the Pacific Northwest. All its output is provided to the Bonneville Power Administration at cost under a formal agreement in which BPA pays the costs of maintaining and operating the facility.

In 1985, Volpentest and Ferguson successfully engineered a merger between the Tri-City Nuclear Industrial Council (TCNIC) and the Tri-Cities Chamber of Commerce, which resulted in the creation of the Tri-City Industrial Development Council (TRIDEC), which had an expanded membership and mandate. Sam Volpentest, now in his eighties, who had been one of TCNIC's founders, remained responsible for Hanford-related projects.

Volpentest and Ferguson, sometimes joined by others, continued their frequent lobbying trips to Washington, DC. By their own count, they made between ten and fifteen trips there a year. Sam provided his reputation and uncanny political instincts, Ferguson, who had by now acquired most of the same contacts as well as many more of his own, contributed his deep technical knowledge and his broad experience to the marketing effort.

The Superconducting Magnetic Energy Storage System (SMES) program began in 1986 and was an important component of the Reagan administration's proposed laser missile defense system. Essentially, SMES was like a giant underground automobile battery but with much higher efficiency and a longer cycle life. Like a car battery, it could be charged and discharged repeatedly. The unit would be connected to a

Bob Ferguson (*center*) announces the creation of TRIDEC during a June 1, 1985, press conference while Sam Volpentest (*second from right*) listens.
(*Robert L. Ferguson*)

utility's transmission or distribution system and would allow for the direct storage of approximately one hundred megawatts of electrical energy without mechanical or chemical conversion processes being needed.[155] When Volpentest and Ferguson heard about the project, they decided that Hanford was a perfect location for it.

In May 1989, after some intense lobbying, it was announced that Hanford was among five sites being considered for a $130 million SMES installation. Not much else was going on at Hanford beyond the construction of the last of the double-shelled nuclear waste tanks, so the two hundred construction jobs, thirty permanent jobs, and annual operating budget of five million dollars were seen as a major boon to the Tri-Cities economy.

The election of President George H. W. Bush in 1988 led to the elimination of many of the Reagan administration's defense programs, and SMES was one of the casualties. The Soviet Union had collapsed. Efforts continued to find funding from other public and private sources for the energy storage component of SMES but without success. Volpentest and Hanford lost another project to changing national priorities.

The Laser Interferometer Gravitational-Wave Observatory (LIGO) was a large-scale physics experiment designed to detect gravitational waves that were believed to have originated hundreds of millions of light years away from Earth during the creation of the universe. Those waves were thought to be so small that they would be roughly equal to one-tenth of a trillionth of the diameter of a human hair. They had first been predicted by Einstein's theory of general relativity in 1916. The proposed observatory would measure these waves using laser interferometers—mirrors suspended at each corner of an L-shaped tunnel two and a half miles long on each side. Precision laser beams in the interferometers were supposed to sense the slightest motion of the mirrors caused by a gravitational wave.

Volpentest somehow found out about the project. Texas was thought to be the leading contender to land the project. "Texas! I'll take care of that," Volpentest responded when he was told about the project. "What is it?"

"It's a Laser Interferometer Gravitational-Wave Observatory."

"What are they going to call it?" Volpentest asked.

"LIGO."

"I'd better write it out. . . . What is it again? Oh, never mind. I don't want to know."

He left for Washington, DC, the next morning.[156] With some well-placed help in Washington, he contacted the project's sponsors at Caltech and MIT and invited them to visit the Tri-Cities where he convinced them the Hanford Site had merit because of its scientific community; it was not just a waste site. The groundbreaking for the LIGO observatory at Hanford took place on July 6, 1994. It was the largest project ever funded by the National Science Foundation at the time. A second observatory is located in Louisiana, and a third was later built in Italy.

No gravitational waves were discovered between 2002 and 2010 when the apparatus was replaced with more sensitive equipment. Then, in 2016, it detected its first gravitational waves. Another first was the detection of a collision of two neutron stars, on August 17, 2017, which simultaneously produced optical signals detectable by conventional telescopes.[157] Over the next two years, LIGO and its twin facilities in Louisiana and Italy detected more than a dozen waves resulting in the collision of black holes in the universe, the collision of two neutron stars that occurred 4.6 billion years ago, and most recently, the first observation of waves that were created when a black hole swallowed a

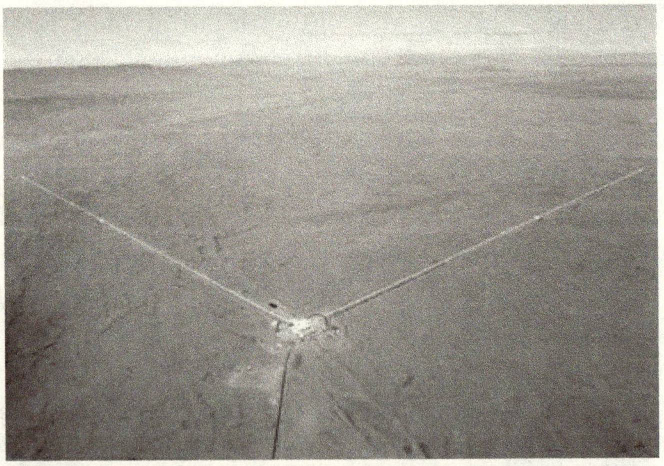

LIGO Hanford observatory. Rattlesnake Mountain (*upper left*) and Hanford Site in background. (*Caltech/MIT/LIGO Laboratory*)

neutron star more than 1.2 billion years ago.[158] The Hanford LIGO site is an example of non-nuclear diversification that promotes science and research, as well as tourism and economic development.

When William R. "Bill" Wiley was named director of PNNL in June 1984, the first African American director at PNNL and only the second named to direct any national laboratory. Wiley was a force to be reckoned with. He was a talented communicator, an excellent salesman, and a hard man to say no to. He was active in the community and deeply involved in the effort to create a branch campus of Washington State University in the Tri-Cities.

Wiley set out to create a unique and world-class scientific capability at PNNL that would not compete with the capabilities of the other national laboratories. The idea that would become the Environmental Molecular Sciences Laboratory (EMSL) came out of a 1986 National Academy of Sciences report that identified scientific challenges relating to energy and the environment that required new fundamental research. By 1988, he had developed a concept for a state-of-the-art research laboratory where scientists and researchers from around the world could undertake research into the world's greatest environmental, health, and energy challenges at the molecular level while still interfacing with the physical and life sciences in an integrated and collaborative manner, using one of the largest super computers in the world.

Environmental Molecular Sciences Laboratory. (US Department of Energy)

Wiley worked with Sam Volpentest and with Washington's congressional delegation—particularly Washington's newly elected senator, Patty Murray—to find $230 million in DOE funding for the project. Wiley wanted the two-hundred-thousand-square-foot laboratory to be built on PNNL's campus. DOE, which was paying for the project, wanted it built on the Hanford Site. A compromise was brokered in which PNNL sold DOE a tract of land on its campus where the project was built. On October 16, 1996, the William R. Wiley Environmental Molecular Science Laboratory was dedicated under blue skies in front of six hundred people on the PNNL campus. Unfortunately, Wiley was not there, having died the previous June.

TODAY, THE MIGHTY COLUMBIA RIVER continues to flow south, past the Priest Rapids Valley, around the Great Horn of the Columbia, by the Wahluke Slope and the White Bluffs, past the Tri-Cities, and on to the sea—the solitary cocooned reactor buildings standing along its bank—almost insignificant in the wide expanse of the majestic landscape, a reminder of a short time in history when momentous occurrences happened there.

That unobstructed flow of the river had almost been blocked. In the mid-1960s, the Army Corps of Engineers began to study the potential of building a new hydroelectric dam across the southern Hanford Reach north of Richland. The proposed Ben Franklin Dam would have helped open the river to navigation all the way to Wenatchee, but at the cost of flooding the Hanford Reach, destroying the salmon spawning grounds, and water levels rising from the reservoir that would be created behind the dam. Environmentalists, fishermen, and even the Atomic Energy Commission objected, the latter because of the impact the higher water table would have on the underground tanks storing nuclear waste. The issue was floated again in the late 1970s with the same result and was finally dropped in 1981.

But the future of the Hanford Reach remained a controversial and hotly debated issue. Everyone wanted the Hanford Reach to be preserved; the issue was who would control it. A coalition of local governments, developers, and irrigators supported by Congressman Doc Hastings sparred with a coalition of eco-friendly congressmen, environmentalists, and fishermen, backed by Senator Patty Murray to promote their very different visions for the protection of the Hanford Reach.

While the primary focus of the battle was on the future of the Hanford Reach corridor, it came to include approximately 194,000 acres of Hanford land that had never been utilized for plutonium production. Because of the nature of the activities at Hanford, most of the site had been virtually undisturbed for thirty years. These included the Saddle Mountain National Wildlife Preserve and the Wahluke Slope Wildlife Refuge, both located north and east of the Columbia River across from the plutonium reactors, and the large Fitzner-Eberhardt Arid Lands Ecology (ALE) Reserve, on the west edge of the site, including a large part of Rattlesnake Mountain. The matter was resolved on June 10, 2000, when Vice President Al Gore, the presumptive Democratic nominee for president, visited the Tri-Cities to announce the creation of the Hanford Reach National Monument. The monument would be operated by another federal agency, the US Fish and Wildlife Service.

The Hanford Reach of the Columbia River as it passes through the Hanford Site. Note deactivated reactor buildings along the river in the left-center of the image. (US Fish and Wildlife Service)

Vice President Al Gore announcing the creation of the
Hanford Reach National Monument on June 10, 2000.
(Doc Hastings)

Only twenty days after Gore announced the creation of the
Hanford Reach National Monument, a large part of it went up in
flames, sparked by a vehicle accident on the site. The weather was
over one hundred degrees, and the hot winds blew at a sustained
speed of twenty miles an hour. In one ninety-minute period, the fire
traveled twenty miles across the Arid Lands Ecology Reserve and
was consuming an average of two thousand acres an hour.[159] Two
days later, on Thursday, June 29, Energy Secretary Bill Richardson
and Congressman Doc Hastings flew out from Washington to view
the situation firsthand. By the time they arrived, the fire had burned
over 190,000 acres and three radioactive waste sites. At least twenty
homes in Benton City and West Richland had been destroyed, and
seven thousand houses had been evacuated. Governor Gary Locke
issued a state of emergency, and nine hundred firefighters using
aerial tankers successfully fought the blaze.

AS CLEANUP PROCEEDED, there was increasing demand for public
access to, and privatization of, the Hanford Site. Hastings had been
trying for years to open public access to Rattlesnake Mountain
over the objections of local Indian tribes and the Fish and Wildlife
Service, which controlled access to the mountain since the creation

of the Hanford Reach National Monument. Similarly, community leaders, including TRIDEC, the city of Richland, and the Port of Benton, lobbied Hastings to force DOE to turn over more than thirteen hundred acres of never-before utilized land adjacent to the city on the southern edge of the site for future economic development purposes. Energy Northwest, the operator of the Columbia Generating Station, asked that another three hundred acres to be transferred to it.

Back in the 1960s, community leaders had embraced the vision of a vast nuclear energy park that would replace plutonium production at Hanford. Now, in 2019, a new generation of community leaders are pursuing a new version of that old dream: a clean, or green, energy complex where research and development, manufacturing, and supporting infrastructure could support vast solar power generation facilities, small modular nuclear power reactors, wind turbine development and manufacturing, and a new generation of bio-fuels building on research already being conducted at Pacific Northwest National Laboratory and Washington State University Tri-Cities.

There was ample precedent to support the land transfer. Much of the Port of Benton's land in North Richland had once been part of the Hanford Site. In 2014, Hastings, then chairman of the powerful House Natural Resources Committee, was able to insert language in the 2015 National Defense Authorization Act—which authorized Hanford funding—to approve both requests. As a result, TRIDEC's Mid-Columbia Energy Initiative, a coalition of seventy-five energy-related Tri-City businesses and a partnership of North Richland landowners including PNNL, WSU Tri-Cities, the Port of Benton, and the city of Richland, are pursuing energy-related projects that could utilize the newly acquired land.

Hastings, along with his counterparts in Tennessee and New Mexico, had been working on another issue that would open parts of the Hanford Site to future tourism. The proposed Manhattan Project National Historic Park would include physical facilities at all three former Manhattan Project sites, including the historic B Reactor and several pre-Hanford sites, including the former Hanford and White Bluffs town sites. The reactor operated for twenty-four years before being shut down permanently in 1968.

The B Reactor had much to recommend it for inclusion in the proposed park. It was already recognized as an engineering and National Historic Landmark. It had produced the first plutonium used in the Trinity test in New Mexico and the Nagasaki bomb. It had also produced the first tritium, used to test the first hydrogen bomb at Bikini Atoll in 1954.

After several failed attempts, Doc Hastings was successful at inserting funding to create the park in the 2015 National Defense Authorization Act (NDAA), introducing yet another federal agency, the US National Park Service, to the Hanford equation. It conducts frequent popular public tours of the reactor and additional tours of the few remaining pre-Hanford buildings in cooperation with the B Reactor Museum Association (BRMA). Tours of the reactor are also available to the passengers of the popular paddle-wheel cruise boats that call at nearby Richland.

School children help a park ranger raise the NPS flag over the B Reactor on November 11, 2015. *(US National Park Service)*

No one knows how the history of Hanford will eventually play out. Cost estimates for cleaning up the Hanford Site are not—and have not been—sustainable from a congressional appropriations standpoint for some time. New technologies may already be available that could decrease the amount of time and cost of completing the cleanup process. New technologies may already be available that could decrease the amount of time and cost of completing the cleanup process.

As this book is being written, DOE is taking steps to decrease the cost of administering the site, such as its recent 2019 decision to combine the two DOE offices responsible for cleanup—Richland Operations and the Office of River Protection—for the first time since 1995. It may also be past time for DOE to review the number of outside contractors working for it at the Hanford Site. Increasing the number of DOE offices and Hanford contractors in the past resulted in bringing more money into the Tri-Cities economy, but as the community approaches three hundred thousand in population and its economy has become more diversified, Hanford is no longer as important to the region's economic future as it once was.

Some portions of the site, particularly the Central Plateau consisting of approximately seven thousand acres where the tank farms and burial pits are located, will never be able to be reused for other public or private use. They will remain under the control of the federal government indefinitely. Over time, the remainder of the site is likely to be used for other purposes, continuing the current trends, consistent with public safety and future government requirements.

Environmental groups, state and federal regulators, and their political constituencies will almost certainly object to DOE's proposals to reduce the cost and time required to clean up the Hanford Site, setting up a classic political test of will between the states, which have the legal authority to regulate what happens at Hanford, and Congress, which has the power to pay for it or not.

The federal government created the Hanford Site, and it has a responsibility to clean it up. It is not appropriate for the government to simply leave, potentially creating another economic downturn in the nearby communities it helped create. The government has an obligation to use some of its potential cost savings at Hanford to help facilitate the transition the site to other job-generating uses, such as financially supporting the creation of a clean energy park or providing funding for education and training for jobs in those new industries that might locate there.

THE HISTORY OF HANFORD presents a mixed legacy. What originally happened there represents a triumph of engineering, chemistry, nuclear medicine, and other research that helped win World War II and protect the nation during the Cold War. In accomplishing those goals, it created an environmental nightmare that remains to this day. In the process, the Hanford Site helped create the fifth largest urban area in the Pacific Northwest—so economically diversified that it no longer needs to rely primarily on what happens there.

Perhaps the most lasting positive legacy of the Hanford Site is the growth and expansion of the Pacific Northwest National Laboratory, still managed for the US Department of Energy by Battelle. With more than four thousand scientists, researchers, and support staff working in basic and applied science, it is the major long-term positive result of the Hanford story. It has become one of the nation's premier national laboratories and remains the only original Hanford contractor to retain its contract. The US Department of Energy's EMSL, located at PNNL,

PNNL campus in 2018. Columbia River and White Bluffs on right, Hanford Site in background. (*Pacific Northwest National Laboratory*)

is a national scientific user facility open to researchers from all over the world. The Bioproducts, Sciences, and Engineering Laboratory (BSEL), located on the campus of the nearby Washington State University Tri-Cities, a leader in bioproducts research, is the result of a joint venture with PNNL. The LIGO observatory at Hanford, along with its sister facilities in Louisiana and Italy, are observing gravitational waves that open a window to the very creation of our universe. Together, they generate spin-off technologies, research, and new job opportunities in the Tri-Cities.

While the Manhattan Project has passed into history, the importance of its role is not forgotten. Fascinating new facts about the project and those who worked on it emerge almost daily. Leading this effort is the Hanford History Project based at Washington State University Tri-Cities. It has inherited DOE's collection of documents, pictures, and artifacts from its earlier operation of the site, as well as has conducted hundreds of oral interviews with former pre-Hanford residents, Hanford workers, including African American workers, and community leaders. Its first book based on these interviews, *Nowhere to Remember*, was published in 2018.

The historic B Reactor and the Hanford Site—important in the telling of the Manhattan Project story—live on, constantly evolving and creating new history with each passing year. They remind us to respect the past, learn from the present, and embrace the future.

ACKNOWLEDGMENTS

So many people have helped us with this book that it is impractical to list them all here. You know who you are, and we appreciate your help more than we can say. Richland and the Tri-Cities are full of people who both have the background and experience and were willing to give liberally of their time and knowledge to assist us with this project.

Some, however, deserve our special recognition because of their help in their various fields of expertise. They include John Fox, Maynard Plahuta, Ron Kathren, Steve Arneson, Tom Moak, Gary Kleinknecht, Bruce Bjornstad, Mike Lawrence, former congressman Richard "Doc" Hastings, Robert Redder Franklin, chief archivist at the Hanford History Project at Washington State University Tri-Cities.

Any errors that remain after the assistance we have received are ours alone.

We are pleased to be working again with Sheryn Hara's Book Publisher's Network team: Julie Scandora, editor; Laura Zugzda, cover design; Melissa Coffman, book design; and Cher Paul, indexer. Chris Picken prepared the various maps. Dr. Delmar Larson, associate professor of chemistry at the University of California at Davis and director of the online LibreTexts Libraries, prepared the diagrams of the atom and fission.

ATOMS TO FISSION

IN 1939, THE HUNGARIAN PHYSICIST, Leó Szilárd, now working in America, and the famous German physicist, Albert Einstein, drafted a letter to President Franklin Roosevelt describing recent research using the element uranium that could cause a nuclear chain reaction and warning that these discoveries could lead to the construction of extremely powerful bombs and that Germany was pursuing this technology. Their letter set in motion what became the Manhattan Project, the development of the Hanford Site, and the construction of the B Reactor at Hanford, the world's first full-scale nuclear reactor. To understand the importance of the Szilárd-Einstein letter, it is necessary to understand the history of atomic research that led to the efforts to build an atomic bomb.

ELEMENTS ARE THE PRIMARY components of all matter found on earth. To date, more than one hundred of these substances have been discovered, but some of those discovered more recently are man-made. The atom is the basic unit of an element, consisting of a nucleus containing one or more subatomic particles, called protons, and a similar number of neutrons. Other subatomic particles, called electrons, orbit the nucleus. Protons have a positive electric charge, and neutrons have no electric charge. The negatively charged electrons are bound to the positively charged nucleus by an energy force created by the opposing electric charges.

The number of protons and neutrons in the atom's nucleus determines the element's atomic weight, or number, the mass of electrons being negligible. The hydrogen atom (H), which has only one proton and one neutron, is the lightest element while the natural uranium-238 atom (U) is the heaviest with ninety-two protons and 146 neutrons.

If the number of protons and electrons is equal, the atom is electrically neutral and generally stable, but if an atom contains more or fewer electrons than its atomic number, it becomes positively or negatively charged as a whole. If the element is naturally radioactive, protons and neutrons can be ejected from the nucleus, leaving behind an element that is different from the original. This process is called nuclear transmutation.

Isotopes are different forms of the same element. They have in common the same number of protons and electrons but differ in the number of neutrons. For example, there are two different uranium isotopes in nature. Uranium-235 has 143 neutrons while uranium-238 has 146 neutrons. Because of the fewer number of neutrons, U-235 is more unstable than the more common U-238 and splits into two or more neutrons and other elements when it is bombarded by other neutrons. When this occurs, the resulting neutrons and other elements weigh less than the U-235. This difference in weight (mass) is converted into heat and energy according to Einstein's famous formula.* This process is called fission. A nuclear chain reaction occurs when more and more U-235 atoms fission, releasing two or three neutrons—a process akin to how rabbits multiply.

THE GREEK PHILOSOPHER Democritus of Abdera and his mentor, Leucippus, lived in the fourth century BC and were among the first people known to record a theory of the atom. The word itself comes from the Greek word *atomos*, meaning indivisible. They theorized that matter consists of separate, solid, eternal, invisible, and intangible unit-particles, which are physically and theoretically indivisible, are different in shape, require space in which to move, but can be moved only by

---

* In Einstein's formula, $E=mc^2$, E stands for energy, m for the mass that is converted into energy, and c for the velocity of light.

physical action. Their theory was based on philosophical and theological reasoning, rather than on any actual evidence or experimentation, which made it difficult to convince their many skeptics, including Aristotle.

It wasn't until 1803—approximately 2,200 years later—that English chemist John Dalton's experimentation and observation provided the first truly scientific theory of the atom as the fundamental building block of all chemical structures. Dalton's theory proposed that everything on Earth is composed of atoms, which form the indivisible building blocks of matter and cannot be destroyed. He concluded that the atoms of an individual element, like hydrogen, are all identical to each other chemically but the atoms of different elements vary in size and mass. He contended that chemical compounds were composed of combinations of atoms in defined ratios and chemical reactions resulted in the rearrangement of those atomic ratios.

A flurry of new research occurred at the end of the nineteenth century. In 1895, Wilhelm Röntgen, a German mechanical engineer and physicist, produced and detected electromagnetic radiation in a wavelength range known as X-rays, or Röntgen rays, an achievement that earned him the first Nobel Prize in Physics in 1901. A year later, a French physicist, Henri Becquerel, discovered that uranium was radioactive without being subjected to electromagnetic radiation. In 1898, the French physicist Pierre Curie and his Polish-born wife Marie Skłodowska Curie discovered an element they called radium. They were the first to use the term "radioactivity." Pierre Curie and one of his students were the first to discover nuclear energy by identifying the continuous emission of heat from radium particles. He investigated the emissions using magnetic fields and determined that some of the emissions were positively charged, some were negatively charged, and some were neutral.

In 1897, the English physicist J. J. Thomson revolutionized atomic research. First appointed as professor of physics at the University of Cambridge's Cavendish Laboratory in 1884, Thomson was an accomplished mathematician and teacher. His research on the conductivity of X-rays on various gases led to his breakthrough discovery of the electron—the first subatomic particle to be discovered.

J. J. Thomson. *(www.firstworldwar.com)*

In 1904, Thomson first suggested a model of the atom that consisted of a sphere of positive matter in which negatively charged electrons were imbedded—like plums in a pudding. Thomson is also credited with finding the first evidence of the existence of isotopes in 1913. His efforts to determine the nature of positively charged particles led to the development of the mass spectrograph to measure the mass of a sample. Two years later in 1906, Thomson was awarded the Nobel Prize in Physics.

ONE OF THOMSON'S most famous students was Ernest Rutherford, born in New Zealand in 1871 at a time when it was still a remote British colony. After attending university in New Zealand, he arrived at the Cavendish in 1895 only a month after Röntgen had discovered radiation. Learning of Becquerel's discovery of radiation emitted from uranium, Rutherford discovered two types of radiation that differed from X-rays. Moving to McGill University in Canada in 1899, Rutherford coined the terms alpha ray and beta ray to describe two of the types of radiation emitted from uranium. In 1903, he was joined at McGill by a young chemist, Frederick Soddy, and together they observed a third type of radiation, which had been originally discovered but not named by the French physicist and chemist Paul Villard in 1900. They named this new type of radiation gamma radiation.

Rutherford found that different quantities of a given radioactive element decay at the same rate. At the time, he had written, "If it were ever possible to control at will the rate of disintegration of the radio elements, an enormous amount of energy could be obtained from a small amount of matter."[160]

The work of Soddy and Rutherford did not go unnoticed. In 1914, the British author, H. G. Wells, who personally knew Soddy, published *The World Set Free* in which he described a continuously exploding device. Wells understood the slow natural radioactive decay of elements like radium continues for thousands of years, and while the *rate* of energy release is negligible, the *total amount* released is huge. Wells used this as the basis for his story.[161]

In 1907, Rutherford returned to England to accept an appointment as professor of physics at the University of Manchester, where John Dalton had revived the atomic theory almost a century before. Rutherford, a physicist, was rather surprised when he was awarded the Nobel Prize in Chemistry, rather than physics, in 1908.

Rutherford performed some of his most famous work at Manchester. A bigger-than-life personality, he was famous for marching around his laboratory singing "Onward Christian Soldiers" off-key. Chaim Weizmann, a biochemist who would become the first president of Israel, was just one of the famous personalities who worked with Rutherford at Manchester. He later wrote that Rutherford would talk "loudly and impassioned about anything, whether he knew anything about it or not."[162]

At Manchester, Rutherford inherited a German physicist named Hans Geiger who, in 1908, had developed a principle underlying what became known as the Geiger counter. Working with Rutherford, Geiger invented an electrical device that clicked at the arrival of alpha particles. Subsequently, Geiger returned to Germany and collaborated with Walther Müller, resulting in the development of a practical gas-filled detector tube that could be used for virtually any type of ionizing radiation, including alpha, beta, gamma, X-rays, and even neutrons.

In 1909, Rutherford, along with Geiger and Ernest Marsden, conducted experiments in which a beam of alpha particles was directed at very thin gold foil. The results were surprising. Nearly all the alpha particles passed straight through the gold foil, a few were deflected at large

Ernest Rutherford at his laboratory at McGill University in 1905.
(*http://wellcomeimages.org/indexplus/image/L0014629.html*)

angles, but only a tiny fraction of the particles—about one in eight thousand—was propelled backwards like a tennis ball bouncing off a solid wall. This result was not at all consistent with Thomson's plum-pudding atomic model.

Subsequently, in 1911, Rutherford developed his own atomic model. He characterized the atom as having a highly dense central nucleus that contained most of the mass, surrounded by electrons moving around it in circular orbits like a small solar system with the number of orbiting electrons exactly the same as the number of positively charged protons in the nucleus.

The Rutherford atom theory was a major step forward but defective in that it could not account for the atom's stability. This problem was remedied in 1913 by the Danish physicist Niels Bohr, who had discovered in 1921 that electrons move in specific orbits around the nucleus. Rutherford's model was further refined in 1916 by Arnold Sommerfeld, who established that electron orbits were elliptical and not circular. The modern symbolic representation of the atom is based on Rutherford's and Bohr's characterization, which shows a symbolic dense central nucleus surrounded by a few orbiting electrons in elliptical orbits.

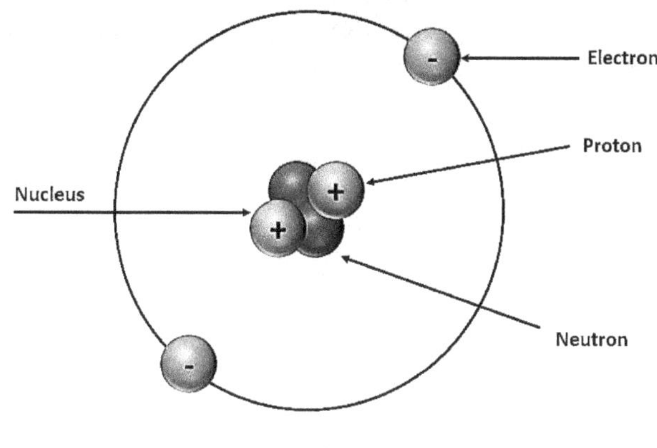

Simplified drawing of a helium atom. *(LibreTexts/Delmar Larsen)*

Rutherford became the director of the Cavendish Laboratory at Cambridge in 1919 where he worked with Niels Bohr; James Chadwick, who discovered the neutron in 1932; and John Cockcroft and Ernest Walton, who later that same year developed a voltage multiplier and used it to create a high-voltage apparatus known as the Cockcroft-Walton machine or accelerator, conducting the first experimentation that could split the nucleus of an atom under controlled conditions.

Rutherford realized there must be positive charge centers within the atom to balance the negative electrons and create electrically neutral atoms. Rutherford's discovery of the nucleus demonstrated these positive charges were concentrated in a very small fraction of the atoms' volume. He was the first to use the term "proton" to describe this phenomenon in 1920.

While Cockcroft and Walton were conducting their experiments at the Cavendish in 1932, an American physicist, Ernest Lawrence, working at the University of California at Berkeley, patented the cyclotron, an early version of a particle accelerator in which charged atomic particles are accelerated in a spiral trajectory to very high energies in a rapidly varying electric field. These accelerators, or atom smashers as they were called, contributed greatly to our knowledge of atomic structure, as well as produced new elements such as plutonium that did not exist in nature.

Lawrence was awarded the Nobel Prize in 1940 for the cyclotron, among other accomplishments, and would become an important figure in the Manhattan Project.

JAMES CHADWICK, who would later become another of Rutherford's students, joined Hans Geiger in Berlin in 1913 where he had hoped to study beta radiation. When Geiger was called up to serve in World War I, Chadwick remained and was interned in a prison camp for the rest of the war. Interestingly, he was able to carry out experimental physics work during his internment and wrote up the results after the war when he returned to England. Chadwick arrived at the Cavendish in 1919.

Chadwick became a leader in British atomic research, working with Rutherford and others on experiments that led to the discovery of the neutron, an important discovery that explained many of the unknowns regarding the structure of the atom and was later essential to the discovery of fission and its applications to nuclear power and nuclear weapons. He received the Nobel Prize in Physics in 1935. In 1932, he worked with Rutherford and others on experiments that led to the discovery of the neutron, making it possible to examine the nucleus of an atom for the first time. His discovery led to his receiving the Nobel Prize in Physics in 1935. In 1941, he was one of the authors of the British MAUD report that was instrumental in the US decision to proceed with atomic bomb.

IN 1934, FRÉDÉRIC JOLIOT and his wife Irène Curie, the daughter of Marie Skłodowska and Pierre Curie, discovered artificial radiation. Building on the work of her parents who had isolated naturally occurring radioactive elements, the Joliot-Curies succeeded in creating artificial radioactivity by bombarding light elements such as magnesium and aluminum with alpha particles and correctly interpreting the results of these experiments. Their discovery was of vital importance because it proved radioactivity is not limited to the handful of elements found in nature and other radioactive materials that could be used beneficially in medical, industrial, and research applications could be created quickly, cheaply, and plentifully. They received the Nobel Prize in Chemistry in 1935.

Niels Bohr in his 1922 Nobel Prize picture. *(www.nobelprize.org)*

ANOTHER OF RUTHERFORD's famous students was the Danish physicist Niels Bohr. Completing his PhD thesis in 1911, Bohr moved to England to study under J. J. Thomson, but Thomson was unimpressed with Bohr, a view that may have stemmed from the fact Bohr had earlier told the great man that he had found errors in Thomson's electron-theory work. One night, Bohr heard Rutherford speak and was so impressed that he requested permission to move his research to Manchester, arriving there in 1912. He studied radioactive research under Hans Geiger while pursuing his studies in electron theory.

Influenced by the work of Einstein and buoyed by Rutherford's encouragement, Bohr published a paper in 1913 in which he hypothesized on a new atomic model that depicted the atom as a small, positively charged nucleus surrounded by electrons that travelled in circular orbits, but with the attraction being provided by electrostatic forces rather than gravity. His theory earned him the Nobel Prize in Physics in 1922.

Bohr later continued his research in his native country at the University of Copenhagen. When Germany occupied Denmark in 1940, Bohr managed to keep his small institute open, but many of his foreign-born researchers left. Bohr was aware of the possibility of using uranium-235 to construct a bomb, referring to it in lectures in Britain and Denmark shortly before the war began, but didn't believe it was technically feasible to separate a sufficient quantity of uranium-235 from natural uranium to make a bomb.

In September 1941, the war in Europe was two years old. Werner Heisenberg, the director of Germany's nuclear program, visited Bohr in Copenhagen. What was said between them remains in dispute, but Heisenberg later claimed he had visited Bohr to let him know that several German scientists believed the production of an atomic bomb was theoretically possible, a potential that placed an enormous responsibility on the world's scientists on both sides.[163]

Then, in 1943, word reached Bohr that he was in danger of being arrested by the Nazis because his mother was Jewish. He sought asylum in neutral Sweden but, after a brief stay, accepted an offer of work in Britain. Leaving his family behind in Sweden, he was spirited out of the country on a three-hour flight to Scotland, lying on a mattress in the freezing bomb bay of a high-flying RAF Mosquito fighter-bomber. Although he had been supplied with a flight helmet, it was too small to fit over his large head, and so he could not hear the pilot order the donning of the oxygen mask when they reached the higher altitudes. Deprived of oxygen, he lost consciousness, recovering fully as the plane descended when it reached friendly skies and landed.[164]

Bohr provided important advice to Britain's top secret "tube alloys" program and later travelled on several occasions to the United States where he conferred with Einstein and J. Robert Oppenheimer, the director of the atomic research facility at Los Alamos, New Mexico. Oppenheimer credited Bohr with acting "as a scientific father figure to the younger men."[165] Bohr responded by saying, "They didn't need my help in making the atom bomb."[166]

CHADWICK'S DISCOVERY of the neutron and the Curies' discovery of artificial radioactivity paved the way for more intensive experimentation into nuclear fission—the process of splitting the atom into smaller parts, and instantaneously releasing far greater amounts of energy than are caused by normal radioactive decay, plus additional neutrons, which could be used to produce more fission and hence a huge explosion if more fissionable material was available—hence, an atomic or nuclear

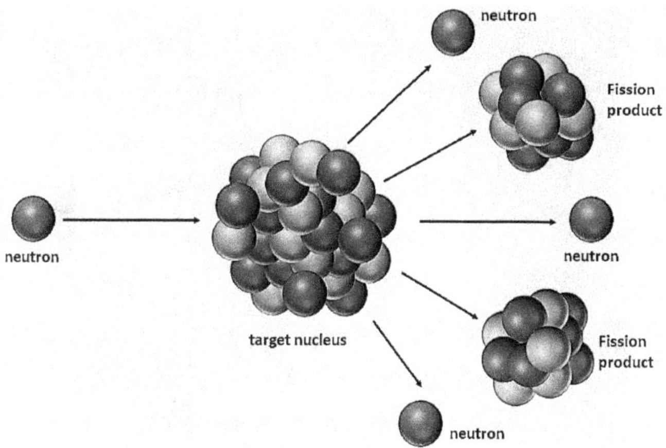

Process of nuclear fission. *(LibreTexts/Delmar Larsen)*

bomb. The resulting fragments, or fission products, are largely short-lived radioactive isotopes whose total mass is slightly less than the original mass of the nucleus that had fissioned and had been converted into energy according to Albert Einstein's equation.167

In October 1934, serendipity favored Italian physicist Enrico Fermi, who had been conducting experiments on the observed phenomenon of radiative capture—the capture of a neutron by a nucleus leading to the creation of a new radioactive isotope one mass unit heavier. By chance, he had placed paraffin instead of lead between the neutrons and the material to be irradiated and was amazed to find the amount of radiative capture was very greatly increased. The paraffin—consisting largely of the light elements hydrogen and carbon—reduced the energy of the neutrons, making them more readily captured by the elements they were irradiating. The result was the first practical production of artificial radioactivity, useful for medical, research, and numerous industrial applications. For this discovery, he received the Nobel Prize in 1938.

After Fermi accepted the prize in Stockholm, he decided not to return to Italy, but rather proceeded to New York City with his family in December 1938. The decision to move to America was prompted by new Italian laws that could have placed his Jewish wife—the daughter of an Italian naval officer—in danger. Once in the United

Enrico Fermi in 1943.
(National Archives, Record Group 434)

States, he was immediately offered posts at five universities and accepted one at Columbia University in New York.

AFTER THE RESULTS of Fermi's experiments were published, the German chemist Otto Hahn and physicist Lise Meitner began conducting similar experiments in Berlin in an effort to understand the process of fission and explain the then-strange radioactive products produced when uranium was bombarded with neutrons. They were joined in this effort by Fritz Strassmann, Hahn's student assistant and co-worker.

Hahn, who had served in World War I and was not a member of the Nazi Party, claimed after the war that he had not agreed with National Socialism or his government's treatment of the Jews, but he decided to remain in Germany.

Meitner was likewise highly regarded by her colleagues, despite great impediments imposed on her career by the political and social order of

Lise Meitner and Otto Hahn in their laboratory in 1938.
(https://www.flickr.com/photos/smithsonian/4405627945/in/photostream)

the time. As a woman, many avenues were closed to her. Accordingly, she had to gain admission to the University of Vienna by an alternative method of preparing for and passing a rigorous entrance examination. Ultimately, she became only the second woman to earn a PhD in physics from the University of Vienna, studying under and working with Max Planck with whom she maintained a lifetime personal and professional association. Unable to obtain a paying job after graduation, her outstanding achievements in quantum physics led to her appointment to professorships with full administrative responsibilities for her own research programs.

Although baptized as a Protestant during early adulthood, her Jewish ancestry led to the loss of her position at the Kaiser Wilhelm Institute, loss of Austrian citizenship, and forced exile in 1938 following the Nazi takeover of Austria. She fled first to Denmark to work with Niels Bohr and then to Sweden but kept in touch with Hahn in Berlin.

In December 1938, Hahn and his assistant, Fritz Strassmann, performed experiments with uranium, which showed that the uranium atom could be split into two smaller atoms, which together weighed less than the original uranium atom, suggesting that the loss of mass must have been converted into energy that might be able to be converted into heat. Hahn, who remained in contact with Meitner in Sweden in violation of the laws against communicating with Jews, wrote to Meitner of their extraordinary finding. With the aid of her nephew, physicist Otto Robert Frisch, Meitner worked out the theoretical physical explanation for what Hahn and Strassman had observed, correctly interpreting Hahn's results to mean the nucleus of the uranium atom had split roughly in half, releasing an estimated two hundred million electron volts and several additional neutrons. They named the process "nuclear fission," after a similar process of splitting cells in biology.[168]

Captured and interned in England at the end of the war, Hahn claimed to be shocked by the announcement that the United States had used a nuclear bomb against the Japanese. He said he had never believed the discovery of fission would have military implications. "I am a scientist," he said, "and like all scientists, am interested only in discovery and not application."[169]

WHEN THE NEWS of Hahn's and Strassman's experiments was published in February 1939, they had an electrifying effect on the entire scientific community. They showed that fission not only released a great deal of energy but also released additional neutrons, which could cause fission in other nuclei of other uranium atoms and possibly a self-sustaining chain reaction that would release an enormous amount of energy. The findings were soon confirmed by Joliot and his co-workers in Paris and by Leó Szilárd, now working with Fermi in New York. Szilárd later remembered he had gone to bed that evening thinking, "There was very little doubt in my mind that the world was headed for grief."[170]

NATURAL URANIUM CONSISTS almost exclusively of two isotopes. It is mostly (99.3 percent by weight) U-238. A much smaller fraction (0.7 percent by weight) is U-235. Since the two isotopes are identical chemically, any process of separating the two or increasing the percentage of the 235 isotope would be extremely difficult, expensive, and time-consuming. Bohr had proposed that fission was much more likely to occur in the uranium-235 isotope than in U-238 natural uranium, and Meitner had been among the first to suggest fission would occur more effectively using slow-moving neutrons. Those findings were confirmed by Szilárd and Fermi, who proposed using a moderator to slow down the neutrons.

By 1939, atomic research that had once been theoretical began to assume real-world consequences as Germany marched into Austria and then Czechoslovakia. How long would it take Germany to produce an atomic bomb? How much time did the Allies have?

The scientists disagreed about what to do with their discoveries. Fermi and his fellow physicists—Szilárd, Edward Teller, and Eugene Wigner—had all objected to publishing the results of their experimentation in an effort to keep their information from falling into German hands, but Bohr had dissented, arguing that secrecy must never be introduced into science.

Fermi had become so concerned with the situation that he had attempted without success to warn the US Navy about the potential military implications of atomic research in a March 16 meeting—the same day German troops marched into Czechoslovakia—and subsequent attempts to interest the military proved unsuccessful.

Another of the scientists' concerns was the possibility that Germany would gain control of the large quantities of uranium ore being mined in the Belgian Congo. None of the scientists had high-level contacts with Belgian officials, although Szilárd remembered his old friend, Albert Einstein, knew Elisabeth, Queen of the Belgians.

Szilárd, Teller, and Wigner first met with Einstein on July 16, 1939, to draft a letter to Belgian officials, the first of several such drafts that found their way into the final letter Einstein would sign on August 2. For his part, Szilárd felt it was improper to contact a foreign government without giving the American government a chance to object. In a July 19 letter to Einstein, Szilárd wrote he had been able to meet with investment banker, former New Deal administrator, and Roosevelt insider Dr. Alexander Sachs. Sachs had cautioned against sending the letter to the Belgian royal family or a US government department: "They wouldn't know what to do with it," he had said.[171] Instead, he would deliver the letter to President Roosevelt if Einstein would sign it. The scientists revised the letter several more times, and by August 15, it was ready for Sachs to deliver to the White House.

Albert Einstein and Hungarian physicist Leó Szilárd drafting the famous Einstein letter. *(US Department of Energy)*

As the crisis over Poland unfolded, Szilárd grew increasingly more impatient. He had heard nothing back from Sachs. Finally, in the last week of September, he and Wigner met with Sachs again and learned he had been unable to arrange a meeting with the president. An appointment was finally arranged for October 11. That meeting takes us back full circle to where this story began.

NOTES

CHAPTER 1

1. Albert Einstein, Letter to Franklin D. Roosevelt, August 2, 1939, Franklin D. Roosevelt Presidential Library, accessed November 1, 2018, http://www.fdrlibrary.marist.edu/archives/pdfs/docsworld-war.pdf.

2. Mindy Weisberger, "Rare Recording Captures Einstein Talking about Music and the Atomic Bomb," *Live Science*, May 3, 2019, https://www.livescience.com/65392-einstein-recording-auction.html.

3. H. W. Brands, *Traitor to His Class: The Privileged Life and Radical Presidency of Franklin Delano Roosevelt* (New York: Anchor Books, 2008), 509.

4. "1938: 'Peace in our time'—Chamberlain," *On This Day September 30, 1938*, BBC Home, accessed July 31, 2018, http://news.bbc.co.uk/onthisday/hi/dates/stories/september/30/news-id_3115000/3115476.stm.

5. Brands, 541.

6. James MacGregor Burns, *Roosevelt: The Lion and the Fox* (Norwalk, CT: Easton Press, 1956), 139.

7. Richard Rhodes, *The Making of the Atomic Bomb* (New York: Simon & Schuster, 1986), 314.

8. Robert Jungk, *Brighter than a Thousand Suns: A Personal History of the Atomic Scientists* (New York: Harcourt Brace, 1958), 109-111.

9. Ibid.

10. Rhodes, *The Making of the Atomic Bomb*, 314.

11. Ibid.

CHAPTER 2

12. Rhodes, *The Making of the Atomic Bomb*, 316.

13. Ibid., 317.

14. Ibid., 332.

15. Ibid., 355.

16. R. L. Kathren, J. B. Gough, and G. T. Benefiel, eds., *The Plutonium Story: The Journals of Professor Glenn T. Seaborg 1939-1946* (Columbus, OH: Battelle Press, 1994), 29; Hewlett and Anderson, *The New World*, 34.

17. Rhodes, *The Making of the Atomic Bomb*, 340-341.

18. Rhodes, *The Making of the Atomic Bomb*, 379.

19. Hill Williams, *Made in Hanford: The Bomb that Changed the World* (Pullman, WA: Washington State University Press, 2011), 61.

20. "S-1 Committee," The Manhattan Project: An Interactive History, Office of History and Heritage Resources, US Department of Energy, accessed August 29, 2018, https://www.osti.gov/opennet/manhattan-project-history/Resources/photo_gallery/s-1_photograph.htm.

21. Frank A. Settle Jr., *General George C. Marshall and the Atomic Bomb* (New York: Praeger, 2016), 40-41.

22. Brands, 679.

23. Ibid., 404.

24. Ibid., 405

25. Ibid., 610.

26. Per F. Dahl, *Heavy Water and the Wartime Race for Nuclear Energy* (Boca Raton, FL: CRC Press, 1999), 279–285.

27. Paul R. Josephson, *Red Atom: Russia's Nuclear Power Program from Stalin to Today* (New York: W. H. Freeman and Company, 1999), 17-18.

CHAPTER 3

28. Cynthia C. Kelly, *The Manhattan Project* (New York: Black Dog

and Leventhal, 2007), 119.

29. Rhodes, *The Making of the Atomic Bomb*, 425.

30. Leslie R. Groves, *Now It Can Be Told: The Story of the Manhattan Project* (New York: Harper and Brothers, 1962), 28.

31. Rhodes, *The Making of the Atomic Bomb*, 426.

32. "Manhattan Project," Wikipedia, accessed September 2, 2018, https://en.wikipedia.org/wiki/Manhattan_Project.

33. F. G. Gosling, *The Manhattan Project: Making the Atomic Bomb* (Washington, DC: US Department of Energy, 2001), 31.

34. Pap A. Ndiaye, trans. Elborg Forster, *Nylon and Bombs: DuPont and the March of Modern America* (Baltimore: Johns Hopkins University Press, 2007), 145.

35. Ibid., 146.

36. David Harvey, *History of the Hanford Site 1943-1990* (Richland, WA: Pacific Northwest National Laboratory, 2000), 5.

37. Rhodes, *The Making of the Atomic Bomb*, 431-432.

38. Harry Thayer, *Management of the Hanford Engineering Works in World War II* (New York: ASCE Press, 1996), 135.

39. Kelly, *The Manhattan Project*, 86.

40. Groves, *Now It Can Be Told*, 67.

41. Ndiaye, *Nylon and Bombs*, 148.

42. Ibid., 165.

43. Ibid., 144.

44. Ibid., 150.

45. Robert L. Ferguson, interview by the author, April 1, 2019.

46. Rhodes, *The Making of the Atomic Bomb*, 119.

47. Kelly, *The Manhattan Project*, 113.

48. "Los Alamos National Laboratory," Wikipedia, accessed August 3, 2015, https://en.wikipedia.org/wiki/Los_Alamos_National_Laboratory.

49. "Los Alamos, NM." Atomic Heritage Foundation, accessed September 6, 2018, https://www.atomicheritage.org/location/los-alamos-nm.

50. John M. Findlay and Bruce Hevly, *Atomic Frontier Days: Hanford and the American West* (Seattle: University of Washington Press, 2011), 17.

51. Harvey, *History of the Hanford Site 1943-1990*, 3.

52. Thayer, *Management of the Hanford Engineering Works in World War II*, **26.**

53. Williams, *Made in Hanford*, 12.

54. Franklin T. Matthias, "Hanford Engineering Works; Early History," address delivered at the Department of Energy Technical Exchange Program, Richland, WA, January 14, 1987, 10.

55. David Smith, "Off the map: the secret cities behind the atom bomb," *Guardian*, May 3, 2018, https://www.theguardian.com/cities/2018/may/03/off-the-map-the-secret-cities-behind-the-atom-bomb-manhattan-project.

CHAPTER 4

56. Bruce N. Bjornstad, "Ice-rafted erratics and bergmounds from Pleiostocene outburst floods, Rattlesnake Mountain, Washington, USA," *Quaternary Science Journal*, v. 63, 2014. 44-59.

57. Bruce N. Bjornstad, *On the Trail of the Ice Age Floods: A Geological Field Guide to the Mid-Columbia Basin* (Sandpoint, ID, Keokee Books, 2006), 5.

58. Gary Kleinknecht, email to the author, October 21, 2018.

59. Click Relander, *Drummers & Dreamers* (Caldwell, ID: Paxton Printers, Ltd., 1986), 46.

60. Hunn, 134.

61. C. Mark Smith, *In the Wake of Lewis and Clark: From the Mountains to the Sea* (Easton, PA: Shore Excursions of America, 2015), 23-24.

62. Gary E. Moulton., ed., *The Journals of the Lewis and Clark Expedition*, Volumes 1-13 (Lincoln: University of Nebraska Press 1983-2001), 5:216.

63. C. Mark Smith, *Congressman Doc Hastings: Twenty Years of Turmoil* (Seattle: Book Publishers Network, 2018), 11.

64. "What About White Bluffs Townsite?" Pacific Northwest National Laboratory, accessed February 16, 2019, https://workbasedlearning.pnnl.gov/pals/resource/cards/whitebluffs.stm.

65. S. L. Sanger, *Hanford and the Bomb: An Oral History of World War II* (Seattle: Living History Press, 1989), 25.

66. Michele Stenehjem Gerber, *On the Home Front: The Cold War Legacy of the Hanford Nuclear Site* (Lincoln: University of Nebras-

ka Press, 1992)12.

67. Findlay and Hevly, *Atomic Frontier Days*, 211.

68. Williams, *Made in Hanford*, 5-7.

CHAPTER 5

69. Cynthia Kelly, *The Manhattan Project* (New York: Black Dog & Leventhal, 2009), ix.

70. "Needed by E. I. duPont de Nemours & Company for Pacific Northwest" (advertisement), *Milwaukee Sentinel*, June 6, 1944, 15, https://news.google.com/newspapers?id=UEMxAAAAIBAJ&sjid=LQ4EAAAAIBAJ&pg=7157%2C1687590.

71. Findlay and Hevly, *Atomic Frontier Days*, 81.

72. Robert Bauman, "Jim Crow in the Tri-Cities 1943-1950," *The Pacific Northwest Quarterly*, Vol. 96, No. 3 (Summer 2005), 126.

73. Thayer, *Management of the Hanford Engineering Works in World War II*, 93.

74. Ibid., 84-85.

75. Findlay and Hevly, *Atomic Frontier Days*, 85.

76. C. Mark Smith, *Community Godfather: How Sam Volpentest Shaped Hanford and the Tri-Cities* (Richland, WA: Etcetera Press, 2013), 75.

77. Findlay and Hevly, *Atomic Frontier Days*, 123.

78. Ibid., 97-99.

79. Thayer, *Management of the Hanford Engineering Works in World War II*, 99.

80. Paul Rogat Loeb, *Nuclear Culture: Living and Working in the World's Largest Atomic Complex* (Gabriola Island, BC, Canada: New Society Publishers, 1986), 122-123.

81. Gerber, *On the Home Front*, 52.

82. Robert Bauman, "Jim Crow in the Tri-Cities 1943-1950," 125.

83. Thayer, *Management of the Hanford Engineering Works in World War II*, 27.

84. Ibid., **29.**

85. Ibid., 89.

86. Ibid., 63.

87. Ibid., 16.

88. Ibid., 29.

89. Ndiaye, *Nylon and Bombs*, 158; Gerber, *On the Home Front*, 35-36.

90. Thayer, *Management of the Hanford Engineering Works in World War II*, **138.**

91. John Fox, email to the author, December 5, 2018.

92. Rhodes, *The Making of the Atomic Bomb*, 498.

93. Williams, *Made in Hanford*, 100

94. Gosling, *The Manhattan Project*, 33.

95. Robert Horgos, email to the author, September 10, 2015.

96. Rhodes, *The Making of the Atomic Bomb*, 603.

97. Ndiaye, *Nylon and Bombs*, 158; Gerber, *On the Home Front*, 156.

98. S. T. Cantril and H. M. Parker, "Status of Health and Protection at the Hanford Engineer Works," Paper 9 in R. S. Stone, *Industrial Medicine on the Plutonium Project*, (New York: McGraw-Hill, 1951), 476-484.

99. Gosling, *The Manhattan Project*, 125.

100. Ibid., 97.

101. Gosling, *The Manhattan Project*, 42.

102. Williams, *Made in Hanford*, 100.

103. John Fox, email to the author, December 5, 2018.

104. Rhodes, *The Making of the Atomic Bomb*, 634-635.

105. Ibid., 131.

106. Groves, *Now It Can Be Told*, 296-297.

107. Rhodes, *The Making of the Atomic Bomb*, 674.

108. Mark Blotz, "When Kodak Accidentally Discovered A-Bomb Testing," *Popular   Mechanics*, July 20, 2016, https://www.popularmechanics.com/science/energy/a21382/how-kodak-accidentally-discovered-radioactive-fallout.

CHAPTER 6

109. Phillips Payson O'Brien, *How the War Was Won* (Cambridge, UK: Cambridge University Press, 2015), 47–48.

110. Tony Holmes, *Janes's Historic Military Aircraft* (London: Harper-Collins, 1998), 120.

111. Rhodes, *The Making of the Atomic Bomb*, 556.

112. "Battle of Okinawa," Wikipedia, accessed February 18, 2019, https://en.wikipedia.org/wiki/Battle_of_Okinawa.

113. Arthur Herman, *Douglas MacArthur* (New York: Random

House, 2016), 611.

114. Rhodes, *The Making of the Atomic Bomb*, 650-651.

115. "Manhattan Project," Wikipedia, accessed October 19, 2018, https://en.wikipedia.org/wiki/Manhattan_Project.

116. Herman, *Douglas MacArthur*, 613.

117. "Manhattan Project," Wikipedia, accessed October 19, 2018, https://en.wikipedia.org/wiki/Manhattan_Project.

118. "Hanford Site," Wikipedia, accessed September 8, 2015, https://en.wikipedia.org/wiki/Hanford_Site.

119. "It's Atomic Bombs," *Richland Villager* and *Pasco Herald*, August 6, 1945, 1; "At Last We Can Say That Name, DuPont," *Richland Villager*, August 9, 1945, 1.

120. "General Electric to Take over Hanford Works," *Richland Villager*, June 6, 1946, 1.

121. Thayer, *Management of the Hanford Engineering Works in World War II*, 85.

122. Ibid., 84.

123. Groves, *Now It Can Be Told*, 59.

CHAPTER 7

124. Simon Sebag Montefiore, *Stalin: The Court of the Red Tsar* (New York: Knopf, 2004), 502.

125. *Public Papers of the Presidents of the United States: Harry S. Truman, 1947* (Washington, DC: Government Printing Office), 178-179.

126. Herman, *Douglas MacArthur*, 799-800.

CHAPTER 8

127. "Report of General Electric Company, Management and Operational Functions of North Richland Construction Camp, For Period of July 1947 through March 31, 1952," Project Services Unit, Project Section, Engineering Department, General Electric, March 31, 1952, no page numbers.

128. David Harvey, *History of the Hanford Site 1943-1990*, 19.

129. Brad Saunders, "The Town That Wouldn't Die," *Pageant*, February, 1971, 139.

130. Jeff St. John, "Happy 40th, TRIDEC," *Tri-City Herald*, March 16,

200, B8.

131. Smith, *Community Godfather*, 175.

132. "Tri-City Nuclear Industrial Council 1963-1883," *Tri-City Herald*, February 13, 1983, E7.

133. Matthew Daly, "Politics Appeals Court: Obama Violating Law on Nuke Site," Boston Globe, August 14, 2013, https://www.bostonglobe.com/news/nation/2013/08/13/appeals-court-obama-violating-law-nuke-site/bzKrnO3oTiuMxHYCTtSOQO/story.html.

134. "Richland Is Human Bonus, Spin-Off of Nuclear Efforts, Says Seaborg," *Tri-City Herald*, June 9, 1968, 3.

135. Gary K. Miller, *Energy Northwest: A History of the Washington Public Power Supply System* (Bloomington, IN: Xlibris Corporation, 2001), 75.

136. Findlay and Hevly, *Atomic Frontier Days*, 133.

137. Robert L. Ferguson, interview by the author, March 30, 2019.

Chapter 9

138. Oregon Department of Energy. *Hanford Cleanup: The First 25 Years* (Salem, OR: Oregon Department of Energy, 2014), vii, accessed January 26, 2019, https://www.oregon.gov/energy/safety-resiliency/Documents/Hanford%2025%20Year%20 Report.pdf.

139. Joel VanEtta, "2000 Join Hands across Columbia in Sign of Unity," *Tri-City Herald*, November 3, 1986, A1.

140. Karen Dorn Steel, "Hanford's Bitter Legacy," *Bulletin of the Atomic Scientists,* 44, no. 1 (January/February 1988), 17-23.

141. Mike Lawrence, email to the author, February 9, 2019.

142. Steel, "Hanford's Bitter Legacy," 16-17.

143. Lawrence, email to the author, January 28, 2019.

144. Lawrence, interview with the author, March 18, 2019.

145. Gerber, *On the Home Front*, 210.

146. Smith, *Community Godfather*, 361.

147. Karen Dorn Steel, "River of Money at the Hanford Nuclear Reservation," *Spokesman-Review*, November 13, 1994, A1.

148. Findlay and Hevly, *Atomic Frontier Days*, 258.

149. Richard "Doc" Hastings, interview by the author, June 7, 2017.

150. Oregon Department of Energy, *Hanford Cleanup*, 85.

151. Robert L. Ferguson, interview by the author, January 9, 2019.

152. John Fox, email to the author, February 9, 2019.

153. Annette Cary, "Hanford Blamed for Most of $110 Billion Bump in Federal Cleanup Costs," *Tri-City Herald*, January 29, 2019, A1.

154. Richard "Doc" Hastings, interview by the author, February 6, 2019.

155. Background paper of unknown origin, "Superconducting Magnetic Energy Storage (SMES): A Critical Dual-Use Technology for the Nation's Military and Industrial Needs," Box 2, SMES, Sam Volpentest TRIDEC files.

156. Gene Astley, interview by the author, February 22, 2013.

157. "LIGO," Wikipedia, accessed February 4, 2019, https://en.wikipedia.org/wiki/LIGO.

158. Claire Reilly, "Your wedding ring came from a neutron star explosion, 4.6 billion years ago." c/net, May 7, 2019, https://www.cnet.com/news/your-wedding-ring-came-from-a-neutron-star-explosion-4-6-billion-years-ago; Annette Cary, "Scientists: Black hole swallowing neutron star perhaps spotted," *Tri-City Herald*, May 2, 2019, A2.

159. US Department of Energy, *US Department of Energy Response to the 24 Command Fire on the Hanford Reservation June 27-July 1, 2000,* October 2000, https://energy.gov/sites/prod/files/2014/04/f15/0011hanf.pdf.

APPENDIX

160. "History of Nuclear Energy," US Department of Energy, DOE NE-0088, 3, accessed August 14, 2018, https://www.energy.gov/sites/prod/files/The%20History%20of%20Nuclear%20Energy_0.pdf.

161. "The World Set Free," Wikipedia, accessed February 27, 2019, https://en.wikipedia.org/wiki/The_World_Set_Free.

162. Chaim Weizmann, *Trial and Error* (New York: Harper & Bros., 1949), 118.

163. Werner Heisenberg, "Letter from Werner Heisenberg to author Robert Jungk," The Manhattan Project Heritage Preservation Association, Inc., accessed August 18, 2018, https://en.wikipedia.org/wiki/Niels_Bohr.

164. Rhodes, *The Making of the Atomic Bomb*, 484-485.

165. Abraham Pais, *Niels Bohr's Times, In Physics, Philosophy and Polity* (Oxford: Clarendon Press, 1991), 497.

166. Ibid., 496.

167. "Nuclear Fission: Basics," atomicarchive.com, accessed August 23, 2018, http://www.atomicarchive.com/Fission/Fission1.shtml.

168. Ruth Lewin Sime, *Lise Meitner: A Life in Physics* (Berkeley: University of California Press, 1997), 236-258.

169. "Otto Hahn, the Nobel-Winning Chemist Whose Discovery Was Used in Hiroshima" (obituary), *New York Times*, July 28, 2016. https://www.nytimes.com/interactive/projects/cp/obituaries/archives/otto-hahn.

170. Rhodes, *The Making of the Atomic Bomb*, 292.

171. Kelly, *A Guide to the Manhattan Project in Washington State*, 41.

BIBLIOGRAPHY

UNPUBLISHED SOURCES

Oral History Interviews

Ferguson, Robert L. Interviews by the author, February 23, May 24, and July 31, 2013; January 31, February 22, March 13, and March 31, 2019.

Recorded Speeches and Interviews

Chamberlain, Neville. "1938: 'Peace for our time.'" *On This Day 30 September 1938*, BBC Home. http://news.bbc.co.uk/onthisday/hi/dates/stories/september/30/newsid_3115000/3115476.stm.
Matthias, Franklin T. "Hanford Engineering Works; Early History," address delivered at the Department of Energy Technical Exchange Program, Richland, WA, January 14, 1987.

Other Unpublished Documents

Johnson, Ben, Richard Romanelli, and Bert Pierard. *Lost in the Telling: The DuPont Company the Forgotten Producers of Plutonium.* Richland, WA: B Reactor Museum Association, 2015.
Tschauner, Candice. *White Bluffs, Hanford Timeline.* 2011.

PUBLISHED SOURCES

Newspapers and Periodicals

Holton, Gerald. "The Migration of Physicists to the United States," *Bulletin of the Atomic Scientists*, Educational Foundation for Nuclear Science, Inc., April 1984.

"Otto Hahn, the Nobel-Winning Chemist Whose Discovery Was Used in Hiroshima" (obituary), *New York Times*, July 28, 2016. https://www.nytimes.com/interactive/projects/cp/obituaries/archives/otto-hahn.

Smith, David. "Off the Map: The Secret Cities behind the Atom Bomb," *Guardian*, May 3, 2018, https://www.theguardian.com/cities/2018/may/03/off-the-map-the-secret-cities-behind-the-atom-bomb-manhattan-project.

Books, Articles, and Congressional Publications

Anderson, C. E. *Keep Your Ducks in a Row! The Manhattan Project Hanford, Washington*. New York: Page Publishing, 2016.

Bauman, Robert. "Jim Crow in the Tri-Cities 1943-1950." *The Pacific Northwest Quarterly*, Vol. 96, No. 3 (Summer 2005).

Bauman, Robert, and Robert Franklin, ed., *Nowhere to Remember: Hanford, White Bluffs, and Richland to 1943*. Pullman, WA: Washington State University Press, 2018.

Bernstein, Jeremy. *Plutonium: A History of the World's Most Dangerous Element*. Ithica, NY: Cornell University Press, 2009.

Bird, Kai, and Martin J. Sherwin, *American Prometheus: The Triumph and Tragedy of Robert J. Oppenheimer*, New York: Vintage Books, 2006.

Bjornstad, Bruce. *On The Trail of the Ice Age Floods (Volumes 1 and 2)*, Sandpoint, ID: Keokee Books, 2006.

Brands, H. W. *Traitor to His Class: The Privileged Life and Radical Presidency of Franklin Delano Roosevelt*. New York: Anchor Books, 2008.

Burns, James MacGregor. *Roosevelt: The Lion and the Fox*, Norwalk, CT: Easton Press, 1956.

Cantril, S. T., and H. M. Parker. "Status of Health and Protection at the Hanford Engineer Works," Paper 9 in R. S. Stone, *Industrial Medicine on the Plutonium* Project, New York: McGraw-Hill, 1951.

Churchill, Winston S. *The Gathering Storm.* New York: Houghton, Mifflin, 1948.

Compton, William M,. and Robert Gilbert, eds., *Memories of Early Atomic Pioneers.* Scotts Valley, CA: CreateSpace, 2015.

Dahl, Per F. *Heavy Water and the Wartime Race for Nuclear Energy.* Boca Raton, FL: CRC Press, 1999.

DeVoto, Bernard. *The Journals of Lewis and Clark.* New York: Mariner Books, 1997.

Findlay, John M., and Bruce Hevly. *Atomic Frontier Days; Hanford and the American West.* Seattle: University of Washington Press, 2011.

Gaddis, John Lewis. *The Cold War: A New History.* New York: The Penguin Press, 2005.

Gerber, Michele Stenehjem. *On the Home Front: The Cold War Legacy of the Hanford Nuclear Site.* Lincoln: University of Nebraska Press, 1992.

Gosling, F. G. *The Manhattan Project: Making the Atomic Bomb.* Washington, DC: US Department of Energy, 2001.

Groves, Leslie R. *Now It Can Be Told: The Story of the Manhattan Project.* New York: Harper and Brothers, 1962.

Hales, Peter Beacon. *Atomic Spaces: Living on the Manhattan Project.* Champaign, IL: University of Illinois Press, 1997.

Harvey, David. *History of the Hanford Site 1943-1990.* Richland, WA: Pacific Northwest National Laboratory, 2000.

Heisenberg, Werner. "Letter from Werner Heisenberg to author Robert Jungk." The Manhattan Project Heritage Preservation Association, Inc. Accessed August 18, 2018. https://en.wikipedia.org/wiki/ Niels_Bohr.

Herman, Arthur. *Douglas MacArthur: American Warrior.* New York: Random House, 2016.

Hunn, Eugene S. *Nch'i-Wána, "The Big River": Mid-Columbia Indians and Their Land.* Seattle: University of Washington Press, 1990.

James, D. Clayton. *The Years of MacArthur: Triumph and Disaster 1945-1964 (Volume 3).* Boston: Houghton-Mifflin, 1985.

Jones, R. V. *The Wizard War: British Scientific Intelligence 1939-1945.* New York: Coward, McCann & Geoghegan, Inc., 1978.

Josephson, Paul R. *Red Atom: Russia's Nuclear Power Program from Stalin to Today.* New York: W. H. Freeman and Company, 1999.

Jungk, Robet. *Brighter than a Thousand Suns: A Personal History of the Atomic Scientists.* New York: Harcourt Brace, 1958.

Kathren, R. L., J. B. Gough, and G. T. Benefiel, eds. *The Plutonium Story: The Journals of Professor Glenn T. Seaborg 1939-1946.* Columbus, OH: Battelle Press, 1994.

Kelly, Cynthia C. *A Guide to the Manhattan Project in Washington State.* Stevens Point, WI: Worzalla Publishing Co., 2018.

———. *The Manhattan Project,* New York: Black Dog & Leventhal, 2009.

Mason, Katrina R. "Something Extraordinary Was Happening Here." In *The Manhattan Project: The Birth of the Atomic Bomb in the Words of Its Creators,* 177-179. New York: Black Dog & Leventhal, 2009.

Mendenhall, Nancy. *Orchards of Eden: White Bluffs on the Columbia River 1907-1943.* Seattle: Far Eastern Press, 2006.

Moulton, Gary E., ed. *The Journals of the Lewis and Clark Expedition,* Volumes 1-13. Lincoln: University of Nebraska Press, 1983-2001.

Nichols, Kenneth. D. *The Road to Trinity.* New York: Morrow Publishers, 1987.

Ndiaye, Pap A. Translated by Elborg Forster. *Nylon and Bombs: DuPont and the March of Modern America.* Baltimore: Johns Hopkins University Press, 2007.

O'Brien, Phillips Payson. *How the War Was Won.* Cambridge, UK: Cambridge University Press, 2015.

Oregon Department of Energy. *Hanford Cleanup: The First 25 Years.* Salem, OR: Oregon Department of Energy, 2014. https://www.oregon.gov/energy/safety-resiliency/Documents/Hanford%2025%20Year%20Report.pdf.

Pais, Abraham. *Niels Bohr's Times: In Physics, Philosophy, and Polity.* Oxford: Clarendon Press, 1991.

Powers, Thomas. *Heisenbeerg's War: The Secret History of the German Bomb.* Cambridge, MA: DeCapo Press, 1993.

Relander, Click. *Drummers and Dreamers.* Caldwell, ID: Paxton Printers, Ltd., 1986.

Rhodes, Richard. *The Making of the Atomic Bomb*. New York: Simon & Schuster, 1986.

Sanger, S. L. *Hanford and the Bomb: An Oral History of World War II*. Seattle: Living History Press, 1989.

Seegré, Gino, and Bettina Hokerlin, *The Pope of Physics: Enrico Fermi and the Birth of the Atomic Age*. New York: Henry Holt & Company, 2016.

Settle, Frank A., Jr. *General George C. Marshall and the Atomic Bomb*. New York: Praeger, 2016.

Sime, Ruth Lewin. *Lise Meitner: A Life in Physics*. Berkeley, CA: University of California Press, 1997.

Smith, C. Mark. *Community Godfather: How Sam Volpentest Shaped Hanford and the Tri-Cities*. Richland, WA: Etcetera Press, 2013.

———. *Congressman Doc Hastings: Twenty Years of Turmoil*. Seattle: Book Publishers Network, 2018.

———. *In the Wake of Lewis and Clark: From the Mountains to the Sea*. Easton, PA: Shore Excursions of America, 2015.

Smyth, Henry D. *Atomic Energy for Military Purposes*. Princeton, NJ: Princeton University Press, 1945.

Stark, Peter. *Astoria: Astor and Jefferson's Lost Pacific Empire*. New York: Harper-Collins, 2015.

Steel, Karen Dorn. "Hanford's Bitter Legacy." *Bulletin of the Atomic Scientists*, 44, no. 1 (January/February 1988).

Toomy, Elizabeth. *The Manhattan Project at Hanford Site (Images of America)*. Mt. Pleasant, SC: Arcadia Publishing Co. 2015.

Thayer, Harry. *Management of the Hanford Engineering Works in World War II*. New York: ASCE Press, 1996.

US Atomic Energy Commission. *The Hanford Story*. AEC-ITT/FSS. Richland, WA: Richland Operations, n.d.

US Department of Energy. *Historic American Engineering Record B Reactor (105-B Building)*, HAER No. WA-164. Washington, DC: DOE, 2001.

———. *History of Nuclear Energy*, DOE NE-0088. Accessed August 14, 2018. https://www.energy.gov/sites/prod/files/The%20History%20of%20Nuclear%20Energy_0.pdf.

———. *The Manhattan Project: Making of the Atomic Bomb*, DOE/MA-0002. Washington, DC: DOE, 2001.

Weizmann, Chaim. *Trial and Error*. New York: Harper & Bros. 1949.

Williams, Hill. *Made in Hanford: The Bomb that Changed the World.* Pullman, WA: Washington State University Press, 2011.

INDEX

105-B Reactor, 84, 107
   See also B Reactor
1100 Area, 89
200 Area, 87, 142–143
200 BeV Accelerator, 128–129
221-T separation plant, 89
300 Area, 89, 121, 143
38th parallel, 118
700 Area, 89

A
accelerators
   200 BeV Accelerator, 128–129
   Cockcroft-Walton machine, 177
   See also cyclotron
Adams, Brock, 140
Adamson, Keith F., 15
Africa, German colonies, 7
African Americans at Hanford, 73, 79–80
Ainsworth town site, 64
Alamogordo NM, 94
Aleutian Islands, 111
All-America City award, 126
alpha radiation, 174
Alsos team, 27–28
Amon, Howard, 68
Amon, W.R., 68
anti-nuclear sentiment, 138, 140
anti-Semitism in interwar Germany, 4–7,
   25, 180, 182–184

Army Corps of Engineers, 33, 160
Astor, John Jacob, 61
Astoria OR, 61
Atlantic Richfield, 128
Atlee, Clement, 112
atom smashers. *See* accelerators; cyclotron
atomic bomb
   deployed against Japan, 103–105
   design, 38, 44–45, 46–47
   Einstein-Szilárd letter, 2–3, 12–14
   genesis of research, 12–14
   hydrogen bomb, 116, 164, 172
   isotopes needed, 38
   other weaponry, 118
   plutonium and uranium compared, 46
   Soviet Union, 116, 120–121
   target cities, 104
   Trinity test, 93–96, 103
   use questioned, 92, 96–97
Atomic Energy Act (1946), 119
Atomic Energy Act (1954), 122
Atomic Energy Commission (AEC)
   opposition to dam at Hanford, 56–57
   regulation dispute, 139
   replaced army at Hanford, 119
   replaced by NRC and ERDA, 138
Atomic Frontier Days (Richland WA),
   123–124

atomic research
  advisory group, 18
  disclosure concerns, 185–186
  early theories, 172–174
  funding, 16–17
  Japan, 28–29
  Nazi Germany, 24–28
  secrecy, 185
  Soviet Union, 29–30
  splitting the nucleus, 177
  United Kingdom, 18–19, 23–24, 30–31
  United States, 15–18, 21–23
  university laboratories, 17
  US-UK liaison, 20, 22–23, 30–31
atomic weaponry, proposed for Korean
  War, 117–118
atomic weight, number, 172
atoms, 171–176
Atoms for Peace, 122
Austria annexed by Germany, 7–8
Austrian Nazi Party, 8

B

B Reactor
  criticality, 107
  in Manhattan District National Historic
    Park, 163–164
  process, 84–87
  shutdown, 120
  run, 90–91
B Reactor Museum Association (BRMA),
  164
B-17 bomber. *See* Boeing B-17 bomber;
  "Day's Pay"
B-29 bomber. *See* Boeing B-29
  Superfortress; *Enola Gay*
B8 experiments, 27
Bard, Ralph A., 103
Basalt Waste Isolation Project (BWIP), 131,
  135, 142
Battelle Memorial Institute, 127, 166
Battle of Leyte Gulf, 101
Battle of the Bulge, 92
Battle of the Somme, 4
Bauman, Robert, 79

Bechtel National, 149
Becquerel, Henri, 174
Belgium invaded by Germany, 16
Ben Franklin Dam, 160
Berlin Airlift, 115
beta radiation, 175, 178
Bikini Atoll, 164
Bioproducts, Sciences, and Engineering
  Laboratory (BSEL), 166
birth rates in Richland Village, 75
bismuth phosphate process, 88
Boeing B-17 bomber, 26, 100
Boeing B-29 Superfortress, 99–101, 104–105
Bogue, Virgil, 64
Bohr, Niels, 28, 176-177, 179-180, 183-185
Bomber. *See* Boeing B-29, *Enola Gay*
Bonneville Dam, 65
Bonneville Power Administration (BPA),
  122, 133, 156
Bradbury, Norris, 95
Brave New World (Huxley), 3
Briggs, Lyman J., 15–17
Britain. *See* United Kingdom (UK)
British North West Company, 57
British Nuclear Fuels Ltd. (BNFL), 148–149
Broughton, William, 59
Building Trade Council, 81
Bush, George H.W., 143, 157
Bush, Vannevar
  atomic research advisory group, 18
  DuPont contract, 43–44
  headed NDRC, 16
  headed OSRD, 18
  Interim Committee, 103
  Manhattan Project, initial organization,
    33–34
  MAUD report, 19
  Trinity test, 94–95
  US-UK liaison, 20
Byrnes, James F., 103

C

C Reactor online, 121
Cable Bridge protest, 140–141
Camp Hanford, 120, 123

See also Hanford Camp
Carnegie Institute, 20
Carpenter Jr., Walter S., 42–43, 108–109
Carter, Jimmy, 129, 138
Cavendish Laboratory, 173–174, 177
Cayuse Indian War, 62, 63
Cayuse people, 58, 63
Celilo Falls, 56
censorship. *See* civil rights of residents and
    employees
Chadwick, James, 31, 95, 177–178
Chamberlain, Neville, 8
charge of subatomic particles, 171-173
chemical separation facilities
    cleanup issues, 151
    at Hanford, 87–89
    X-10 (Oak Ridge), 45, 49
Chernobyl nuclear accident, 136, 140
Chiang Kai-shek, 116
Chicago Milwaukee St. Paul and Pacific
    Railroad, 67
Chicago Pile-1. *See* CP-1 reactor
China, 116-117
Chinese families, segregation, 80
chronology, iii–xxx
Church, Gilbert P. "Gil," 49–50, 83
Churchill, Winston
    formed government, 23
    government fell, 112
    Hyde Park meeting with Roosevelt,
    22–23
    Quebec Conference, 31
Ciano, Galleazzo, 8
civil rights of residents and employees
    censorship, 69, 76, 78
    North Richland, 123
    Richland Village, 74-76
    segregation, 73–74, 79–80
Clark, William, 57-58
Clayton, William L., 103
cleanup
    1989 cost estimate, 143–144
    1993 cost estimate, 147
    2000 cost estimate, 149
    2006 cost estimate, 150

cleanup, *continued*
    2007 cost estimate, 150
    2016 cost estimate, 151
    2019 cost estimate, 143, 152, 165
    2023 deadlines, 151
    administration, 154–157, 165–166
    changing Hanford culture, 145–146
    coming to Hanford, 139–145
    contractors and challenges, 145–154
    costs and consequences, 143–145
    environmental concerns, 165
    Nuclear Cleanup Caucus, 148
    responsibility, 165
    schedule, 154
    Tri-Cities economy, 154–157
    work suspended, 150
    See also nuclear waste
Clinch River, 35
    See also Oak Ridge TN
Clinton, Bill, 147
Clinton Engineer Works, 36
    See also Oak Ridge TN
Cockcroft, John, 177
Cockcroft-Walton machine, 177
Cold War
    ending, 137–138
    HEW expansion, 120-123
    inception, 114–118
    Richland residents, 123–126
    Tri-Cities economy, 128–129, 134–137
Columbia Basin Project, 66
Columbia Generating Station, 155–156, 163
Columbia University, 20-21, 33
Committee for the Scientific Survey of Air
    Warfare (CSSAW, UK), 18
communism, early period, 3
community education campaign, 141–142
Compton, Arthur
    Interim Committee, 103
    Met Lab (Chicago), 21, 22, 40, 86
    on Oppenheimer, 46
Compton, Karl T., 103
Conant, James B.
    atomic research advisory group, 18
    headed NDRC, 18

Conant, James B., *continued*
Interim Committee, 103
MAUD report, 19
US-UK liaison, 20
construction worker housing
Camp Hanford, 120, 123
Hanford Camp, 71–74, 82
See also employees
contamination, 143, 147
See also nuclear waste
cooling, reactors compared, 87
Corps of Discovery, 60–61
Cosmos Club, 20
Cox, James M., 11
CP-1 reactor (Chicago), 22, 40–41, 82, 107
Cuban Missile Crisis, 118, 122
Curie, Irène, 178
Curie, Marie Sklodowska, 173, 178
Curie, Pierre, 173, 178
cyclotron
Japanese research, 28
Lawrence's Nobel Prize, 177
patented, 177–178
Soviet research, 29
Czechoslovakia, Munich Agreement, 8

D
D Reactor online, 91
Daladier, Édouard, 8
Dalton, John, 173, 175, 205
"Day's Pay" B-17 bomber, 76–77
Democritus of Abdera, 172–173
Department of Energy (DOE), 128, 138,
166–167
a dollar, DuPont reimbursement, 43,
107–109
Donation Land Claim Act, 63
Douglas Aircraft, 128
Douglas Laboratories, 132
DR Reactor online, 120
Drake, Francis, 58
drought at Hanford Reach, 65
du Pont, Lammot, 42
Dunkirk, British evacuation, 16

DuPont
getting started at Oak Ridge, 40–42
groundbreaking at Hanford, 71
HEW site development, 82
Matthias' coordination, 81
Oak Ridge contract, 43–44
One Dollar reimbursement, 107–109
relationship with Met Lab, 44
relinquished control of HEW, 119
on Richland Village, 74
role in atomic bomb announced,
106–107
withdrawal from Manhattan Project,
107–109
dust storms, 77–78

E
E = mc², 172n
East Prussia, targeted by Germany, 9
Eastern Europe, post-WWII, 113–114
economy, world, post-WWI, 4
Einstein, Albert
disclosure concerns, 185–186
left Nazi Germany, 7
work with Bohr, 180
See also Einstein-Szilárd letter
Einstein's formula, 172n
Einstein-Szilárd letter, 1–3, 4, 12–14, 85,
171, 186
Eisenhower, Dwight, 118, 122
electric power generation, 122, 132–135
electromagnetic isotope separation, 18, 21,
35–37, 43
Y-12 plant (Oak Ridge), 37–39, 42
electrons, 171–173
element 94: plutonium, 17–18
elements, explained, 171–172
employees
attraction, retention, 71-72
construction worker housing, 71–74, 82,
119–120, 123
health and safety, 89
hired for cleanup, 145
layoff, 150, 154
working conditions at Hanford, 77–80

See also civil rights of residents and
    employees
Energy Northwest, 156, 163
Energy Research and Development
    Administration (ERDA), 138
engineers, conflicts with physicists, 90-91
England. *See* United Kingdom (UK)
Enola Gay, 104
entertainment at Hanford Camp, 73
Environmental Molecular Sciences
    Laboratory (EMSL), 159–160, 166
Environmental Protection Agency (EPA),
    139, 143
espionage, Soviet on UK and US, 30
Euro-American explorers, 57–59, 66–68
European Recovery Plan, 115

F
F Reactor online, 91
fascism, early period, 3
Fast Flux Facility (FFTF)
    Cold War economy, 136
    located at HEW, 129–130, 132
    shutdown, 142
"Fat Man"
    compared with "Little Boy," 44–45
    further deployment, 103–105
    Nagasaki bomb, 105
    Trinity test, 45, 92–97, 107
Federal Bureau of Investigation (FBI), 47,
    76
Federal Power Administration, 138
Ferguson, Robert L. "Bob"
    advocating for SMES, 157–158
    advocating for Tri-Cities economy,
        155–157
    Hanford cleanup, 140
    management viewpoint, 148
    on project cost, 150
    rebranding TCNIC, 137
    WPPSS head, 134–135
    on Yucca Mountain decision, 132n
Fermi, Enrico, 46
    artificial radioactivity, 181–182
    B Reactor run, 90–92

Fermi, Enrico, *continued*
    disclosure concerns, 185
    first self-sustaining nuclear reaction,
        40, 43
    fission research, 184, 185
    Interim Committee, 103
    Met Lab (Chicago), 22, 86
    Trinity test, 94–95
    Uranium Committee, 16
Findlay, John, 76
First World War. *See* World War I
Fish and Wildlife Service, 145, 162
fission, defined, 172
fission research, 24–25, 180–181, 184–185
Fitzner-Eberhardt Arid Lands Ecology
    (ALE) Reserve, 161
Flyorov, Georgy, 29
Fort Nez Perce, 62
France
    declared war on Germany, 1, 9
    invaded by Germany, 16
    Munich Agreement, 8
    post-WWII, 115
Franck, James, 96
Franco, Francisco, 7
Frisch, Otto Robert, 18, 184
Ft. Astoria, 61
Ft. Nez Perce, 62–63
Ft. Walla Walla, 62–63
Fuchs, Klaus, 30, 93
Fuels and Materials Examination Facility
    (FMEF), 130
Fuller, Murrey, 126
Fulton, Robert, 13
fusion bomb. *See* hydrogen bomb
Fusion Materials Irradiation (FMIT), 130

G
Gable Mountain, 53, 55, 87, 131
gamma radiation, 174
Gardner, Booth, 144
gaseous diffusion isotope separation, 21, 35,
    38–39, 43
    K-25 plant (Oak Ridge), 38–40
Geiger, Hans, 175–176, 178, 179

Geiger counter, 175
General Electric Company (GE), 107, 119, 127
German Army Ordnance Office (Heereswaffenamt), 24
German Communist Party, 6
Germany
    1948 blockade, airlift, 115-116
    atomic research, 24-28
    defeated, 93
    divided, 114
    invasions, 7-8, 14, 16, 18, 26
    Kristallnacht, 6-7, 12
    non-agression pact with Soviet Union, 8-9
    WWII declared, 9
Gillenwater, Kelso, 137
Gingrich, Newt, 148
Gold, Harry, 30
gold standard, post-WWI, 4
Gorbachev, Mikhail, 137
Gore, Al, 161-162
Gorton, Slade, 140
Grand Coulee Dam, 50, 65
graphite creep, 120
graphite reactor, 22, 42, 140
Gray, Robert, 59
Grays Harbor County, 133
Great Britain. *See* United Kingdom (UK)
Great Depression, 4, 11
"Great Patriotic War," 112
Great War. *See* World War I
Greece, 115
green energy complex (Hanford), 163
Greenwalt, Crawford
    B Reactor run, 90
    DuPont at Oak Ridge, 43-44
    on DuPont-Met Lab relationship, 44
    liaison with Met Lab, 82
    member of evaluation team, 43
Gregoire, Christine, 144
groundwater contamination, 147
Groves, Leslie R., 83
    bomb research (Smyth report), 30
    briefing Truman, 92-93

Groves, Leslie R., *continued*
    cancelled Y-12, 42
    courting DuPont, 41-42
    on building internment camps, 80
    on DuPont one dollar reimbursement, 109
    on enemy research, 27
    "Little Boy" targets considered, 93
    Manhattan Project leader, 33-40
    relationship with Matthias, 81-82
    relationship with scientists, 46
    on retaining employees, 78
    on Richland Village, 74
    Trinity test, 93-94
Guam captured, 101
Gun Site (Los Alamos), 48

H
H Reactor online, 120
Hahn, Otto
    B8 experiments, 27
    captured, 27
    discovered fission, 24
    fission research, 182-184
Hall, A.E.S., 49-50
Hall, Theodore, 93
Hanford Camp, 71-74, 82
    See also Camp Hanford
Hanford Engineer Works (HEW)
    Cold War expansion, 120-123
    contractors, 107, 127
    ground broken, 106
    named, 50
    no congressional oversight, 80-82
    reactor shutdown, 126-127
Hanford Federal Facility Agreement and Consent Order. *See* Tri-Party Agreement (TPA)
Hanford Field, 77
Hanford Generating Plant, 122-123, 132-137
Hanford History Project, 167
Hanford Irrigation and Power Company, 67
Hanford Laboratories, 121
Hanford Reach, 56, 57, 61, 65

Hanford Reach National Monument, 55–57, 154, 161–164
Hanford region
    ancient inhabitants, 57
    climate, 67
    Euro-American explorers, 57–59
    Euro-American settlements, 66–68
    geology, geography, 53–57
    land claims, 58–61
    land grants, 64–68
    missionaries, fur traders, 61–64
    Native Americans, 57–64, 162
Hanford Site WA
    B Reactor online, 84–87
    B Reactor run, 90–92
    chemical separation facilities, 87–90
    chosen, 48–50
    cleanup area, 154
    cleanup on the horizon, 139–145
    employee conditions, 77–80
    GE becomes prime contractor, 107, 119
    groundbreaking, 71
    HEW management, 80–84
    infrastructure built, 82–84
    land acquisition, 68–69
    location, 56
    mixed legacy, 166–168
    nuclear waste repositories, 130–132
    Pasco as staging area, 71
    post-closure land use, 163–166
    purpose announced, 106
    Richland Village, 74–77
    site development, 71–77
    support facilities, 89–90
    Trinity test, 94–97
    waste management focus, 142
Hanford WA
    history, 67–68
    town dissolved, 69, 71
Hansen, Edith, 69
Happy Valley TN, 39-40
Harrington, Willis, 41
Harrison, George L., 103
Hastings, Richard "Doc"
    on 2019 revised cleanup estimate, 151
    on cleanup, 148–150
    on future of Hanford Site, 162–164
    Manhattan Project National Historic Park, 164
    Nuclear Cleanup Caucus, 148
    Office of River Protection, 148
Hazardous Materials Management and Emergency Response Training Center (HAMMER), 146
hazardous waste mgt, *See* nuclear waste
healthcare at Hanford Camp, 73
heavy water reactor, 21–22, 26
Heereswaffenamt (German Army Ordnance Office), 24
Heisenberg, Werner, 25–27, 46, 180
helium atom, 177
Herman, Arthur, 117
Hindenburg, Paul von, 5
Hirohito, Emperor, 105
Hiroshima, Japan, 103–104
Hitler, Adolph, 4–9, 26, 93
H.K. Ferguson Company, 39
HMS *Chatham*, 59
Homestead Act, 65
Hoover, Gilbert C., 15
housing shortages, 77
Hudson's Bay Company, 63
Huxley, Aldous, 3
Hyde Park meeting, 22
hydrogen bomb, 116, 164, 172
    See also atomic bomb

I

Ice Age in NW North America, 53–54
Inchon, Korea, 116–117
Indians. *See* Native Americans
Interim Committee, 103
Intermediate-Range Nuclear Forces Treaty, 137
internment camps, 80
Iran, post-WWII, 113
irrigation in Hanford region, 65–67
isolation, at Hanford, 49, 77–78
isolationism, US, post-WWII, 113
isotope separation

electromagnetic, 18, 20, 35–37, 42
electromagnetic, Y-12 plant (Oak Ridge),
    37–39, 42
gaseous diffusion, 21, 35, 38–39, 42
gaseous diffusion, K-25 plant (Oak
    Ridge), 38–39
NRDC mandate, 16–17
Radium Institute (Leningrad), 29
thermal diffusion, 20, 28
thermal diffusion, S-50 plant (Oak
    Ridge), 39–40
isotopes, generally, 172, 174
    See also U-235
Italian Club (Seattle), 125
Italy
    Munich Agreement, 8
    Mussolini's march on Rome, 5
    post-WWII, 115

J
Jackson, Henry M. "Scoop," 125, 127, 129,
    134, 140
Japan, 101–103, 105
    atomic research, 28–29
Japanese families, segregation, internment,
    80
Jefferson, Thomas, 59 - 60
Jews, interwar discrimination, 4–7, 25, 180,
    182–184
Johnson, Lyndon B., 126–127
Joint Center for Graduate Studies, 126
Joliot, Frédéric, 178, 184
"Jumbo," 95
Jungk, Robert, 13

K
K-25 gaseous diffusion plant (Oak Ridge),
    38–49
Kaiser Wilhelm Institute, 26, 184
K-East Reactor, 122, 143
Kelly, Joyce R., 126
Kennedy, John F., 122–123
Kennewick Man, 56
Kennewick WA
    population increase, 135–136
    segregated housing, 79–80
Kennon, George, 114
King, William Mackenzie, 30
Kodak, 95 - 96
Kokura, Japan, 104–105
Korea, post-WWII, 114
Korean War, 117–118, 121
Kristallnacht, 6, 12
Kurchatov, Igor, 29
K-West Reactor, 122, 143
Kyoto, Japan, 104

L
Laliik, 55
land claims, 58–61
land grants, 65–68
land use, post-closure, 163-165
Laser Interferometer Gravitational-Wave
    Observatory (LIGO), 157–159, 166-
    167
laser missile defense system, 157
law enforcement, at Hanford, 75
Lawrence, Ernest,
    cyclotron, 177–178
    Interim Committee, 103
    isotope separation, 37–38
    MAUD report, 19
    plutonium research, 17–18
Lawrence, Mike
    on cleanup cost, 149
    preparation for cleanup, 139–141,
        144–146
    resigned, 145
League of Nations, 7, 11
Lee, Glenn, 125
Leucippus, 172–173
Lewis, Meriwether, 60–61
Lewis, Warren, 43
Lewis and Clark expedition, 57, 60–61, 64
Libby, Leona Marshall, 90
"Little Boy"
    compared with "Fat Man," 44
    first uranium bomb, 93
    Hiroshima bomb, 104–105
"Little Boy" *continued*

targets considered, 93
U-235 provision, 40
Locke, Gary, 162
"Long Telegram," 114
Los Alamos NM, 48
atomic bomb design, 38, 44–45
first plutonium delivery, 89
secret city, 48
site chosen, 47–48
Louisiana Territory, 59–60
Luxembourg invaded by Germany, 16
Luzon liberated, 103

M
MacArthur, Douglas
on Hiroshima bombing, 104
Japanese surrender, 111
Korean War, 117–118
named Pacific commander, 102
Mackenzie, Alexander, 60
MAD (mutually assured destruction), 122
Magdeburg, Germany, 7
Magnuson, Warren G., 125, 140
Manhattan Project
bomb design comparison, 44–46
DuPont management, 40–44
DuPont withdrawal, 107–109
early information released, 141–142
established, 33–34
genesis, 2
Hanford chosen, 48–50
Hanford History Project, 167
Los Alamos site chosen, 47–48
Oak Ridge site chosen, developed, 35–40
Oppenheimer chosen, 46–47
secret cities, 50–51
transition to AEC, 119
Truman briefed, 92–93
Manhattan Project National Historic Park,
164
manifest destiny, 59
Mao Zedong, 116
Mariana Islands invaded, 101
Marietta GA, B-29 assembly plant, 100
Marsden, Ernest, 175

Marshall, George C. (Gen.), 18, 22
Marshall, James C. (Col.), 33
Marshall Plan. *See* European Recovery Plan
mass spectrograph, 174
Matthias, Franklin T. "Fritz"
choosing Hanford, 49–50, 65
on "Day's Pay," 76–77
first plutonium delivery, 89
HEW responsibility, 81–83
relationship with Groves, 81–82
Trinity test, 94–95
MAUD Committee (UK) report, 18–20, 178
measles epidemic, 63
Mein Kampf (Hitler), 5
Meitner, Lise
discovered fission, 24
fission research, 182–185
gender, religion issues, 183–184
Met Lab (Chicago)
choosing Hanford, 49
created, 40
graphite reactor, 21
questioned use of bomb, 97
relationship with DuPont, 44, 82
researchers, 86
team members, 22
Metallurgical Laboratory. *See* Met Lab
(Chicago)
Metropolitan Edison, 134
Mid-Columbia Energy Initiative (TRIDEC),
163
missionaries, early NW, 61–64
Müller, Walther, 175
Munich Agreement, 8–9, 12
Murray, Patty, 160-161
Mussolini, Benito, 5, 8

N
N Reactor
Cold War economy, 137
nuclear power, 132–133
online, 122–123, 127
shutdown, decommissioned, 147

N Reactor, *continued*

similarity to Chernobyl reactor, 140
waste storage, 143
Nagasaki, Japan, 105, 164
Napoleon, 60
National Academy of Sciences (NAS), 151, 159
National Bureau of Standards, 15
National Council on Radiation Protection, 89
National Defense Authorization Act (NDAA), 148, 164
National Defense Research Committee (NDRC), 16, 18, 94
National Environmental Policy Act (NEPA), 139
National Historic Landmark, 164
National Park Service, 164
National Recovery Administration (NRA), 1
National Science Foundation, 158
National Socialism, early period, 3
Native Americans
Cayuse people, 58, 63
community stakeholders, 145
history in the Pacific Northwest, 57–64
local residents, 50
Nez Perce people, 58, 60
Palouse people, 58
Rattlesnake Mountain, 55, 162
River People, 58
Walla Walla people, 58
Wanapum people, 58, 63, 66, 68
Yakama people, 57
Natural Resources Committee (US House), 163
Nazi Germany. See Germany
Nazi Party, beginning, 5
Ndiaye, Pap A., 42
Netherlands invaded by Germany, 16
neutrons, 171–172
New Deal launched, 11
Newlands Reclamation Act, 65
Nez Perce people, 58, 60
Nichols, Kenneth, 35, 95
Niigata, Japan, 104
Nishina, Yoshio, 28

Nixon, Richard, 129
Nobel laureates
Bohr, Physics, 179
Chadwick, Physics, 178
Compton, Physics, 21
Fermi, Physics, 181
Franck, Physics, 96
Joliot and Curie, Chemistry, 178
Lawrence, Physics, 177
Röntgen, Physics, 173
Rutherford, Chemistry, 175
Thomson, Physics, 174
Nootka Sound trading post (Spain), 58
Norsk Hydro heavy water plant, 26
North Atlantic Treaty Organization (NATO), 120
North Richland worker housing, 120
North West Company, 61–62
Northern Pacific Railway, 63-65
Norway invaded by Germany, 26
nuclear chain reaction
B Reactor, 86
early research, 18, 22, 29, 184
Einstein-Szilárd letter, 2, 171
explained, 172
first, 41, 43, 45, 90, 107
theorized, 16
Nuclear Cleanup Caucus, 148
nuclear energy, 103, 140
nuclear energy park, 132–135
nuclear fission, 181, 184
Nuclear Regulatory Commission (NRC), 132, 138
nuclear research. See atomic research
nuclear transmutation, 172
nuclear waste
BWIP, 131, 135, 142
Hanford waste, 142–143
high- and low-level treatment, 147–148
high-level reclassification, 152–154
legislation, 139–140
management viewpoint, 149
NAS review, 151
radioactive liquid waste, 88

nuclear waste, *continued*
   repositories, 130–132
   vitrification, 147–148, 150–151, 153
   See also cleanup
Nuclear Waste Policy Act (NWPA), 130–131
Nuremberg Laws enacted, 6

O

Oak Ridge TN
   isotope separation facilities, 36–40,
      42-46, 48
   secret city, 47-48
   site chosen, developed, 35–40
Obama administration, 132
Office of River Protection, 148, 165
Office of Scientific Research and
      Development (OSRD), 18, 94
oil crisis, 138
Okinawa captured, 101–102
Oliphant, Mark, 18–19, 31
Omaha NE, B-29 assembly plant, 100
one dollar, DuPont reimbursement, 43,
      107–109
Operation DOWNFALL, 102
Operation OLYMPIC, 102
Oppenheimer, J. Robert
   selected by Groves, 46 47
   Interim Committee, 103
   Trinity test, 94
   work with Bohr, 180
Oregon Territory created, 63
Oregon Trail, 62, 63

P

Pacific Northwest National Laboratory
      (PNNL), 127–129, 136, 163, 166
Pacific War, 101–105
Palouse people, 58
Paris, German occupation, 16
Paris Peace Conference, 3
party politics in US, post-WWII, 117
Pasco Kiwanis Club, 108–109
Pasco WA
   choosing Hanford, 50
   Lewis and Clark, 60

Pasco WA *continued*
   named, 65
   population increase, 135
   segregated housing, 74, 79
   staging area for Hanford Site, 71
Pash, Boris, 27
Pearl Harbor, 33, 100, 111
Pehrson, G. Albin, 74
Peierls, Rudolf, 18, 31
Perry, Matthew, 111
Philip, Robert E. "Bob," 125
Philippines invaded, 90, 92, 101
physicists, conflicts with engineers, 90-91
Planck, Max, 183
plum pudding model, 174, 176
plutonium
   compared with uranium, 46
   "Fat Man," 45
   first delivery, 89
   named, 17–18
   Oak Ridge reactor, 45–46
   shipped from Hanford, 147
   two production techniques, 21–22
   waste storage, 143
Plutonium Finishing Plant, 120–121, 143
plutonium production reactor
   criticality, 107
   Hanford chosen, 49-50
   pilot, 45
   site requirements, 49
poisoning, B Reactor startup, 90–91
Poland, targeted by Hitler, Soviet Union, 9
poliomyelitis, 11
Potsdam Conference, 95, 112–114
Price, Melvin, 128
Project Y (Los Alamos), 48
Prosser WA, 74
protons, 87, 171–172, 176
PUREX plant, 122, 146, 151
Pusan, Korea, 117

Q

Quebec Conference, 30

R

radiation, early research, 174–180
radioactive liquid waste, 88
radioactivity
    decay, 175
    natural, 172
    term coined, 172
radium discovered, 173
Radium Institute (Leningrad), 29
Rattlesnake Mountain, 53, 55
Reagan, Ronald, 131, 137–138, 157
REDOX plant, 121, 151
Referendum 40, 140–141
Reichstag fire, 6
Rhineland, reoccupied by Germany, 7
Rich, Nelson, 68
Richardson, Bill, 162
Richland Community Council, 124
Richland Operations Office, 145, 166
Richland Village
    DuPont withdrawal, 107
    under GE control, 119
    Hanford employee housing, 73–77
    HEW housing, 82
    self-government, 124–126
Richland WA
    choosing Hanford, 50
    climate, 65
    incorporated, 125
    independence, 124–126
    nuclear energy park, 132
    recession, 127
    secret city, 50–51
    settled, 68
    town dissolved, 68, 71
RIKEN Institute, 28
River People, 58
Rocky Flats CO, 121
Röntgen, Wilhelm, 173
Roosevelt, Eleanor, 10
Roosevelt, Franklin D.
    approved DuPont contract, 43
    approved initial facility exploration, 20
    approved nuclear research, 20
    authorized Grand Coulee Dam, 65

Roosevelt, Franklin D. *continued*
    background, early career, 9–11
    death, 92, 102
    elected to first term, 11
    elected to second term, 11
    Hyde Park meeting with Churchill,
        22–23
    Japanese American internment, 80
    on the Munich Agreement, 8
    New York governor, 11
    orders nuclear research, 14
    poliomyelitis, 11
    Quebec Conference, 30
    secretary of the navy, 10
    Social Security Act, 11–12
    on the United Nations, 113
Roosevelt, Theodore, 10
Rosellini, Albert, 125
Russell, Robie, 144
Russia
    early claims in NW North America, 58
    See also Soviet Union
Rutherford, Ernest, 46, 174–178

S

S-1 Committee (of OSRD), 20-22, 33
S-1 Section (of OSRD), 18
S-50 thermal diffusion plant (Oak Ridge),
        39–40
Sacajawea, 60
Sachs, Alexander
    disclosure concerns, 186
    Einstein-Szilárd letter, 1–2, 4, 12–13
Saddle Mountain, 53, 55
Saddle Mountain National Wildlife
        Preserve, 161
safety record at Hanford, 73, 88–89
Sagebrush Annie, 67
Saipan captured, 101
Savannah River SC, 146
"Screw Nevada Bill", 132
Seaborg, Glenn, 17, 132
Seattle WA, B-29 assembly plant, 99-100
Second World War. *See* World War II
secret cities, 51

security at Hanford, 72, 79
segregation
    at Hanford Camp, 73–74
    at Hanford Site, 79–80
    See also civil rights of area residents
seismic concerns, 150
self-government, Richland area, 123–126
Site Y (Los Alamos), 48
Skidmore, Owen & Merrill, 36
Smohala, 58
Smyth, Henry D., 30
social activities in Richland Village, 75-76
Social Security Act passed, 11
Soddy, Frederick, 174–175
soil contamination, 147
Somervell, Brehon, 34
Sommerfeld, Arnold, 176
Soviet Union
    arms race, 137
    atomic bomb, 116, 121
    atomic research, 29–30
    collapse, 13-138
    early Russian claims in NW North
        America, 58
    espionage on UK and US, 116-117
    invaded by Germany, 18
    non-agression pact with Germany, 9
    post-WWII objectives, 111–114
Spain, land claims in NW North America,
    59
Spanish Civil War, 7
Special Committee to Investigate the
    National Defense Program, 80–81
Speer, Albert, 25,-26
Spokesman-Review (Spokane), 147
Stagg Field, 22. *See* CP-1 reactor (Chicago)
Stalin, Josef
    on the atomic bomb, 29–30, 114-116
    European Recovery Plan, 115
    knew of bomb, 92
    Potsdam Conference, 112
Stimson, Henry L.
    atomic research advisory group, 18
    briefing Congress, 22
    briefing Truman, 92–93

Stimson, Henry L., *continued*
    chose bomb site, 104
    HEW oversight, 81
    Interim Committee, 103
stock market crash, 4
Stone and Webster, 33, 35-37
Strassman, Fritz, 25, 182–184
subatomic particles, 128, 171
Sudentenland annexed by Germany, 8
Sunnyside WA, 74
super bomber. *See* Boeing B-29
        Superfortress
Superconducting Magnetic Energy Storage
        System (SMES), 157–158
support facilities, 89
Swanson, Mel, 108–109
Szilárd, Leó
    disclosure concerns, 185–186
    fission research, 183, 185
    left Nazi Germany, 6
    Met Lab (Chicago), 22, 86
    questioned use of bomb, 96–97
    Uranium Committee, 16
    See also Einstein-Szilárd letter

T
T Plant online, 91
tank farms, 147, 150, 165
Tapteal, 60-61
Teller, Edward, 46
    disclosure concerns, 184
    Einstein-Szilárd letter, 1
    left Nazi Germany, 7
    on Soviet bomb, 116
Tennessee Valley Authority, 122n
Test Bed Initiative (TBI), 153
"The Hill". *See* Los Alamos NM
thermal diffusion isotope separation, 20, 28
    S-50 plant (Oak Ridge), 39–40
Thompson, David, 57, 61, 64
Thomson, George Paget, 18–19
Thomson, J.J., 173–174, 176, 179
Three Mile Island, 134, 136
Tizard, Henry, 18, 24
TNX project (Oak Ridge), 44

Tojo, Hideki, 28
transuranic (TRU) waste, 142–143
Tri-Cities
    consolidation attempts, 136
    economy during cleanup, 154–157
    recession, 127–129, 135–136, 154-155
Tri-Cities Chamber of Commerce, 156–157
Tri-City Herald, 125, 137
Tri-City Industrial Development Council
    (TRIDEC), 137, 156
Tri-City Nuclear Industrial Council
    (TCNIC)
    becomes TRIDEC, 137, 156–157
    Cold War economy, 136
    on funding cleanup, 152
    name, 134
    on nuclear energy park, 132
    nuclear waste repositories, 130
Trinity test, 92–97
    DuPont, 107
    espionage, 30
    people present, 94–95
    plutonium bomb, 45, 103
    similar to Nagasaki bomb, 105
    Soviet espionage target, 30
Tri-Party Agreement (TPA), 143–144, 147
tritium, 130
Truman, Harry
    approved bombing Japan, 103
    becomes president, 92
    briefed on Manhattan Project, 92–93
    Interim Committee, 103
    Potsdam Conference, 112
    response to N. Korean invasion, 117–118
    response to Soviet bomb, 116
    Senate Special Committee to
        Investigate the National Defense
        Program, 80-81
    signed Atomic Energy Act, 119
Truman Doctrine, 114-115
Tube Alloys program (UK), 19, 180
Turkey
    post-WWII, 113
    Truman Doctrine, 115
turnover among Hanford employees, 72, 77

U
U-235
    bomb research, 179–180
    "Little Boy," 40, 44–45, 93
    RIKEN Institute, 28
    U-238 compared, 37, 172, 184
    See also isotope separation
underground repository. *See* Yucca
    Mountain
unemployment, Tri-Cities economy, 136
unions at Hanford Site, 76, 82, 134
United Kingdom (UK)
    atomic research, 18–19, 23–24, 30–31
    collaboration with US, 23–24
    early claims in NW North America, 58-
        59, 62
    Munich Agreement, 8–9
    post-WWII objectives, 114
    US-UK research liaison, 20, 22–24
United Nuclear
    HEW contractor, 128
United States (US)
    atomic research, 15–18, 21–23
    claims in NW North America, 59, 62
    collaboration with UK, 23–24
    interwar isolationism, 12
    post-WWII objectives, 111–114
    Soviet espionage, 116
uranium
    B Reactor process, 85–87
    compared with plutonium, 46
    isotopes, generally, 172, 174, 184–185
    UK research, 18–19
    See also isotope separation; U-235
Uranium Committee, 16–18
Uranium Section (OSRD), 18
Uranverein ("Uranium Club"), 24
Urey, Harold, 21
US Army Air Corps, 99
US Navy Seabee battalions, 101
USS *Missouri*, 111

V
Vancouver, George, 59
Versailles, Treaty of, 3, 6–7, 11

Vietnam War, 118
Villard, Henry, 63-64
Volpentest, Sam, 125–127, 140
   advocating for EMSL, 160
   advocating for LIGO, 158
   advocating for SMES, 157
   advocating for Tri-Cities economy,
      155–157
   on cleanup funding, 148
   HAMMER training facility, 146
   on nuclear waste repositories, 130–131
   on TCNIC name, 134

W
Wahluke Slope, 56
Wahluke Slope Wildlife Refuge, 161
Walla Walla people, 58
Walla Walla WA, 62
Wallace, Henry, 18, 20
Wallula Gap, 54, 62
Walton, Ernest, 177
Wanapum people, 57–58, 63, 66, 68
War of 1812, 62
War Production Board, 34, 72
Washington Group International, 149
Washington Public Power Supply System
    (WPPSS)
   collapse, 135-136, 142, 155
   electric power generation, 133–136
   Energy Northwest, 155, 156
Washington State University, Tri-Cities
    campus, 126, 159, 163, 166
waste. *See* nuclear waste
Waste Receiving and Processing Facility,
    146
Waste Treatment Plant (WTP), 147–149
water treatment, 147
Watkins, James, 143, 145
Watson, Edwin M. "Pa," 12–16
weather, climate at Hanford, 77–78
Webb, Julian H., 95-96
Weimar Republic, 5
Weizmann, Chaim, 175
Wells, H.G., 175
Wells, Sumner, 9

Westinghouse at Oak Ridge, 36
White Bluffs WA
   choosing Hanford, 50
   climate, 65
   settled, 65–67
   town dissolved, 68, 71
Whitman, Marcus and Narcissa, 63
"Whoops," 134
Wichita KS, B-29 assembly plant, 100
Wiehl, Lloyd, 68
Wigner, Eugene
   designed B Reactor, 85, 90
   disclosure concerns, 185
   Einstein-Szilárd letter, 1, 2
   left Nazi Germany, 7
   Met Lab (Chicago), 22
Wiley, William R. "Bill," 159–160
Williams, Roger, 74
Wilson, Charles, 107
Wilson, Woodrow, 10
Wishram Native settlement, 56
WNP-2 nuclear power plant, 155–156, 163
World War I, aftermath in Europe, 3–4
World War II, 9, 91-92, 111

X
X-10 Pilot Plutonium Reactor (Oak Ridge),
    45, 49, 87
X-ray radiation, 173

Y
Y-12 electromagnetic separation plant (Oak
    Ridge), 37–39, 42
Yakama people, 57
Yakima River, 58, 60, 65
Yalu River, 117
Yasuda, Takeo, 28
Yom Kippur War, 138
York, 60
Yucca Mountain, 131–132, 139, 152, 154

ABOUT THE AUTHORS

ROBERT L. FERGUSON

Robert L. ("Bob") Ferguson has more than sixty years of experience in the field of nuclear energy and managing nuclear waste. His nuclear career started with General Electric at the Hanford Engineering Works where his final assignment was as a reactor physicist and operating supervisor at the famous B Reactor. He is a former deputy assistant secretary for Nuclear Programs within the US Department of Energy and former managing director for the Washington Public Power Supply System (now Energy Northwest). He is responsible for building the Fast Flux Test Facility, a government test reactor for the Breeder Reactor Program, and the Columbia Generating Station, a commercial nuclear reactor still in operation on the Hanford Site in eastern Washington. He served as president of the Tri-City Nuclear Industrial Council and its successor, the Tri-Cities Economic Development Council. He is a graduate of Gonzaga University in physics, the Oak Ridge School of Reactor Technology, and the Federal Executive Institute.

Robert L. ("Bob") Ferguson

For excellence in his field, Ferguson has been recognized with the Gonzaga University Alumni Merit Award and featured in Who's Who in America and Who's Who in Corporate America. In 2018, he received the Albert Nelson Marquis Lifetime Achievement Award by Marquis Who's Who.

Ferguson was one of three private citizens who successfully sued President Obama and the Nuclear Regulatory Commission for illegally shutting down the Yucca Mountain nuclear waste repository and is the author of two books based on government mismanagement of nuclear waste and spent nuclear fuel. www.bobferguson-legacymatters.com

C. MARK SMITH

C. Mark Smith

C. Mark Smith spent forty years managing economic development organizations at the local, state, and federal level, including eight years as regional director of the federal Economic Development Administration for the eight western states, and is a graduate of the Federal Executive Institute. He is a Fellow Member and Honorary Life Member of the International Economic Development Council and received a Lifetime Achievement Award from Washington Governor Gary Locke in 2004.

He is the author of four books and numerous magazine articles of history, biography, and politics, receiving the John M. McClelland Jr. Award from the Washington State Historical Society in 2011 for the best article to appear in their journal, *Columbia*, and the 2015 Murray Morgan Award for Preserving and Communicating Local History from the Tacoma Historical Society. He is a graduate of the University of Puget Sound, served eight years on its board of trustees, and received its Lifetime Achievement Award in 2011. www.cms-author.com.

ABOUT OUR PARTNERS

B REACTOR MUSEUM ASSOCIATION (BRMA)

BRMA WAS FORMED IN 1991 with the sole purpose of preserving the B Reactor as a historic landmark for people to visit. At that time, the DOE intended to somehow dispose of or cocoon the shutdown production reactors. BRMA is a dedicated group, consisting mostly Hanford engineers who lobbied hard to save the B Reactor, the first large-scale reactor, which introduced the atomic age. They worked through the various engineering societies to get designations as a historic technical landmark and persuaded the DOE not to cocoon the reactor. This was the BRMA's major achievement.

Then they joined with Los Alamos—which had wanted to become the national park—and Oak Ridge to lobby for a three-location national park. Tours of the B Reactor began almost a decade ago, and in addition to providing the docents, BRMA developed and made a number of models and displays used at the reactor building. They also developed video interviews and lectures and various items for sale in the gift shop near the visitor center.

HANFORD HISTORY PROJECT (HHP)

THE HANFORD HISTORY PROJECT at Washington State University Tri-Cities is an archive and curatorial repository focusing on the Hanford Site and the Tri-Cities region. It administers the Department of Energy's Hanford Collection, partners with Northwest Public Television for an oral history project focused on the Manhattan Project and Cold War–era Hanford workers, and houses numerous collections donated by the community. The Hanford History Project provides academic and historical gateways for students and the general public.

CPSIA information can be obtained
at www.ICGtesting.com
Printed in the USA
LVHW021247150422
716296LV00008B/297